How to Get More Done in Less Time

JOSEPH D. COOPER

1962

Doubleday & Company, Inc.

Garden City, New York

T
58
.C67

Acknowledgments

These individuals:

MR. ELLSWORTH C. ALVORD, attorney at law, Alvord & Alvord, Washington, D.C.

DR. HURST R. ANDERSON, President, The American University, Washington, D.C.

MR. JACK S. BLACK, sales manager, U. S. Photo Supply Co., Washington, D.C.

MRS. MIRIAM BALLER, registered representative, Sutro Bros. & Co., Washington, D.C.

MRS. MARLYLEE P. BUCHLY, Silver Spring, Maryland

HON. MICHAEL V. DISALLE, Governor, State of Ohio

MR. OSBORN ELLIOTT, editor, *Newsweek*

DR. LOUIS FETTIG, Philadelphia

DR. C. RICHARD A. GILBERT, Washington, D.C.

HON. BARRY GOLDWATER, United States Senator

MR. ERIC JOHNSTON, President, Motion Picture Association of America

MR. FRED JOINER, Bureau of National Affairs, Washington, D.C.

MR. F. R. KAPPEL, President, American Telephone and Telegraph Co.

DR. CHARLES L. "CHUCK" LAPP, Professor of Marketing, Washington University, St. Louis, Mo

MR. JAMES LUTZ, President, McCrory Corp.

MR. ROBERT E. MACK, the American Airlines

MRS. JANE P. McKNEE, Washington, D.C.

HON. JOHN W. MACY, JR., Chairman, U. S. Civil Service Commission, Washington, D.C.

DR. ALEX F. OSBORN, Chairman, Creative Education Foundation, Buffalo, N.Y.

MR. CHARLES H. PERCY, Chairman, Bell & Howell Co., Chicago

BISHOP JAMES A. PIKE, San Francisco

MR. ELMO ROPER, President, Elmo Roper & Associates, New York City

MR. IRVING RUDD, partner, Sutro Bros. & Co., Washington, D.C.

MR. HAROLD F. SMIDDY, Vice President, General Electric Co., New York, N.Y.

MR. FRANCIS D. TAPPAN, Assistant to the Vice President, North American Aviation, Inc., Los Angeles

Mr. Stephen G. Thompson, Vice President for Public Relations, Webb and Knapp, Inc., New York City

Mr. E. Charles Woods, U. S. Bureau of the Budget, Washington, D.C.

Mr. James C. Worthy, Republican Citizens League of Illinois, Chicago

Mr. Harold Zelko, Professor of Speech, Pennsylvania State University

These publications for the copyrighted materials cited:

The American Salesman, 355 Lexington Ave., New York 17, New York "Where to Find the Minutes You've Misplaced," by W. Guy Laird, March 1961; also, excerpts from reports of round tables and for other brief references

Bell Syndicate, synopsis of story in Drew Pearson column, March 13, 1961

Doubleday and Co., *The Compleat Practical Joker,* H. Allen Smith, 1953

Dun & Bradstreet Co., "The Myth of the Overworked Executive," originally published in *Dun's Review and Modern Industry,* February 1961.

Farm Chemicals, "Organize Your Time," O. C. Merritt, August 1960

Harper & Brothers, *Sparks off My Anvil,* James R. Adams, 1958

Harper's Magazine, "Writing the 'Inside' Books," John Gunther, March 1961

Medical Economics, "Busiest Solo Practice I've Seen," Horace Cotton, August 1, 1960; "75 Office Visits a Day—and He Practices Good Medicine," Garrett Oppenheim, February 27, 1961; "Telephone Hours? No More for Me!" Stanley I. Wolf, M.D., May 23, 1960; also for other brief references

The New York *Times Magazine,* "Thoughts about Thought in High Places," Dean Acheson, October 11, 1959

Public Administration News, "Barriers Preventing Delegation," Dr. Richard B. Cravens and Dr. Addison Duval, Spring 1961

U. S. Air Force, Management Course for Air Force Supervisors

Preface

At lunch one day Harold Kuebler, my Doubleday editor, put a problem to me. He asked how one can keep on top of the mass of details that never stop coming and how, in spite of them, one can push ahead on the main tasks, each of which may take hours and hours of work.

On the backs of envelopes, then, we drew diagrams of work weeks and workdays. We discoursed on various psychological approaches. We noted general principles. When we were done, Harold looked up, smiled, and said:

"Now—there's a book we might do!"

The indirect origins of this book go back to early years when I first heard the famous saying that if you wanted to get a task done, you should ask the busiest man to do it. It was then I noted that those who turned out the least work were usually the ones who seemed to have the least time.

I proceeded, then, to adapt to my own needs the techniques used by successful men of action whom I was privileged to observe. Eventually, I was asked to develop techniques for planning, scheduling, and controlling the time of people whose work was not of a routine nature. These techniques, included in this book, have served me well—as they have served others and as they can serve you.

You can learn to get more done in the same time or as much done in less time. The choice is yours. You can also learn to get the important things done on time, especially those things others depend upon, thereby conserving and amplifying your stature as a man of action.

Finally, you can learn to use your every waking hour constructively and fruitfully. Here, too, the choice is yours, although I hope your schedule includes time for leisure, reflection, and a recharging of your batteries.

This counsel is included because of an admonition given me: "Can't you tell people that they should work to enjoy life; not that they should work harder to find more time for more work? Can't you tell them to find more time for their families, for culture, and for recreation?"

This challenge was put to me at a meeting with members of the Capital chapter of the National Secretaries Association. They had seen men whose life was their work and *vice versa*.

Of course, the ladies are right. There are some, however, for whom the chase itself is the thrill of living and working. That's their way of life and it is not likely that such people can change.

Now, returning to the matter of what you can do with the information in this book, I hope you will not expect dramatic results merely from a first reading. You must actually *do something*. Try out at least one idea that fits your situation and your personality. Perseverence and patience then must be your watchwords as you develop new workways and make habits of them. You then can try out other ideas offered in this book.

Although the return for your effort may be immediately impressive, the greater likelihood is that you will take your biggest gains in small increments. You will be surprised at the value of a minute, when added to other minutes. Elihu Burritt, the learned blacksmith, said: "All that I have accomplished, or expect, or hope to accomplish, has been and will be by that plodding, patient, persevering process of acretion which builds the ant-heap, particle by particle, thought by thought, fact by fact."

JOSEPH D. COOPER
Chevy Chase 15, Maryland

Table of Contents

How to Get More Done
in Less Time

I

What's a Minute Worth?

At age nine John Quincy Adams wrote to his father:

". . . My thoughts are running after birds' eggs, play and trifles, till I get vexed with myself. Mamma has a troublesome task to keep me studying. I own I am ashamed of myself. I had but just entered the third volume of Rollin's History. . . . I am determined this week to be more diligent. I have set myself a stint to read the third volume half out. . . .

"I wish, sir, you would give me in writing some instructions with regard to the use of my time, and advise me how to proportion my studies and play, and I will keep them by me, and endeavor to follow them."*

The boy Adams had faced a problem not unlike that of countless millions of students before and after him. What distinguished him from most, however, was his eagerness to do something about his problem. At an early age, therefore, he was already displaying the traits of character which were to lead to his becoming President of the United States.

While the problem of using time effectively has always been with us, the ways in which we have approached it have under-

* From the quotation in *Profiles in Courage,* by John F. Kennedy (New York: Harper and Brothers, 1955).

gone great change, keeping pace with the development of economic man. The deadlines of primitive man were probably associated with such controlling factors as the approach of nightfall or the changing of the seasons. Today's deadlines are expressed in terms of the number of sales calls made or patients examined in a given day, the completion of a project to meet a customer's deadline, the completion and filing of a report or tax return by a given date, or the catching of an airplane which is to carry you to a distant city where you are to make a speech the same evening.

Nowadays, we so often hear the expression "time is money." This is an abbreviation for "getting more accomplished in the same period of time." It is with the latter that we will be concerned throughout this book.

HOW TO VALUE TIME

Practically everybody who makes a living takes it for granted that it pays to make the best use of one's time. We need not belabor the obvious. What may not be so obvious, however, is the way in which little moments of time, here and there, build up into sizable amounts over a day, a week, a month, a year, a lifetime. It may not be so obvious, also, that the same hour may have different values at different times of the day. That same hour, used judiciously at the beginning of a project, may save many more hours later on.

The Arithmetic of Odd Moments

Can you spare a minute—and have you ever thought how much it is worth? A minute by itself is not worth very much, unless it is that extra minute needed to catch a plane or train or that critical minute sooner that would have caught someone before he left the office. These, of course, are moments of *timeliness*. They are a matter apart from our arithmetic of odd moments.

Suppose you save a minute a day for an entire work year. Theoretically, this would net four hours of saved time, but I challenge anyone to pin down any really measurable return from these few hours.

If you can save as little as ten consecutive minutes a day, you begin to cross the threshold of the worthwhile. Ten minutes saved each workday will net more than one full week of productivity each year, assuming a standard work week of five days of eight hours each. In the average lifetime, ten minutes saved each workday adds up to one additional year of productivity.

Offhand, this seems worthwhile, but I suggest that we ignore it and that we try for bigger stakes. After all, even though saving ten minutes should be about as easy as eating apple pie, for most of us, the amount is too small to prove anything one way or the other.

The Bigger Stakes

Can you derive from each working day at least one additional hour of productive accomplishment? This is a great deal, as we shall see. There are few of us, indeed, who cannot achieve at least this much if we really try. It can be done by better work planning, making better use of personal helpers, avoiding interruptions, sharpening one's skills of conferring, reading, and writing, and by improving one's skills of concentration, among others.

Perhaps you should not answer the question until you have read through this book. It may suggest ways of saving time— or using it more effectively—which have not occurred to you.

What's it worth to save that single hour a day, on the average? In a normal lifetime, one hour saved each day of a five-day week is worth six years of productive effort!

How you use this time is up to you. If you are now working longer hours than you would like, your aim might be to get as much done in fewer hours, using the savings for the family, leisure, and self-improvement. If greater productivity or greater earnings are goals, you can use the techniques presented in this book to help you achieve more in the same time.

The Proper Use of Time

Up to now we have considered the worthwhileness of time savings as they accumulate throughout the day. The uses of time have differential values. They can be analyzed in terms of the familiar questions of what, why, where, when, who, and how. As we course through this book, we will raise these questions—although not necessarily under those brief labels—and we will attempt to provide answers to them. Meanwhile, to make our point we will sample the questions briefly.

What you do and how much time you allocate to it should be your first concern. You should know whether your activities are spread too thin so that you fail to get the best return for your efforts or whether concentration on too few things results in a failure to exploit your potentials. You need to know the sources or the nature of your time losses.

Whatever you do in your work at least should be justified by a constructive answer to the question *why*. If what you are doing does not contribute to worthwhile goals of the enterprise or to the achievement of personal goals, you might as well spend the time in relaxed reflection.

Where you spend your time relates to the question of place. That is, is it more worthwhile for you to be in one place as against another? Where can you make your greatest contribution? As a sales manager, should you be spending more of your time in the field among your men, providing the leadership they require? As a salesman, should you consider spending more time in the upstate territory because it has not received much of your attention lately, or should you work closer to home base because it is more convenient to do so or because the territory is a little richer closer to home? As a plant-operating executive, should you be spending more time away from your desk in closer touch with operations where your presence can be felt and where you can obtain a more realistic and more direct understanding and appraisal of what is going on? As a researcher, should you burrow into the second- and third-hand accounts that you will find in libraries, or should you use them as clues to the primary sources of your working materials and ideas?

When you do things may pay off in terms of increased productivity immediately, or it may be a matter of "a stitch in time saves nine." Is an hour for creative thinking, early in the day, worth more than later when you're on the droopy side in mind and body? If you are planning an engineering project or if you are building a house, will you save time with an early start on procurement of "long-lead" items?

Who engages your time? Is your clientele sufficiently remunerative? Does your clientele give you the spread or breadth of experience you desire? Are you providing a balanced distribution of your time among your subordinates? Are some people taking too much of your time?

Finally, *how* effectively are you using your time? Have you established the right environment for yourself? Are you subject to interruptions by visitors and by the telephone and, if so, what are you doing about it?

Time of itself is neutral. It is available equally to the rich and to the poor, to the big and to the small. What matters is how well you use your time for the greatest return, whatever your objectives might be.

WHOSE PROBLEM

Unless you are among the top performers in your business or profession, the chances are that you could do better, that you *could* find that extra hour of productivity.

Even this challenge does not go far enough. Top performer Charles H. Percy, chairman of the board of the Bell & Howell Company, wrote me: "The art or science of managing time so that every minute is productive is not one in which I feel I have become proficient enough to serve as an example. It is a subject to which I have given a good deal of thought, however, and I believe that in the past ten years there is evidence of some progress." His comments on how he attempts to manage his time in a typical day are quoted in a later chapter.

A Universal Problem

The effective use of time is not alone the problem of men at the top, even though their treatment of it may be of interest to the rest of us. It is a problem for all who must *organize or control* their own use of time, including those who must meet deadlines or turn out work in spite of conflicting pressures or interruptions, those who must see the most clients in a limited period of time, and those who are self-starting producers of creative work. It is a problem for executives, physicians, lawyers, engineers, outside salesmen, writers, executive secretaries, and foremen and supervisors, among others.

Of course, it is the peculiar problem of people who are successful in any line of endeavor, for the higher they move up the ladder of achievement, the more conspicuous they become as targets for those who wish to share their success. Hence, it is the problem of the ambitious ones who want to learn how to govern their activities so that they, too, may reach their higher goals.

The symptoms of ineffective planning and use of time may be found within ourselves. You have ample opportunity for self-improvement if you are constantly slipping deadlines, if you cannot find time for people to see you, if you cannot cover your territory adequately, if you wind up the day with a sense of frustration and a feeling that you have not accomplished anything, or if you feel that your work is a succession of crash deadlines and crises. If you recognize these symptoms or others like them, you are fortunate in this respect: you are conscious of a need for improving the ways in which you use your time. A sense of awareness is the first step. You can intensify this awareness by comparing your performance with that of others, especially those who have a demonstrated record of successful performance.

Some Comparisons and Contrasts

In every walk of life the difference between the successful and the unsuccessful ones lies, *in large measure,* in how well they organize their work and their time schedules.

Let's take salesmen, for example. My friend Jack Black, who has been selling in the photographic field since 1953, said,

"The difference between the good salesman and the man who never seems to get through his calls each day begins in the morning. It is so easy to talk yourself into a late start when you don't have to punch a clock. The opportunities for frittering away your time literally throw themselves in your path throughout the day. Much of your time is lost riding around the downtown section, getting in and out of parking lots. Another bundle of your time is lost trying to telephone ahead for appointments. One of the biggest time-eaters is the coffee-break with dealers and with friendly competitors.

"These are only a few of the things that eat up your time as you get around. There are so many others, like calling upon a dealer only to find him out or, if he is in, having to wait away much of your time. These examples scarcely scratch the surface.

"From my own experience and from observing the top producers I can say that we all too often can find excuses, but deep down we know that when we slip, in the long run it's due to our own failure to plan and make the best use of our time. A lot of our lost time is unavoidable—a part of our way of life—and we know it. Still, the determined salesman learns how to trim away a good part of this waste. He knows that if he can squeeze in another call each day, that's about 250 more calls a year, and that's a pretty big base from which to draw much greater dollar earnings.

"With this thought in mind I become more conscious of time. I learn to fend off invitations for coffee. I plan my call schedules so as to spend the least possible time in traveling from one dealer to another. I find other productive things to do when I have to wait until the dealer is ready to talk to me."

Let's shift now from the time problems of a man on the move to a man who spends most of his time behind a desk. Clarence B. Randall, a former board chairman of the Inland Steel Company, has written much about the problems of the executive. His comments about the self-appointed overworked executive could almost serve as a table of contents for this book.* Mr. Randall said: "Here is how you will know him: His desk is a mess. Papers are strewn across it in wild disarray, creating the

* "The Myth of the Overworked Executive" by Clarence B. Randall. Reprinted by special permission from *Dun's Review and Modern Industry*, February 1961. Copyright, 1961, Dun & Bradstreet Publications Corp.

impression that every important corporate transaction comes to him for approval. Yet if you should discreetly make a few spot-checks, you would find that many of the letters and memos which he paws through to find the one you are after were there last week. They will be there next week, too. . . . He seldom goes out to lunch, but has a sandwich and a glass of milk brought in. This adds to the build-up. . . .

"In his hand when he leaves the office at night is the inevitable bulging briefcase. He would no more be caught without that mark of martyrdom than he would be seen without his trousers. True, many of the papers in it have already made a great many round-trips without being disturbed. . . . "He is greatly given to travel, rushing about on planes, briefcase in hand, as though the number of miles flown in a year were any criterion of effective effort. Physical activity gives him a proud sense of doing. Often a long-distance call, if prudently planned and intelligently carried through, would fully answer the purpose, but that would some-how downgrade the whole transaction. Nor does he ever achieve much by correspondence, since he has never learned to express himself cogently and persuasively in a letter.

"What little responsibility he bears, he shares with no one. To simplify his day by delegating to juniors the routine clerical part of his tasks would deflate his ego. . . . If something takes him away from his desk, whether for an hour or for a week, every-thing stops. . . .

"He is chronically late for all engagements. When a staff con-ference is called, he bustles into the room fifteen minutes after it has begun, wearing an air of preoccupation which is intended to suggest to his colleagues that it is generous indeed for a man who bears such manifest responsibility to take time for such lesser matters at all.

"In his office he is rude to visitors. He keeps them waiting beyond the time set for the engagement, partly because his aware-ness of his surroundings is so low that he is actually not conscious of the passage of time, and partly because by delaying others he reminds himself once more of his own importance.

"They, of course, know him well, and expecting such treat-ment, arrive late, thus introducing irregularity into both his schedule and theirs. They know, too, that he will not cut his telephone. He will make them listen to boring conversations that are completely unrelated to what they have come to discuss."

In contrast to all this hustle and bustle which produces very little, Mr. Randall paints a verbal image of a highly productive executive whose performance is characterized by a serenity which is evident even in periods of turbulent action and conflict.

"This quality is never lacking in the truly great executives of American industry. They must, of course, have fine minds and strong wills. Yet the power of their personalities finds expression through order and a self-discipline so immaculate that it is seldom apparent as a separable trait of character.

"For example, they practice precision-timing in all of their movements, though they do it unobtrusively. They are, quietly, always on time. They thus cause others to adopt punctuality as a way of life without ever declaring themselves about it.

"When a visitor is shown in to a good executive, he finds before him a clean desk and behind it a man who is at ease, who makes him feel that this is the call he has been waiting for, and he listens attentively. Yet, subtly, the man behind the desk is in control of the interview all of the time and knows how to terminate it without giving offense.

"The good executive also has a plan for his day. He knows what things have to be accomplished if the required tempo is to be maintained, and times himself accordingly.

"Throughout the day, with deliberate speed he moves from one task to the next, making his decisions resolutely when he senses the matter has consumed the maximum period that can be allotted to it. . . .

"He works a full day, though not an overly long one. When the normal quitting time comes, except for those sudden emergencies which no man can control, he will walk promptly out of his office with a sense of satisfaction at what he has accomplished. And in closing the door, he will put it all behind him. . . .

"Then, in company with his family and neighbors, he turns with high enthusiasm to other challenging interests that are totally unrelated to his daily routines. When he comes back to his job, both his body and his mind have been refreshed."

HOW TO SOLVE TIME PROBLEMS

While we like to use examples that demonstrate the successful practices of others, it is risky to attempt to apply them directly to our individual situations. One man's food may be another's poison. What works for the man next door, in the same line of work, may not fit your situation at all.

The approach in this book will be to take general situations and to analyze out of them the essential ingredients which need to be made applicable to individual situations. We shall avoid simple formulas which often may bring about more harm than good if they are not used with care.

The Danger of Oversimplifying

There is a famous bit of advice for which Charles Schwab, president of Bethlehem Steel Company, was reported to have paid $25,000 to efficiency expert Ivy Lee. Schwab had complained that he was not getting things done. He wanted some advice that would help him become more productive.

Lee offered him this advice: "Write down the six most important tasks you have to do tomorrow and number them in order of their importance. Now, put this paper in your pocket and the first thing tomorrow morning look at item one and start working on it until it is finished. Then tackle item two in the same way; then item three, and so on. Do this until quitting time. Don't be concerned if you have only finished one or two. You'll be working on the most important ones. The others can wait. If you can't finish them all by this method, you couldn't have with any other method either; and without some system, you'd probably not even have decided which was the most important.

"Do this every working day. After you've convinced yourself of the value of this system, have your men try it. Try it as long as you wish, and then send me a check for what you think it is worth."

Now, I think this is pretty good advice but I cannot believe that Mr. Schwab followed the advice exclusively. For example, everyone has a host of small chores and responsibilities which must be cared for if they are not to build into big problems or cause difficulties for others, thereby generating counterforces. Mr. Schwab must have had his share of them and, being a man of action, he must have budgeted time for them.

There is a great temptation to seek the simple formula to solve our manifold problems. It is, however, a dangerous pursuit unless qualified by the full realization that *nothing is as simple as it seems*. When you propose to follow advice, including that given in this book, you must ask yourself how it fits your situation and how it does not.

You look for the core of the idea and then, you do not merely *adopt* it; rather, you *adapt* it to your own situation. There is only the slightest difference in the spelling of the two words but there is a world of difference in their implication.

The Elements of a Time Plan

There are two ways to use this book: one is to adapt to your own needs any of the ideas contained in the individual chapters. The other is to establish for yourself a total way of life; that is, to provide for the timely and speedy disposition of all of one's responsibilities. Put still another way, your goal should be to engineer your working goals and methods so that you obtain a maximum return from your use of time.

The chapters in this book group themselves into the following four categories:

1. *Self-organization:* Working on the right things, working under a plan that makes all activities "fit together," assigning priorities and time values for activities.

2. *Psychological factors:* Getting off to a good start, motivating oneself to be productive, matching physical and creative tasks to variations in your energy cycle, learning to concentrate.

3. *Operating skills:* Working through others, managing one's paper work, saving time in conversations and conferences, coping with interruptions, reading and writing rapidly, learning to do more than one thing at a time.

4. *Special conditions:* Using time effectively "on the road" or away from the office, working effectively at home.

II

Where Does Your Time Go?

If you are not getting as much done each day as you think you should, you will know it. The symptoms are quite common: people still to be seen, letters yet remaining to be answered, urgent projects not yet touched, work to be done at night after dinner, telephone calls to be made or returned, a sinking feeling of futility, and the despairing fatigue that is an accompaniment of frustration. You may have had a busy day but this is not the same as a productive one. All kinds of "busy work," interruptions, and unforeseeables might have stalled the accomplishment of the things you set out to do that day.

Then, too, you might have had little to do and yet your day might have come to an unfinished close. As C. Northcote Parkinson said, "Work expands so as to fill the time available for its completion."

Where does the time go?

You can't really tell when you are in the midst of it all. You need to get a perspective on yourself. Somehow you must detach yourself from your daily activities and see the patterns of time usage and abusage.

You can do this with the aid of some of the check lists contained in this chapter. You can use some of the suggested forms to keep count of the way you spend your time. If you prefer—and if you have someone available to do this—you can have someone else keep track of your time. This can be an enlightening experience. You will find out where you are spending too much time and where you are spending too little. You will discover the most important sources of interruption and how much of your time they take up. You will discern the patterns of your work and whether or not they make the most efficient use of your time.

Even as you immerse yourself in this self-analysis, you will begin taking benefits. Rolf Nordling, former president of the French National Management Committee, told of his experience with members of the management of his own company as they engaged in this self-analysis. ". . . Something rather strange happened. Starting on the third day of the analysis, the number of useless actions decreased. The majority of my associates then happily applied the conclusions they had reached. Since then, we have been disturbed much less by telephone calls, useless visits, etc., which have been replaced with prearranged visits."

Thus, the most important way to begin using time more effectively is to take stock of oneself—to see the patterns of one's own activities. There is nothing magical or difficult about it. Instead of looking at individual acts or instances, you add them up and see them in bunches or patterns.

The following, then, is the sequence of this chapter:

1. First we will set up a framework of the main purposes for which we use time. This will help us in analyzing how we spend our time. It will also be helpful in planning the use of our time.

2. We will look at critical slippage points. These will be check lists for self-inventory of the ways in which we lose time. They can be used introspectively without actually making a work count.

3. Several methods for recording the use of time will be presented. These will be for use by the individual himself or by others.

4. Finally, we will have some further thoughts on how to value time.

ELEMENTS OF TIME USAGE

Practically all jobs include the following elements of time usage:

1. Creative time.
2. Preparatory time.
3. Productive time.
4. Overhead time.

These elements are present whether you are an industrial executive, a government administrator, an outside salesman, an independent writer, an engineer, a doctor, or a lawyer. Only the proportions vary.

This is only one way of analyzing your time. You can set up almost any other categories or sets of categories. For example, you can analyze the distribution of time between inside contacts and outside contacts. These are so broad, however, that you will need to subdivide them further. Ernest Dale and Lyndall F. Urwick subdivided the time of executives into the three main categories of representation, initiation, and administration. Since administration accounted for 60 per cent of the total effort, it was further subdivided into forecasting, planning, organizing, direction, co-ordination, control, and communication.

Yet another way to analyze your time is to divide your activities into fixed, semiflexible, and variable. The fixed items are those about which you cannot do very much; the semiflexible ones are those over which you have some degree of control; while the variable ones are those over which you have fairly complete control. Personally, I think this analytical approach is more suited to work engineering and planning.

Creative Time

Over-all creative time is that which pertains to your own work planning. This includes long-range plans and short-term goals and targets. It means: "How will I set up this project to get it done in the shortest possible time with the least cost and effort?" It means: "Where should I put the greatest emphasis in my selling efforts? What territory should I cover next week? Shall I concentrate on certain kinds of prospects in preference to others? How many calls will I be able to make tomorrow and in what sequence?"

Creative time covers anything you do that relates to planning your work, organizing it, and evaluating your own performance. It is the thinking part of the job rather than the doing part. In some jobs thinking or creative activities occupy a greater percentage of time than in others. Generally speaking, the higher the level of responsibility, the greater will be the percentage of time spent creatively.

Some jobs are almost entirely creative. This brings up a rather tricky distinction. The creative engineer, writer, economist, or other analytical type should make a distinction between creative planning and evaluation of his tasks, as such, and the creative performance of his job. In other words, if you are engaged in writing, this is creative activity. If you plunge into writing without adequate planning, you are not likely to be as productive as you would be if you did a better job of planning, outlining, and scheduling before sitting down to dictate. Similarly, if you are an engineer, you are more likely to finish within the scheduled time if you first develop a project plan which would provide for early attention to long-lead items and intermediate accomplishment targets, among others.

Thus, while problem-solving and analytical activities are creative in themselves, they are not likely to be included within your estimate of creative time unless they relate to the planning and evaluation of your work tasks themselves.

There is a famous quip that starts with an apology for having written a long letter. The explanation given is that it would have been much shorter had the writer had more time. This might be the case for some people, but I think that for most of us the fault lies not in having more time but in not allocating some of the available time for a little preplanning before starting to write the actual letter. If this were the procedure to be followed, the shorter letter would take less time than the unrehearsed longer letter.

If you are not spending sufficient time on creative activities, the likelihood is that you are not operating under a tight performance schedule. The products of your work are liable to be loosely organized with much waste and slippage of effort. Like the long, rambling letter, you are likely to have much backtracking, rework, and discarding of false starts.

Preparatory Time

Preparatory time is the "setup" phase of work. It includes whatever you might have to do to arrange your work for a prompt start or for readiness to meet a visitor, client, or prospect. This would include having all of the facts you will need, organizing your briefcase or sample case, reading medical or technical reports beforehand, ordering and having on hand the necessary test equipment, providing oneself with adequate supplies and writing materials, etc.

In a sense, the very detailed scheduling or arranging of one's immediate activities constitutes a phase of preparation. Thus, to arrange one's schedule for the next day or to straighten out one's desk or organize one's correspondence is not so much creative effort as it is preparatory effort.

If you do not allow sufficient time for preparatory work, you will suffer by doing the necessary as part of the work task itself. A clear example of time loss is when you steal time from a presentation or sales talk in order to organize or arrange your materials. The prime time is with the prospect himself. Preparatory activity done in front of him makes a poor impression in addition to reducing the available time for constructive presentation.

If you do not prepare in advance, you may lose time in waiting for things to be brought to you to enable you to get on with the work. Apart from the dead loss of waiting, there is a stop-and-start loss that results from the breaking of continuity. As with insufficient creative time, failure to allow preparatory time inevitably results in rework, slippages, and waste effort.

Sometimes an entire effort can be lost through failure to spend just a few extra minutes in getting organized. There is the case of the attorney who worked far into the night to prepare for an important meeting the next day. When he settled himself in the airplane for his trip to a distant city, he found, to his consternation, that he had left his night's work behind.

Productive Time

Productive activities and the time you spend on them are the hard core of your work. They constitute the things which earn ʲor your employment.

ɹium time. The other categories of time
expected to enhance the return from
me. Thus, a salesman may not be able
or three hours a day, on the average,
ʲith business prospects. Whatever else
uld aim at getting as much advantage as
ɔontact hours.
ʲenient balance between productive time
on the other categories of time usage.
ɹarry them beyond a point-of-no-return.
you spend too little time on creative,
ad activities, your productive effective-
ɹiminished. The allocations of time for
stated. You must find your own ideal

Thus, if yoɹ   ɔntains a great deal of routine activity, the chances are you wɹɹ need to spend comparatively little time on creative work. The percentage of the latter will tend to increase as the tasks become more varied and original. Variety of any kind will tend to increase the percentages of creative and preparatory effort.

Productive time may be divided into regular productive activity and emergency or unscheduled productive activity. The problem here is that in spite of crises or unanticipated tasks, the regular work must be done. If you have too much nonregular activity, this may be evidence of a lack of planning on your part or on the part of others or it may point to the need for a realistic determination as to whether you can do both your regular work and the crisis work.

Many organizations relieve this problem by setting up trouble-shooting jobs to assure that the ordinary work continues without delay. Practically every job, however, has its share of unanticipated work demands. The ordinary solution is to estimate the time which should be allotted for such activities and then leave room for them in the weekly schedule. This will assure that when you spend time on them, you will still be able to get your regular work done.

Overhead Time

Overhead activities relate to your work as a whole as well as to your position in the organization and in the community. If they pertain to specific duties or tasks, they are more likely to be creative or preparatory activities. Overhead activities include your general correspondence and reports, your office housekeeping and paper work, personnel relations and public relations. Of course, any of these duties could also be your main line of work. If so, they would have overhead activity on top of them. For example, if you are in the public-relations business, you may be promoting the interests of your client or your employer but then, over and above that, you would be spending time on personal public relations to enhance your own effectiveness or to improve your business-getting capability.

It is very easy for public relations activities to get out of hand. The more successful you become or the higher you go on the management ladder, the more conspicuous a target you become for people who want your help. Not to mention the demands for money contributions, you'll be asked to participate in fund drives and a variety of civic-improvement activities. You will be asked to attend breakfasts, lunches, and dinners. If you hold a prominent position, you'll be asked to give talks. If these are not budgeted so that they do not exceed a fixed percentage of your time, they will eat into your very livelihood.

Nevertheless, many corporations expect their executives and other responsible personnel to participate in charity, civic, and other public-service projects. A few years ago *Management Methods* magazine published a survey of time given by executives to such activities. Of the executives who were queried, 93 per cent gave varying amounts of time. The number of hours per month varied as follows: under 10 hours, 60 per cent; 11 to 20 hours, 12 per cent; 21 to 30 hours, 20 per cent. Then, in answer to the question, "How many of these hours occurred during business time?", the respondents stated: under 5 hours, 52 per cent; 6 to 15 hours, 36 per cent; 16 to 25 hours, 7 per cent; and over 25 hours, 5 per cent. Thus, it can be seen that time spent on public-relations activities can become very consuming.

Nevertheless, in some types of work, participation in community affairs is an important part of business-getting. Certainly this is true of professional fields where ethical standards prohibit direct solicitation. It is also true for businessmen and salesmen, because their opportunities increase as their contacts with other men in the community are broadened.

If you are an independent operator, you can determine for yourself just how much of your time you are willing to devote to outside activities. You can spend a great deal of time and money and lose a great deal of income and yet feel the effort worthwhile. Thus, it cost Dr. Franklin W. Yeager almost $6000 to hold the post of president of the Texas Medical Association for a year. As reported by *Medical Economics* magazine, Dr. Yeager said it was worth it. "The benefits in years to come," he said, "and the honor of the post offset all the expenses."

For Dr. Yeager, this was a personal judgment based upon the values that he assigned to such activities. Another physician might not consider the effort anywhere near as rewarding. Moreover, his income level might be such that he could not afford to absorb the loss. It is a question for each person to decide in accordance with his own circumstances.

POINTS OF SLIPPAGE

The preceding discussion relates to patterns of time usage to assure that you have the right balance in your work program. As we saw, either too much or too little of a certain kind of activity could be wasteful.

Now we should look at some of the more specific ways in which we fail to make the best use of our time. I have grouped these under several headings, as follows:

1. Time lost in getting started.
2. Time lost through disorganization.
3. Time lost through diversion.
4. Time lost through excessive involvement.
5. Time lost in paper work.

Each reader must find in the check list and comments which follow those items which pertain particularly to his situation. I cannot overemphasize that each person's situation, compared with others within the same occupational grouping, calls for individual analysis and adaptation. Certainly, there will be even more pronounced differences between different kinds of work.

A production foreman finds that he is largely the agent of the situation. He has a line to keep moving, ever mindful of the costs of "down time" due to a failure in supply, maintenance, personnel, or breakdown of equipment. His work is characterized by a tremendous amount of stop-and-start activity. Thus, Charles R. Walker, Robert H. Guest, and Arthur N. Turner told, in *The Foremen on the Assembly Line,* of Foreman Pat, a typical supervisor, who took part in 387 separate observable incidents in a day, each lasting from a fraction of a minute to several minutes. It would be unfair to label all these interactions, whether from other section foremen, from his superiors, or from his employees, as being interruptions. In his case they are characteristic of his job, so he must plan around them, his goal being to assure that he allows sufficient time, without interruption except for crises, for other activities.

A typical salesman builds his work schedule around his calls. These are his actual encounters with his customers or sales prospects. As we have already noted and will see in other parts of this book, a surprisingly small part of the salesman's day is actually spent in direct contact with the customer. Of course, we are talking here of the outside salesman rather than the retail store clerk. The salesman, then, will be looking for opportunities to increase the amount of call time available to him without doing so at the expense of his creative and preparatory work. He will look for evidences of wasteful travel and inefficient utilization of his time between calls. Since a great deal of the time may be spent waiting to see his prospects, he will be alert to suggestions for recapturing some of this time and putting it to productive use.

A physician has an entirely different problem in that his clients come to see him unless they have emergencies at home or in the hospital. One of the physician's problems is to train his patients to respect his time by being prompt for their appointments and by not engaging in unnecessary conversation.

Because the physician earns his money from his use of his professional capabilities, any time spent in subprofessional work or in clerical work detracts from his earning capability. Hence, the typical physician with a full practice finds himself increasingly preoccupied with efforts to have his subprofessional and secretarial aides take over as much as possible of his nonprofessional duties.

The typical executive has many of the problems of the physician in that he is pressed by people who wish to see him or talk to him over the telephone. He also finds that he must make effective use of the techniques of delegation. Unlike the physician, he has certain longer-range work programs which he is always trying to accomplish. While people are important to him also, he must keep his contacts with them under "budgetary" control so that he can get other work done. Because he is a veritable communications center, he will be interested in techniques for improving his skills in written and oral communication so that he will be able to read and write more in less time and make more judicious use of conference time.

The creative worker, whether he be a writer, a researcher, a creative engineer, or an economist, is preoccupied less with people than with information. Much of his time goes into the organization of his work. He can save a great deal of time by arranging to have information come to him rather than to have to go out after it. He learns that it is important to become skilled in rapid reading and writing. It is important that he learn how deeply to go into subject matter, especially to avoid going beyond a point of no return. For him, it is important to master the art of concentration.

We see, then, that while the elements of effective time usage are common to practically all kinds of work, the specific emphases and applicabilities will vary with individual jobs and personalities.

Time Lost in Getting Started

Do you:
      rise early or late?
      linger in bed before rising?
      prepare the night before?

read the paper in the morning?

linger long over an extra cigarette or coffee at breakfast?

The early hours are the most precious for people who think. They are the hours when, for most people, the mind is clearest and energies are at their best. This premium time should be used for activities which will yield a comparable return.

Activities which do not require use of critical or creative faculties should be performed the night before or deferred until later in the day. A cursory reading of headlines and stock-market reports should hold you until the evening.

The moments spent in dalliance, lingering, and climbing off the morning cloud, can add up to fifteen minutes, thirty minutes, or a full hour, depending on your personal habits.

Now that we have you out of the house and on your way to start work, do you:

stop off to socialize before you reach your desk?

take your morning coffee before starting?

do personal work before doing your livelihood work?

read newspapers, trade journals, unimportant reports, and information documents the first thing?

The wastage here divides into two categories: (1) the cumulative time lost from the best part of the day through dalliance and (2) the uneconomical use of time on chores which do not require the best of your morning mind.

As you move through the day you will be picking up new problems and activities, each of which calls for a fresh start. Do you:

socialize between tasks?

start slowly because of a lack of interest?

procrastinate because of other interests or a lack of motivation?

bumble into a task without first thinking it through, thereby wasting effort through re-do?

Losing Time through Disorganization

Do you personally:

handle too many *different kinds of duties?*

sell too many *different types of merchandise or service?*

cover too many *different kinds of work problems or client problems?*

supervise too many *people who bring a variety of problems* to you?

The central idea here is that it is much easier to do more of the same than to readjust to entirely different problem situations. The creative and preparatory activity that goes into a single line of effort can be reused or adapted for more of the same. As you diversify, you do so at the risk of using a disproportionate amount of your time in creative, preparatory, and overhead activities. Moreover, you subject yourself to a greater mental and physical strain.

There is some fine balance point between diversity and complexity on the one hand and utter simplicity on the other. This, however, is something to be evaluated by each person in the light of his own situation and his own capabilities. If, however, you feel that you are holding on to too many strings simultaneously or that you are wearing yourself out by readjusting to too many different kinds of challenges, it is a signal that you need to do something to simplify your mode of operation. At the very least you may need to group or cluster your activities.

Are you:

spending time on the right problems?

working on things that contribute to your work goals?

trying to sell to the right prospects? serving the right kind of clientele?

Have you "qualified" the things you do, before you do them, to make sure they are worthwhile? Do they fit in with your work goals? Is the effort likely to be worthwhile? The word *worthwhile* is the key criterion.

Assuming you *are* working on things of importance, do you:

assign priorities to your tasks in accordance with their importance?

allocate time to all your responsibilities to assure that your productive time is in balance with and supported by creative, preparatory, and overhead activities?

schedule the best time to do work to assure that priorities are met and that you make the best use of your energies?

anticipate possible crises and the methods for handling them?

allow enough time in your schedule for the average amount of unanticipated urgencies, crises, and unscheduled time demands?

do you provide for productive continuity in your work at your desk by protecting yourself against interruptions?

These questions pertain to the planning of your work and to the order and sequence in which you do things. If you take things as they come, without fitting them into an over-all time budget and schedule, you will work harder than would be the case with a little planning. You will otherwise lose time and return-for-effort as a result of the inevitable disorder and disproportion in your activities.

An important aspect of work planning is to find ways of getting more work done through improved methods and the assistance of others. Do you:

delegate to others—if you have such help—those tasks which they can do in support of your more important or more profitable activities?

use modern tools and facilities which yield greater outputs in the same period of time?

Time Lost through Diversion

During your *important production* hours, do you:
do personal shopping?
make stock-market analyses?
pay personal bills and otherwise manage personal finances?
indulge personal hobbies?
socialize personally or by telephone?
engage in professional and personal improvement activities?

That these personal diversions lose time may be obvious, but not so obvious may be the cumulative amount of time lost as well as the brutal sacrifice of prime working time.

Equally important are the slippages in your use of time through unnecessary business conversation. Do you:
attend unnecessary (for you) conferences and meetings?
spend too much of your time with visitors?
make or receive too many telephone calls?

These time-eaters can consume more of your productive time

than you might imagine. One way to control them is to budget your time for the priorities. Another is to screen them ruthlessly, applying standards of value.

People on the move, especially outside salesmen, have a different problem. Instead of being the recipients of pressure (other than from the sales manager!), they seek time with others and, in so doing, they are subject to a variety of time slippages. If you are in this category, do you:

> arrange your travel schedule to cover as much territory as possible?

> plan your engagements ahead, as much as practicable, to assure actual contact with your prospects?

> have alternative tasks to do while waiting?

> have alternative calls to make in event of a broken interview?

Time Lost through Excessive Involvement

Although spending excessive time with visitors or in conferences or on the telephone can be regarded as diversion of effort, these should also be considered from the standpoint of going beyond the point of return.

Do you:

> bring an interview or conference to a close when further talk seems fruitless?

> "sample" the sellability of a prospect to avoid wasting time on an unlikely situation?

> dig too deeply into factual research, in pursuit of details, after having already obtained the key important facts?

> work too long on a problem so that you obtain decreasing return from your efforts?

In each of these situations you might think of some case where the further effort *did* yield a good return. Thus, every salesman has one or more anecdotes about the unlikely prospect who proved out with a tremendous order. Did you ever hear the story of the man in rough bluejeans who paid greenbacks cash for a Cadillac after receiving a frowning and skeptical reception? If you are inclined to use this "you-never-know" philosophy, consider these two points: (1) in general, you'll be ahead if you work on the law of averages rather than on sweepstakes possibilities; (2) make generous use of the sampling technique to avoid deep involvement in fruitless situations.

Time Lost in Paper Work

The paper-work dragon grows ever larger in modern business. You must ever be alert to economies in reading, writing, record-keeping, and reporting, not merely to get ahead but to keep abreast of your situation.

In reading, do you:

> screen your reading materials, to weed out unnecessary or unproductive matter?

> skim the surface of the reading matter for the main ideas, pausing to read selectively?

> practice rapid-reading techniques to improve both speed and comprehension?

Few of us can ever hope to read as much as we'd like. Many of us don't like to read at all. Whether you want to cover more in the same time or do the minimum in less time, the same techniques are applicable.

To get more writing done in the time available, do you:

> make simple outlines for letters, memoranda, and reports; more detailed outlines for major writing tasks?

> use a simple, direct style of communication, getting right to the point?

> make use of form letters, form paragraphs, and other "boiler-plates" for your routine correspondence?

People who object to outlining may say, "I'm too impatient; I must jump right in." With a little practice and a stop watch you may find that the preliminary analysis of what you want to say will give you a shorter and better product in less time.

In your procedural paper work, do you:

> eliminate work done out of habit, which no longer serves any useful purpose?

> streamline paper work, cutting out nonessentials?

> combine forms and records, making one paper serve more than one purpose?

> avoid record-keeping in anticipation of highly unlikely circumstances?

HOW TO COUNT TIME

In the series of check lists through which you have just gone, you should have found some or many ideas for self-improvement, but this in itself may not tell you truly how well you spend your time. Until you *actually take count* of where your time goes and for what and with whom, you are likely to underestimate or even overlook important slippage points in your use of time. In addition to pinpointing specific areas for self-improvement, you should take a reading of the total stream of activity in which you are at the center.

Some rather simple techniques can be used to keep track of time usage. We'll discuss these, as well as some slightly more advanced sampling and analysis methods. Before getting into the procedural aspects we first should cover certain problems of self-consciousness on your part and how they might affect results.

Ideally, you should have some outside means of monitoring your every working hour and minute and what you do and with whom. Since this is not feasible, you must either keep a record of your own activities or have someone else do it for you. In either case this creates an awareness on your part of your being observed. This awareness brings about some measure of adaptive behavior. In other words, as you begin taking stock of yourself or know that others are, you do things to improve your performance so that you do not obtain a true reading of how you operate under typical conditions without being observed. Personally, I don't think this matters too much. Whatever improvements you make are that much to the good, but you are still likely to overlook some of the most important areas of which you may not even have been conscious until you see the results of the survey and analysis.

Commenting on his experiences with the survey of executive use of time, Sune Carlson said: ". . . Indeed, even had the executives wanted to change their behaviour, they did not have much chance to do so. The conduct of their working day is determined only to a small extent by themselves, and it is difficult to change it without making considerable alterations in the organizational structure of which they are a part. . . . I always thought of a chief executive as the conductor of an orchestra, standing aloof on his platform. Now I am in some respects inclined to see him as the puppet in a puppet-show with hundreds of people pulling the strings and forcing him to act in one way or another."*

In effect, then, if you are a busy person, you will not have time to become overly conscious of yourself. Quite apart from this consideration, since you are a busy person you will want to make use of existing records and observational techniques without adding to them, whenever possible.

The Tools of Time-counting

The two basic types of recording forms may be called "chips" and "logs." The chip is an individual notation slip or card on which you make all of your entries for a single recorded incident. Later, all of the chips are collated in whatever sequence or combination may be desired. The advantage of the chip is its sheer simplicity, because you can carry a supply of slips or cards wherever you go and pull another one for a notation each time you want to make a record. This may be much more convenient for you than filling in a bigger composite form.

The log is a ruled form having a number of column headings across the top of the sheet under which individual entries are made. Each incident is recorded as a single line of entries. You can have one comprehensive log designed to obtain all the information about every use of your time or you can have a basic work log supported by a series of subsidiary logs such as a telephone log, visitor log, interruption log, etc. You can, if you prefer, have special-purpose logs, such as these or any others, in order to study one phase of your activity at a time.

The third basic paper-work tool in studying your time is a recap form on which to enter consolidated totals on a week-by-week basis as well as on a total-period-of-study basis.

Your analyses can be made, of course, on ordinary blank stationery.

The accompanying illustrations show a variety of analyses

* *Executive Behaviour* (Stockholm: C. A. Strömberg Aktiebolag, 1951), p. 52.

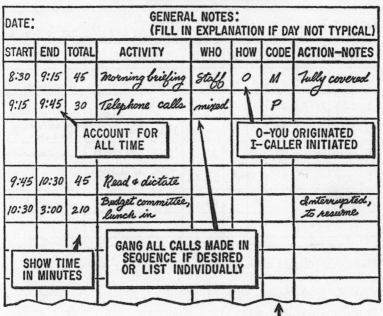

TIME INVENTORY FOR GENERAL USE

DATE:			GENERAL NOTES: (FILL IN EXPLANATION IF DAY NOT TYPICAL)				
START	END	TOTAL	ACTIVITY	WHO	HOW	CODE	ACTION—NOTES
8:30	9:15	45	Morning briefing	Staff	O	M	Fully covered
9:15	9:45	30	Telephone calls	mixed		P	
9:45	10:30	45	Read & dictate				
10:30	3:00	210	Budget committee, lunch in				Interrupted, to resume

ACCOUNT FOR ALL TIME

O—YOU ORIGINATED
I—CALLER INITIATED

SHOW TIME IN MINUTES

GANG ALL CALLS MADE IN SEQUENCE IF DESIRED OR LIST INDIVIDUALLY

SUGGESTED CODE:
C—INDIVIDUAL DISCUSSION OR CONFERENCE
D—READING & DICTATING CORRESPONDENCE
R—READING & STUDYING
M MEETING
P—TELEPHONE CALL
S—SIGNING CORRESPONDENCE
NOTE: VARY TO SUIT OWN SITUATION

Suggested form to account for all your time use. Make your own code to suit your own work situation. Use only during a typical work period. Analysis is made by adding time totals under each code letter.

forms which you can use or, if you prefer, you can make your own.

Whenever possible, existing reports and records should be used —even simple desk calendars and appointment sheets.

An interesting account was given to *The American Salesman* by William B. Pierce, vice president for sales of the Allegheny

TELEPHONE (OR VISITOR) LOG

	START	END	TOTAL	IN	OUT	WHO	PURPOSE	COMMENTS
DATE: *Monday, Aug. 17*						NOTES: (MENTION ANY UNUSUAL ACTIVITY)		
1	8:50	8:55	5	✓		Shaw	Asked for meeting	Arranged
2	8:55	8:57	2		✓	Hendrick	Notified re mtg.	
3	9:30	10:15	45	✓		Roman	Who stuck John!	5 minutes would have done it
4	10:20	10:35	15	✓		Albert	Boss: chit chat	unavoidable
5	10:47	10:50	3		✓	Denton	Told to arrange review	
6	11:07	11:07	–	✓		Rapp	unspecified	call back
7								

Use to supplement overall time analysis or for selective analysis.

Ludlum Steel Corporation. Mr. Pierce outlined a "scientific way to sell more in the same time" which was used by his company. Three forms are used: a customer-evaluation form, a time-reporting form, and a quarterly summary. In order to compare amount of time spent in relation to customer volume, at least once a year the salesmen fill out the evaluation form. They group their customers in three categories of buying volume while a fourth group includes prospects and their potential buying power. For each account, the salesmen enter the estimated number of calls and total contact time expended. Another form is used to report how the total amount of time available to the salesmen is spent. Worktime is divided into fifteen-minute units. The salesmen enter the names of the companies and individuals visited and the products which were discussed. The quarterly form summarizes the total contact time by product and type and size of user. From an analysis of this form the salesman can recapitulate his calls per day, the amount of time spent on the average for each call, how much business resulted from each call on the average, and the relationship between selling and non-selling time. He can also make additional analyses from the recorded data.

OUTSIDE SALESMAN'S TIME FINDER

DATE: *Monday, Aug. 17*				
START	END	TOTAL	WHO—WHAT—WHERE—NOTES	CODE
7:50	8:30	40	En route to Kroger Co.	T
8:30	8:50	20	Wait for R. K. Allison, busy	W
8:50	9:30	40	Present new combination special. Get reaction to new products	S
9:30	9:40	10	Call ahead to Simpson to confirm delayed schedule	P
9:40	10:00	20	En route to Simpson	T
10:00	10:30	30	New special. Market reaction	S
10:30	12:00	90	Drive to Frederick, Md.	T
12:00	12:45	45	Lunch	D
12:45	1:00	15	Walk to McAllister's	T
1:00	2:00	60	Present full line	S

NOTE: Each job has its own time-using elements. Outside salesman can make time notes using code such as this: *T*—Travel; *S*—Sell; *W*—Wait; *P*—Telephone; *D*—Dine; *X*—Personal. This form can fit on easily pocketable 4 x 6″ card. Analysis would be made of time totals under each code letter. Effort would be made to reduce time taken on non-selling activities where greatest slippage is found.

The Representative Study Period

In conducting the study you need to select a representative period. This should be as typical as possible of the average condition of work throughout the year. Hence, you would want to avoid any unusual periods of work concentration or of seasonal or cyclical variations. Obviously, if a man is in a series of all-day sales meetings which will be going on for a full week, any survey conducted that week will not produce any helpful information. Similarly, the study should not be conducted at any time when there is any unusual or heavily concentrated activity which is not typical.

The length of the study is another matter. I have seen recommendations that the study should be conducted for a period of at least twelve weeks. Undoubtedly this would provide a very sound basis for analysis, but one might question whether the records would be kept faithfully for that long period of time, and if they were to be kept, the costs would then be questionable.

For all practical purposes, a maximum of four weeks should be sufficient. In his study of executives Sune Carlson, who recommended not more than four weeks, found a tendency for executive recording to trail off after one or two weeks. Of course, if all or most of the recording is done by someone else, such as a secretary who is given the assignment to do this as part of her regular duties, you could conduct a survey for as long a period as you desire. I assume, however, that most time records will be kept directly by the person himself.

Self-Analysis Techniques

When the individual keeps his own records, they should be designed as simply as possible so as not to add to his existing time burdens as well as to assure that he will keep them fully and accurately. Naturally, you can control this to a maximum extent with employees whose time may be subject to detailed control, but with independent individuals who are not subject to anyone's control or who occupy senior posts in an organization, more compelling incentives are needed. Harold Lasswell, professor of law at Yale University and noted political scientist, said, "If more 'practical' men are to make better records, two requirements must be met. First, a question must be asked that seems to them worth answering. Second, a procedure must be available that does not interfere with this work."

A very simple approach for record-keeping by an individual is to concentrate on a few items at a time—even one item at a time. Thus, Lasswell reported on a government bureau chief who wanted to know the source of all the pressures for his time. In his pocket he kept a single four- by six-inch card with the letters *IN* in the upper left corner and *EX* in the upper right corner. Under the one he would list each personal contact involving someone internally. Under the other he would list each external contact. Each day he would begin using another card. He found that nine out of ten of his contacts were internal. This brought him to a sharp realization that he was not spending enough of his time on outside activities. The same nine-out-of-ten findings were made by the executive secretary of a trade association, so he also changed his work mix for obvious reasons. On the other hand, a college president had more than half of his entries under the *EX* column with the remainder concentrated on the board of trustees and one dean. This had been provoking the resentment of the rest of the faculty. With the insight afforded him by this analysis the president rearranged his affairs so that he thereafter spent more of his time with more members of his faculty.

Following are several suggestions pertaining to the making of time entries:

1. Carry your entry cards or chart with you at all times.

2. If you are using a travel diary, expense diary, call report, or pocket or desk calendar, devise a system of notations for entry on these. Be sure to take the diary or report form with you on your trips.

3. Make your notations immediately after each incident. If you do not, you are bound to forget many details and your record will be of limited value, if any.

4. Make your entries sufficiently specific, while keeping them short, so that you will recall just what they mean if you want to refresh your memory weeks or months afterward.

5. Record the smallest interruptions in your time. These are very important because they interrupt your continuity of thought and activity.

6. Subdivide long periods of time on extended tasks so that you will be able to report on the specific kinds of work in which you are engaged. For example: creative or preparatory work, the specific productive work, reading, writing correspondence, reading and signing, participation in conferences, telephone conversations, etc.

Use of an Observer

In view of the cost—and for other obvious reasons—a close observer would be used to record and analyze the time of an individual only when the individual is a very busy and important person, particularly if he functions at a top level of organization. The observer would be used when the individual is so busy that his time cannot be diverted into self-analysis. Another justification is when a deeper insight is needed into the individual's operations than can be provided by simple self-analysis.

The most convenient approach, at least in keeping the records, is to use a secretary. In his own survey of executives Sune Carlson reported that the secretary was used in addition to personal assistants, the telephone-exchange operator, and even porters in order to record the goings and comings of executives as well as their activities in the office itself. The secretary, naturally, is the one who is supposed to know most about her superior's activities. It should not require very much more work on her part to make additional notes for survey purposes. Moreover, if she has a smooth working relationship, she can move in and out of his office without seeming to intrude as she finds out what is going on. She can also ascertain whatever additional information she needs with a minimum number of questions.

When a Boswellian approach is used, in which the observer practically lives with his subject, you introduce the added complication referred to above of a personality who might affect the conduct of activities. If he is present at all times, he can make the subject and his visitors very conscious of themselves.

In conducting a survey of the time of an administrator in the U. S. Department of Agriculture, the analyst was authorized to examine every detail of the business of the executive by reading his daily mail, listening to telephone conversations, and sitting in on interviews and staff conferences, etc. He filled out a separate form for each contact and at the end of each day obtained evaluations by the executive of the time spent on each contact. A form was attached by the secretary to each piece of incoming mail, and evaluations were made by the executive as he considered the letters. The analyst detached the sheets from the mail when it reached him on its way out of the office, and added other descriptions to the forms in order to have complete information on these mail contacts.

The following results were attributed to the survey and the discussion which followed it:

"1. Analysis of time expended enabled the administrator to adjust his working schedule to spend more time on the more important matters.

"2. The administrator appointed assistants to act as his representatives on committees and wherever else possible. These steps cut down immediately demands upon the administrator's time and paved the way for future conservation of time by increasing the prestige of the assistants in departmental circles.

"3. The administrator's secretary exerted a greater effort to send callers to persons other than the administrator for information and advice. (A guide was prepared for this purpose listing names and the subject-matter each individual could best handle.)

"4. The administrator reduced interview time by getting to the 'roots of business at hand as quickly as possible' and terminating interviews as soon as possible in a genial yet business-like manner.

"5. The secretary followed a closer sifting process in deciding what written material should be brought to her chief's attention.

"6. Greater authority was delegated to assistants. Authority was delegated for final approval of most personnel actions, travel authorizations, reports, and minor purchases to assistants.

"7. Staff conferences were directed toward a better understanding of policies so that assistants could make more decisions independent of the administrator and in line with their own definite responsibility.

"8. The administrator's morale improved and his work efforts were more effectively applied."

Group Time Analyses

Work-sampling techniques have been employed to assist entire categories of professional and administrative employees to understand, from their own records, how they are using their time. This is, of course, the kind of study that ordinarily would be conducted by a member of a methods-analysis or efficiency-engineering staff. There is some danger, however, in using such techniques with professional and administrative personnel because of the implication that they are being treated in much the same way as office clerical workers and production employees in the labor grades.

MORE ON HOW TO VALUE TIME

In conducting your analyses you may want to assign dollar values to time lost or to time spent on various activities. If you are in a service division or in a general overhead or administrative position in which you are not directly producing income, the task is quite simple because all you need do is divide the total number of work hours into the weekly, monthly, or annual rate of pay in order to find an actual hourly rate to charge against specific activities. If this is your situation, then this part of the chapter is not applicable to your own position. In fact, it is aimed mostly at people who sell their services in exchange for fees or who earn commissions, such as outside salesmen.

Value of Productive Time

To find your productive time, keep track of the total number of hours spent over a period of time on actual selling of service or in direct contact with the customer and divide these hours into your total earnings for a corresponding period of time. This gives you the amount which you earn, on the average, per hour. Then, each hour expended in actual productive activity must earn that amount or, if it earns less, it must be made up by higher earnings in other hours.

It is well known, for example, that outside salesmen may average from two to four hours a day in actual contact with their customers. One survey of farm chemical salesmen showed a range of two and one-half to three hours of actual contact, based upon a survey of 3375 salesmen. Other surveys have shown more or less time on the average. W. Guy Laird, general sales manager of the Maybury Shoe Company, made some computations based upon an average of four hours a day of actual selling time, while admitting that this was a little high. For a fifty-week year, this would mean 1000 hours of actual selling. With a yearly salary of $10,000, the salesmen would then have to produce an average of $10 for each hour of selling time.

The $10 yardstick would then be related to both selling time and *certain* aspects of nonselling time. Assuming that the salesman could reduce his creative, preparatory, and overhead activities to the very minimum, any time not spent in either these activities or in direct selling would constitute additional time available for selling. It would be fair then to assign a potential value of $10 an hour to most of the wasted time.

To dramatize the cost of this wasted time, Laird prepared this table, as published in *The American Salesman:*

THE HIGH COST OF A MISSING MINUTE

To show what those precious four hours of selling time per day are made of, this table gives the worth to you (it's even more to your company) of each 60-second interval. If your annual earnings are:

$6000,	every minute is worth				$.10, or a newspaper
$8000,	"	"	"	"	$.13, or a cigar
$10,000,	"	"	"	"	$.17, or a bus ride
$12,000,	"	"	"	"	$.20, or two phone calls
$15,000,	"	"	"	"	$.25, or a loaf of bread
$20,000,	"	"	"	"	$.33, or a gallon of good gas
$25,000,	"	"	"	"	$.42, or a half-dozen eggs

Laird also listed a number of time-consuming activities that could be done at other times, together with a bill for each. The "reader's estimate" is your estimate of your own time loss and its cost.

"1. Office time: Visiting, talking shop, doing paper work that could be done at home, and generally acting like a 'big shot.' *Thirty minutes a day or $5.* *Reader's estimate:* —————————.

"2. Personal phone calls: They cost money when made during working hours.

Ten minutes a day or $1.66.
Reader's estimate: —————————.

"3. Personal shopping: Under this heading come errands run for the wife.
Ten minutes a day or $1.66.
Reader's estimate: —————————.

"4. Paying personal bills: Or going to the bank during working hours. How about paying bills and banking by mail?
Ten minutes a day or $1.66.
Reader's estimate: —————————.

"5. Coffee break: Here's one of those exorbitant prices quoted at the beginning of the article.
A minimum of fifteen minutes a day or $2.50.
Reader's estimate: —————————.

"6. Car servicing: It pays to have it done at night instead of during the day.
About 50 minutes a week or ten a day or $1.66.
Reader's estimate: —————————.

"7. Shoe shines: Probably about three a week; many salesmen shine their own shoes at home or have them done on the way home after business hours.
Fifteen minutes or $2.50 three times a week.
Reader's estimate: —————————.

"8. Hair cuts: Every ten days to two weeks—about one hour including the trip to the barber shop. How about Saturdays for this?
Five minutes a day or 85¢.
Reader's estimate: —————————.

"9. Haphazard telephoning: Looking up each number at the time called instead of listing in a notebook all the numbers to be called during the day. Forgetting to keep plenty of dimes on hand.
Ten minutes a day or $1.66.
Reader's estimate: —————————.

"10. Small talk: Doing too much visiting with customers instead of getting into the sales story fast. Some men who make calls of one hour's duration have found they can easily cut them to 50 minutes. Salesmen who make 30-minute calls might try whittling them to 25 minutes.
About 40 minutes or $6.66.
Reader's estimate: —————————.

"11. Sloppy presentations: By rehearsing the presentation at night, a salesman can cut out the wasted words and the say-nothing sentences. Again, he'd find his calls getting shorter.
Ten minutes a day or $1.66.
Reader's estimate: ————————.

"12. Lunch time: This is a hard one to figure. Doctors say it's not healthy to be on the go every noon hour. But when a salesman doesn't have a date, he can occasionally make a long jump on the road around noon, stopping to relax in a diner for a short time.
Ten minutes a day or $1.66.
Reader's estimate: ————————.

Laird's recap on time saved in this array adds up to 175 minutes or more than 2¾ hours a week. Acknowledging that not every salesman can *boast* of this record and that these savings may not be potentially possible for each, he singled out for particular attention Item 10, small talk; Item 12, lunch time; and Item 5, the coffee break. He estimated that these would yield about $10 a day, $50 a week, or $2500 a year in added potential earnings.

Value of Indirect Time

Because we put the burden of direct value on productive time, this does not mean that creative, preparatory, or overhead time has no value. To evaluate them you need other criteria. They must be measured in terms of their contribution to direct effort. Perhaps it is easier to evaluate them from a negative stand-point. That is, what would be the consequences of a failure to support direct time? How much of a decrease would there be in the effectiveness with which you use your direct time if you try to increase it at the expense of essential indirect time?

Value of Time Remaining

One interesting way to value time is in terms of the amount of time remaining to you to get things done. You rarely think of this when you are a very young person, but as you get older you start thinking of the probable number of years remaining to you in which you can conduct an active life. Then you may start budgeting those years so as to get as much done as possible in them. A political official holding some office who knows the expiration of his term will also budget his activities in the light of time remaining. Probably many a reluctant bachelor has planned his activities in terms of time remaining as he approached the day of the marriage vow!

This is of very practical importance in the planning of project time when you know that you must meet a fixed, irreconcilable deadline. You have so much to do and as you approach the deadline you have less and less time in which to get it done. This could be minutes, hours, days, weeks, months, or years, depending upon the magnitude of the project. There may be no second bite at the apple. You must produce or you are in default.

Instead of assigning a monetary value, the criterion is one of remaining opportunity. When you look at the situation in this light, it acts as a powerful incentive to make the best use of every possible moment of time remaining.

SUMMARY

Time moves forward regardless of how we use it. The challenge for you is to obtain the greatest return on your use of time through the manner in which you divide your effort and the sequence in which you do things. Most effort can be assigned to one of these categories: creative work, preparatory work, productive work, and overhead work. All these must strike a balance with each other or productivity will suffer. If productive hours must be increased, this should be accomplished through more efficient accomplishment of indirect activities and through elimination of time slippages in all activities.

It is easy enough for any of us to find opportunities for self-improvement merely through running down check lists of difficult points of time slippage. This, in itself, may not give us a true picture of our total use of time inasmuch as most of us are prone to estimate poorly on how we ourselves use time. For a more accurate estimate, you need to find some means of detaching your observational self from your operating self. One way to do this is to keep certain simple operating records. Another is to have someone observe and record your activities. The more likely procedure for most of us will be to do our own recording.

Finally, each of us needs a yardstick with which to value his utilization of time. This may be one's hourly earnings with a factor for overhead. For people who make their living through selling products or services, the criterion would be average earnings for each productive hour and the objective would be to put as many recovered hours as possible into earning hours.

III

The First Rule: Organize Yourself

The most difficult part of organizing oneself is that tricky bit which calls for you to jump out of your skin and see yourself as you are. While looking for a way in which to explain this, I came across an Air Force training outline subtitled "How to Get the Work Out."* In it appeared this interesting case example:

YOU CAN'T WASTE A SECOND

Mr. Carl was a hard-working supervisor. He had enough personnel in his organization to accomplish the workload. In spite of this, his work was rarely done on time. One day, Carl excused himself from the chief's staff meeting stating that he just had to get back to the job. The chief decided to spend the next morning with him.

Next morning when the chief arrived, Carl was talking on the phone, and at the same time, signing some forms. He interrupted the phone conversation to greet the chief and, still holding the phone, called to the secretary: "Mary, these forms are signed."

Carl, talking again on the same phone call, thrust the signed

* *Management Course for Air Force Supervisors*, Conference Outline 10, How to Plan Work, Part 3. "How to Get the Work Out," for sale by the Superintendent of Documents, Washington 25, D.C., twenty-five cents.

forms toward Mary as she entered. His movement pushed a disorderly pile of papers off the corner of his desk. The papers were scattered on the floor by a breeze from an open window and Mary started picking them up. Carl shouted: "I'll think about it and call you back, Oliver." Then said to Mary: "Don't pick them up, you'll just mix them worse." He scooped up a paper that was on his desk and handed it to the chief. "There's Don Pitt's idea of how to save about half the time we spend on processing. Wish we had time to try it out. What do you think of it?"

Mary came to Carl's desk.

"Bill Evans wants to know if he can start on that priority job right now," said Mary. "Tell him to wait," said Carl. "I haven't time to finish training him, and I just can't trust him to start a job that important without checking it myself."

While Carl was picking up and sorting the papers, Mary brought in some forms. "Mr. Carl, you just signed those on the line for the major's signature, so I typed them over."

"Too much to do," muttered Carl, glancing at the chief as he signed. "If you sign them now I'll take them to the major right away," said Mary, reaching.

"I'll take them," said Carl. "The major might want to ask me about them."

Carl explained to the chief: "Don and Bob can't do a thing till I run these through. I'll be right back." He dashed out. In a minute he stuck his head in the door. "I forgot to tell you, Mary, don't type that report till I read it. We can get the due date backed up a day. See if the chief wants some coffee. I won't have time for any."

And he dashed away again, but before he went he said to the chief: "No use Mary typing that report twice. Anybody as busy as I am knows you can't waste a second."

If you were Carl, you might not see the errors you were committing, but being an outside observer you can readily see the utter disorganization of his methods, the lack of planning, the failure to delegate, and the addiction to minutiae. If you were Carl's chief, you undoubtedly would advise him to "straighten up and fly right!"

When it comes to evaluating yourself, however, the chances are you do not see things quite so clearly. *There are very few of us, however, who cannot make some time-saving improvement in our work methods.* Why is this so generally true? The most important reason is that we are creatures of habit; we tend to keep on doing things the same way even though conditions have changed. Another reason for wasteful work organization is that your job content might have grown "like Topsy" without ever really having been planned or rationalized. A third source of error in your work mix or priorities is that you may be doing things you like to do or that others press you to do rather than those you should do.

Other personal work problems include: performing tasks no longer necessary; doing things that others could do more efficiently or economically; doing things in the wrong sequence; working with the wrong people; performing unnecessary steps in a task; and failing to use more modern methods and equipment.

Regardless of the kind of work you do, you may find some or all of these faults present. Work simplification and methods improvement in the office have been regarded as techniques used to introduce economies and efficiencies into clerical work. Both the need and the method, however, have applicability even at the very highest levels. Former Secretary of State Dean Acheson said:

"It is hard to get reliable data on the matters which now occupy the time of 'the very highest echelon.' Of course, they vary with the men involved, their physical and mental vitality, their powers of concentration, their resources of knowledge, experience and wisdom. Their tasks are difficult ones. This cannot be altered. Our present question is: is their time well spent? If not, is the remedy 'reorganization in the very highest echelon?'"

While mindful of the total pressures upon the time of high personages, Mr. Acheson continued:

"No one knows better than I that the published appointment list of the President or a Cabinet officer is only that one-tenth of the iceberg which appears above water. But even a short study of the sample given makes two points clear: first, at least half the appointments are wholly unnecessary; and, second, those which are necessary are neither very time-consuming nor exhausting."*

So we have moved from the clerical level to the highest and we have found the preoccupation with one's work organization ever present. Were we to direct a telescope toward people in

* "Thoughts about Thoughts in High Places," New York *Times Magazine*, October 11, 1959.

other kinds of work, such as doctors, lawyers, writers, and outside salesmen, among others, as we shall do later, we would find elements of the problem in common.

The important thing is that almost anyone can do something about these problems, working them out silently, without outside help. He can inventory his tasks, evaluate them, and make basic improvements.

This effort should lead to a total work plan, rather than individual task improvements alone. The benefits of a work plan, faithfully followed, are these:

1. Working on worthwhile tasks.
2. Assigning priorities correctly.
3. Allocating correct proportions of time to different tasks.
4. Accomplishment of tasks within deadlines.
5. Reaching of quotas and goals.
6. Avoidance of waste effort.
7. Achievement of greater flexibility.
8. Elimination of tasks others should do.
9. Improvement of personal relationships resulting from improved output.

The aggregate effect should be to expend less energy getting the most important things done—or getting more done—in less time with more work satisfaction.

The results of such self-improvement might not be as good, in many cases, as would be the case if a management consultant were used. At least the cost would be absorbed and, not unimportant, one need not sacrifice his desire for privacy.

By asking yourself a few simple questions—mostly "why?"—you can become your own consultant. It would be wrong to suggest that you could achieve the same objectivity, but the question will enable you to obtain amazing insight into your personal operations, if you really desire this.

If you work for others, your duties and responsibilities might be spelled out in a position description. By mere inspection of it you can make a mental comparison between what is written down and what you know you are doing. If the position description is currently correct, you might recognize immediately the things on which you are not spending enough time, those on which you are spending too much time, and those which you are neglecting completely.

There is no substitute for a written record of how you actually spend your time. For this purpose, you can use the forms and techniques described in Chapter II, "Where Does Your Time Go?" Keeping a written record is essential because if you rely upon your memory you are bound to overlook many small elements.

Without being an expert on methods-improvement techniques, the very fact of your new self-consciousness will make you aware of opportunities for saving time and eliminating wasteful activities. On the whole you may be better off to refrain from changing anything until you have completed your self-inventory. A not-too-important reason for this is that you should really get for yourself as faithful a compilation as possible. That is, you ought to find out how really good or bad you are! A more important reason is that if you begin to preoccupy yourself with improvement during the period of inventory, you will be adding a time factor which, in itself, will affect the results of your inventory.

SHORT COURSE IN WORK PLANNING

Now that you have your working data, you need to refresh yourself as to your bases of comparison. These are the targets for which you are striving, whether they are project targets, service targets, or volume targets, depending upon the kind of work you do. Against these you will review all of the things you actually do in order to eliminate any that do not contribute to your work goals. The remainder you will want to simplify or improve.

Your Work Targets

Your work targets give you a clue to where you must put the emphasis and what you must omit or place in suspension.

A project target usually relates to some kind of developmental or creative activity. That is, by a certain date you must have assembled something, written a report or proposal or other lengthy document, or achieved some intermediate milestone in a work project. If you are on schedule, you can afford to be doing other things or even to take on a few additional ones. If you are behind schedule, you must look first to things that you can set aside until you catch up and then for ways of accelerating what you are doing, both through putting in more effort and through streamlining or simplifying your work methods.

In some forms of work, including those in which you serve a clientele, whether internal or external, your work load is not subject to your own control. People come to see you, they call for information, or they send you "cases" to be processed. Your objective, in this kind of work, is to eliminate unnecessary preliminaries and windups. Through careful management of conversation, elimination of unnecessary writing, and through use of the most modern, streamlined methods and equipment, you should be able to fit more into the day or have more time available for other tasks.

The output target serves as a standard of efficiency. You handle a certain number of cases a day, see a certain number of prospects each day on the average, write so many thousands of words a day, or otherwise satisfy some kind of productivity standard. The standard may be one that you engineered for yourself, it may be common to your profession or work, or it may be an achievement goal that you have set for yourself. Thus, you may have been making fifteen sales calls a week while your self-imposed quota may be twenty calls. Your analysis of activity will be sharpened by a search for the extra time to convert into a greater number of sales calls.

Work Screening

In your first screening of your activities you would earmark for *elimination* any tasks or steps which do not contribute at all to your work goals or which are marginal. Next you should identify tasks which seem worthwhile but which more appropriately should be transferred to others or delegated to subordinates. Then you should note for set-aside any activities which are not now timely or which can be deferred in favor of more pressing matters.

After your first go-around, add up what you have eliminated and take a count of what is left over. If you have not cut out enough, go over all of your tasks once more, making more critical judgments and giving the benefit of the doubt to fewer activities. You may find the going much rougher and you will need to be more ruthless, as you will ask yourself, in each case: What will I really contribute and how much is it worth? What will I really lose if I cut this out? Can I achieve my main goals without doing this?

Personal-Methods Engineering

Up to now we have been eliminating entire tasks. From here on the savings in time and effort must come out of the simplification or improvement of tasks which you will continue performing. Six different approaches which you might try singly or in combination are: (1) eliminate, (2) combine, (3) rearrange, (4) modify, (5) substitute, and (6) standardize.

The first thing you do is break the task down into each step, in order of performance. Be sure to include everything you read, everything you fill in, and everything you write. Everything you handle is a step. So is every review, every new entry, every new signature. Then, with open mind, you challenge each step with the familiar questions why, what, where, when, who, and how?

The *elimination* of a step is an easy improvement. The step is one that serves no useful purpose. Nothing is lost (or not very much) if you drop it.

When you *combine* steps, you are really eliminating one or more of them. For example, you might take two forms which have differences and similarities. The forms are sufficiently related, used for substantially the same purpose, so that you can combine them into one, thereby saving duplicate effort. Reviews are a favorite candidate for this kind of saving. Unless certain intermediate reviews along the line of progress are needed as a condition for moving forward, they might be eliminated by combining them into a final review. The idea is that once you pick up and put down whatever it is that you are doing, you might as well get as much out of this handling as possible.

When you *rearrange,* you look for methods of performing which save time later on. This has to do with the sequence of steps. That is, what is the most logical order in which to do things? Rearranging also takes in improved layouts. Should working tools or materials be closer at hand or should they be laid out in a different way?

When you *modify,* you change the way in which you do things. You perform the same task but you do it differently. The improvement should give you a better product, a less costly product, or one that takes less time to produce.

When you *substitute,* you take out one element and replace it with another without changing the characteristics of the whole other than to get better performance. It is like taking a baseball or a football player out and replacing him with a man from the bench.

To *standardize* is to make common. You take things which you do often and you arrange to do them the same way every time, with differences in your method only when there are corresponding differences in the situation.

Now, of course, you would not take everything you do and subject it to the same searching analysis. This would be self-defeating. Your methods analysis in depth should be made only for the most important items, such as those which take up the most time, occur most frequently, require most effort, control other phases of work, or are most fatiguing.

In adopting new work methods, be careful not to copy the practices of others without making sure that they are suited to your own needs and personality. Commenting on this point, Joseph Giacalone, Philadelphia sales manager of the Container Corporation of America, said, "You can't impose a standard method of selling upon a salesman personality. . . . Individual differences come to light when a salesman who has been successful on an account gets transferred. His replacement may act entirely differently from the first man, yet achieve the same goal."

The American Salesman magazine held a round-table discussion with sales managers representing a half-dozen different companies on the subject, "How to Unclutter Your Work Calendar." The round-table group considered so-called nonessentials which could be eliminated but agreed that what might be a nonessential for one account might be very important in order to book an account with another. Speaking of socializing, for example, William C. Roher, district sales manager, Plastics Division, The Spencer Chemical Company, said: "Doesn't it get back to what the salesman has in front of him all the time, his objective? Chitchat or anything else is essential if it contributes to the sale."

Summarizing the discussions of the participants in the round-table, the editors of *The American Salesman* said: "They looked at the salesman's total activities and tried to determine which ones don't pull their weight, which ones don't contribute toward the job of selling. Then, they suggested ways to eliminate these non-essentials. Each salesman's judgment, round-table participants said, will vary according to his personality, his product and the type of customer relationship he's building. Within this flexible framework, he can set up a yardstick to measure effectively the productivity of his own activities."

Over the years, the professions such as law and medicine had resisted mightily the intrusion of professional managers with ideas about the application of scientific management techniques. The typical lawyer or doctor could not see how someone not a member of the respective profession could make any worthwhile contribution, especially since each man's practice was so highly personalized. This has been changing. Professional management consultants have been gaining wider acceptance among physicians. More recently, law-office management has started to come under professional attention.

For a professional man, the greatest emphasis is put on maximizing the amount of time he has available to service the greatest number of clients. This really is no different than the efforts made by the typical salesman to maximize the number of face-to-face contacts with customers or prospects and to derive the greatest return from them.

A noteworthy case of one physician, Dr. Earl T. McGhee of Dalton, Georgia, was reported by Garrett Oppenheim in *Medical Economics* magazine. Dr. McGhee is a general practitioner who sees seventy-five patients a day all by himself. "He practices medicine of a high order," said Oppenheim. "His patients will vouch for him as both a doctor and a friend."

In spite of the brisk pace with which Dr. McGhee proceeds, the visitor is impressed with a seemingly unhurried operation. Everything contributes to this: the décor, the arrangement of the furniture and filing cabinets, the businesslike but unhurried pace of the uniformed aides.

"Through this bustling serenity," said Oppenheim, "the doctor moves into an examining room where a young mother and her daughter are waiting for him. 'Hello, Mrs. Harrison!' he exclaims with a show of pleasure. 'And how's Debbie?' Debbie has an earache and has been vomiting. The doctor questions her, examines her, and writes a prescription while his nurse gives an injection. 'How's school?' he asks. 'Did that essay of yours win a prize?' The visit is finished in three minutes. The doctor moves to the next room. Here he burns off a wart. Four minutes. Then he returns to his consultation room and spends ten minutes talking over the problem of schooling with the parents of a retarded child."

Anyone not familiar with this physician's practice might question the quality of his work. Oppenheim quoted Dr. Loyd C. Yeargin, one of Dr. McGhee's colleagues in Dalton.

"Earl McGhee's office is no factory, I assure you. We work together, and we look after each other's patients at vacation time, so I know. The quality of McGhee's work is well above average. He just doesn't fool around at it. He makes a diagnosis, treats, and moves right on to another room where the next patient is waiting for him. And what an easy manner! You never realize how fast he really moves!"

Apparently, this quiet control of an active situation seems to be characteristic of successful men in many fields. "This quality is never lacking in the truly great executives of American industry," said Clarence Randall, quoted in Chapter I of this book. His description of the effective executive, with a few name references inserted, might just as well have applied to Dr. McGhee, as described by Garrett Oppenheim.

Apart from his friendly manner, his interest in his patients, and his quiet control of each situation, these additional techniques help Dr. McGhee devote the very maximum of his time to his professional tasks:

1. He delegates all duties that can be performed to his satisfaction by someone else, whether it be obtaining equipment for his own use, handling finances, setting fees, administering treatments, or performing the myriad other subprofessional and administrative tasks.

2. He treats two to four patients at a time, moving into an examining room to work on another patient, for example, while the one he just left is waiting for an anesthetic to take effect.

3. He uses preprinted forms to communicate standard information to his patients, whenever practicable.

4. He makes extensive use of any medical equipment that will pay off in greater speed and efficiency.

5. He refers patients freely when he feels that they can get better care in the hands of a specialist.

6. He avoids assisting at surgery whenever he can gracefully do so and whenever this is consistent with good doctor-patient relationships.

7. He works strictly within a schedule governing both his work and leisure hours.

While the preceding example brings out the techniques of a specialized professional, with some changes in setting and terminology it could just as well have described the situation of most other professionals and executives; certain basic approaches are universally applicable.

THE STRATEGY OF EMPHASIS

One of the most important aspects of work-planning lies in putting one's best efforts into those things which will yield the greatest return for the time, energy, and cost. This is what the physician did when he shucked away all duties and responsibilities that others could perform—even the duty of planning his work system—so that he could put the greatest emphasis on the professional tasks that only he could perform. Undoubtedly, his personality had much to do with his effectiveness.

Each type of work, each level of work, and each job environment will govern, in its peculiar way, just how one should order his activities for greatest effect.

Three Main Types of Work

Keeping the intended readers of this book in mind, it seems to me that they fall naturally into three main groupings: situation-handling, clientele-handling, and outside-handling. Admittedly, these couldn't fit all cases. You might need to adapt or interpolate for your own situation.

The *situation-handlers* include most executives, writers, journalists, independent business people, consultants, and analysts, among others. They are concerned with taking new situations, analyzing them, developing approaches to solving them, and then carrying them out. While they may come in contact with a great variety of people, in person, by mail, and by telephone, they are preoccupied with keeping this to a minimum in order to get out their other developmental work. Their work is characterized by a thrusting upon them of many unanticipated problems, interruptions, and special situations, all clamoring for attention. A task begun is not necessarily brought to completion; it may be held in abeyance while other information or ideas are forthcoming or while others complete steps, in turn, which permit successive actions to be contemplated and consummated. At times their work may call for great concentration. If it is not done in the office, the work often may need to be completed at home. Avoidance of interruption is a great preoccupation.

A very important approach to time control for such people is personal work planning leading to a carefully controlled time budget. Depending upon the specific character of the work, the technique of delegation should be used to the utmost, and particular stress should be laid upon avoidance of interruptions. If much of it is involved in the work, the techniques of oral and written communication as well as the techniques for mastering the mounds of reading matter should be improved.

Clientele-handlers, for the purpose of this discussion, include doctors, lawyers, case-handlers, and any others who receive visitors and inquiries. For some, the work calls for an immediate diagnosis of the situation, a tentative or deferred conclusion if not an immediate one, and some form of action in behalf of the client. For others, notably in the case of the law, visits with clients are interspersed with periods of research, study, and creativity. One frequently hears the cry, "All I have to sell is time." Hence, the main effort must be expended on those things which directly or indirectly lead to a profitable return. A man with time on his hands would do whatever he could for himself but as he becomes busier, he begins thinking of having others do his lesser tasks, restricting himself more and more to those which make the best use of his professional talents.

The *outside-handler* category consists mainly of outside salesmen but it also covers, in large measure, all others who are on the move, who call upon others or go from place to place in pursuit of their work. In common, they are beset with problems of time losses in travel, waiting, and broken interviews or appointments. A salesman must concentrate on getting the greatest possible return from his selling hours. Therefore, he arranges his schedule to take care of his creative, preparatory, and overhead work during nonselling hours. He spends much of his time planning to avoid time losses in his personal routing and in calling upon the wrong prospects. He learns how to have activities in reserve in case he has to wait or in case he has a broken appointment on his hands. He allocates time for his paper work during nonselling hours, mindful of the consequences of letting this work build up.

Level of Work

Within each type of work, as one moves up the line or becomes more successful in his practice, his work mix changes and he also becomes more selective in choosing and accepting work. The man in an organization finds that he devotes greater proportions of his time to thinking, evaluating, planning, and representation. He spends less time in direct performance by himself. The carrying out of his work is assigned through division of labor to department heads and special assistants. The resources and supporting facilities of the organization become geared to his working needs and convenience.

Individual workers, such as top professionals, become more selective as to the types of work they take on. They begin concentrating on those things which pay the most and are most gratifying to do. The salesman goes after the more profitable accounts, whether they yield the biggest orders or whether they yield a constancy of orders.

The professional man can add assistants who handle the work on which there is a lower return. He can also assign subprofessional and administrative tasks to supporting aides, as already described. If his practice is too successful, he can raise his fee level. This may reduce the number of clients but it might not necessarily reduce his income. In fact, it might go up!

Dynamic Qualities

The dynamic or static qualities of the work will also have an important influence on how you organize for it. Is there a great deal of start-and-stop activity due to interruptions? If so, major emphasis must be placed on obtaining privacy. Are there many interactions with outside groups, visitors, business prospects, employees, and others? If so, these time-consuming contacts must be rigidly budgeted in order to conserve as much time as possible for productive effort.

Are situations constantly undergoing change, thereby calling for revisions in your working approaches? If so, you might need to allocate more time to fact-finding and forecasting so that you can anticipate trends and changes.

Are you breaking ground on many new kinds of work or projects at about the same time? If so, you will find the starting effort for each much more taxing and time-consuming than if you keep doing more of what you have already been doing. You may want to limit your involvement in new activities until you achieve a measure of stability in what you have already undertaken. The same applies, in the main, to activities in which there are many intangibles and unknowns. Getting the facts to run these down is in itself time-consuming. Additionally, as you clarify the situation, you will find yourself wiping out what you may already have done or assumed. The new information or experience may set you on a new course of action. Hence, with highly dynamic, volatile, or intangible situations, you will want to organize your time on a basis of tentative involvement and maximum flexibility so that you can change your course at will.

SUMMARY

The first step in making the best use of your time is to organize yourself. You must start with some clear identification of your work goals, assigning values or importance to them. Then, you can use these as a basis for reviewing the worthwhileness of everything you do.

Now, begin working on the nonessentials. In the light of your important goals and current targets, eliminate any activities which do not yield a material return for your efforts. If, after your first go-around, you find that you have not eliminated much, tighten up on your criteria and go down the list once more.

The next phase of personal work simplification is to examine each task with a view toward achieving economies in one or more of the following ways: eliminate, combine, rearrange, modify, and substitute work steps or methods.

After you have simplified, you should standardize your ways of doing things that recur. This will reduce to a minimum the creative and preparatory work that goes into performance of a nonstandardized task.

Above all, do not adopt some stereotyped method of work which did well for others. This is the fallacy of one man's meat being another man's poison. You must personalize your work plan in the light of your own personality, the environment and situations in which you work, your level in the organization, the resources available to you, your professional or selling attainments, and the dynamic or static qualities of your work. From an understanding of these you will find the personal guidance that will enable you to put the emphasis in your work planning where it belongs.

IV

How to Save Time by Looking Ahead

In the preceding chapter we were concerned mostly with an initial "shakedown" of current activities. This means the elimination of nonessentials, the simplification of the remaining activities, and the placing of emphasis upon a way of doing things in accordance with one's own working conditions. Now we will look into some of the ways in which you can make the best use of your time by thinking ahead. Largely, this is effectiveness in personal planning.

Our emphasis in this chapter will be on personal planning as distinguished from group or enterprise planning. A man at the head of an organization or one of its activities may have responsibility for *over-all* planning for his area of responsibility, but this is another matter, so far as this book is concerned. Here we will be concerned only with the planning of one's personal tasks—one's personal work program.

For our purposes, also, we will not cover, here, short-term planning covering brief periods of up to a week or so. These come more under the heading of *scheduling* and will be taken up in subsequent chapters.

We will cover here:

1. The role of personal planning.

2. How to take on new tasks.
3. How to limit your outside activities.
4. How to plan a project.

THE ROLE OF PERSONAL PLANNING

What is a plan?

A plan is a course of action for reaching a goal, starting from now or from any predetermined time in the future.

Without planning, things may be done on a hit-or-miss basis. In the same vein, planning is an effort to make every hit count.

A budget is a plan. It reaches into the future to anticipate conditions which will be then encountered. It allocates resources in accordance with the assumptions about future conditions. Under an intelligently administered budget you would proceed according to plan but you would also verify the future as it becomes the present. Thereby, you would either confirm the accuracy of your budgeting or you would modify it. So, also, with any other kind of plan.

What It's Worth to Look Ahead

Whether you are evaluating your work, as already discussed, or looking ahead, you must have defined goals, the things you aim to achieve. The process of planning, as such, forces you to look at your goals with some sense of realism. You must prove them out by laying out the specific steps through which you must go, supported by adequate resources, to achieve your goals. By laying out your course on paper, you avoid costly missteps or attempts to reach goals which are not really attainable.

As you work out the sequencing of steps to achieve goals— your action blueprint—you also identify intermediate goals or targets. These serve as checking points on a timetable. Knowing when intermediate steps must be accomplished, you can take the long-lead actions which will put you in a state of readiness at the proper time.

The individual with a variety of projects on which he may be simultaneously engaged, as well as one who is pursuing a number of separate goals at the same time, must have a defined basis of operating if he is to avoid confusion. If you are blocked temporarily on one, or when you must shift quickly to another, you can make the changeover without loss of time, because you have already figured out what to do about the new project at that particular stage. As a corollary to this, you can work on a wider range and variety of tasks and goals if each is supported by its own blueprint for action.

If you have defined your goals and supported them with plans, you have something to communicate to others with whom you work. Then you can work co-operatively with the least misunderstanding. As an additional by-product, others who know of your interests may volunteer things to you, whether they be related opportunities and materials or merely suggestions as to sources of information. They may also contribute useful ideas and experiences which will save time for you.

How Far Ahead to Look

The number of goals and plans you can manage wisely will depend mainly on the time and energy available to you. Identifying the longevity of our goals gives us some sense of priority and timeliness. In business life we are accustomed to designations such as the following:

> Long-range goals — 3 to 5 years or more
> Intermediate goals — 1 to 3 years
> Short-term goals — 3 months to 1 year
> Current goals — 1 week to 3 months

Oddly, planning for the near-term and planning for the long-range are both easier than planning for intermediate goals. Near-term planning, which includes the last two categories, must be quite specific. The unknowns are likely to be fewer in number as compared to planning for the more distant future. You see quicker results from your planning efforts if you are able to correct just as quickly. On the other hand, long-range planning is sufficiently generalized so that you need not be encumbered by the obligation of being specific.

Executives, researchers, writers, engineers, and others who are concerned with developmental and creative work will be concerned with long-range planning as well as with intermediate and closer planning. In some measure, just about all of us should be concerned with long-range goals and the plans for achieving them in such areas as self-improvement, the building of a reputation, and the building of a personal following, among others.

People who work in terms of sales quotas, case loads, and the servicing of a clientele will also have long-range goals but they will be heavily preoccupied with their more immediate and short-term goals, plans, and schedules.

Consider the salesman. For his coming year, he may set up an earnings goal. This obliges him to evaluate his total performance as well as all of his opportunities so that he can come up with a plan for achieving the earnings goal. He might go even further and say that within a period of five years he wants to build from an earnings of $10,000 to an earnings of $17,500. This becomes his major goal, which must be supported by subsidiary goals and plans.

One subsidiary plan might be to work out a more thorough and economical coverage of his entire territory. Another plan might prompt his ingenuity in getting more repeat business. Still another plan might be devised for locating new prospects and selling new customers. Even this could be subdivided. He might want a plan to go after only certain kinds of customers to whom he might sell only certain kinds of products. Another approach might be to divide the plan for achieving greater acceptance for certain kinds of products or services because, even though they may be "low-ticket" items, they offer the prospect of repeat bread-and-butter business. And so on.

Some Key Elements of Personal Planning

The very act of picking your objectives or goals in itself presupposes that you have the capability of reaching them. You cannot really know if the goal is obtainable unless you have first worked up a plan for reaching it or have had prior experience in reaching for a similar goal. Then, you might estimate capability based upon your prior experience.

In planning you are constantly making assumptions as to conditions you will find in the future and as to the consequences of actions to be taken in the future.*

You will need to know the limiting and fixed factors which must be incorporated into your plan: the time in which you must achieve your goal, the resources available to you, the obstacles, the unknowns, and the anticipated actions of others which might affect what you are doing. You must be able to characterize the volatility or stability of the situation. The less you can pin things down or the more you expect change to occur frequently, the more you must arm yourself with alternative courses of action. That is, you must be able to anticipate the ways in which your plan might have to be changed, even as you perform under it.

At last you are ready to build your road to Mecca—on paper— brick by brick. In a paper exercise you use prior experience, either your own or that of others. If there is no available experience, you try to simulate it by analogy to other things of which you have knowledge.

Now, having completed your first draft of the plan, can you say that it is feasible? Can it be achieved in the light of the resources and time available and do you, personally, have the capability of achieving it? This last could be the decisive element which you must be willing to face just as frankly as possible.

If you have difficulty either as to feasibility or desirability, you might want to go over the plan to see what alterations could be made in it in order to make it worthwhile to go ahead. You might also want to alter your goal in some way or to increase it or decrease it.

Finally, because of all the uncertainties in planning for the future, you will identify logical check points in your plan for purposes of future control. As you approach the check points, you will evaluate your progress and make revisions in the plans wherever necessary.

* For an extended discussion of techniques for forecasting events as well as the behavior of people, see Chapter XII of *The Art of Decision-Making*, "Crystal-Balling the Future," by the same author (Garden City, N.Y.: Doubleday and Company, 1961).

HOW TO TAKE ON NEW TASKS

A very common aspect of personal planning grows out of the question of whether or not to take on a new task. We must start with the assumption that you have a full schedule and that to fit in something new requires that something else be phased out or that you find room, somehow, to squeeze in the new.

What so often happens is that we commit ourselves for something that we must do in the future, thinking that the future will take care of it itself or that somehow we will be able to absorb the work load. This is particularly true of outside commitments and speeches, which we will describe below as a separate problem. When the time for making good on a commitment rolls around, we so often find that we must ask for delays or postponements or else take drastic measures to make good.

Estimating Your Going Work Load

One solution is to estimate your basic work load—what you can expect week after week or month after month—as well as your estimated contingency load. The latter consists of the unforeseen new problems, activities, and work loads which must be added on top of the basic work load. Although individually the contingency items might not be identifiable, this does not really matter. You are more concerned, in any event, with the aggregate amounts of time on the average. Hence, to be able to predict your contingency load, you keep records over a period of time, identifying the unforeseeables and the amount of time each took. From there it is easy to get an average. Of course, in applying the average to the future, you might want to make adjustments for special conditions that you might anticipate.

Estimating Time for New Tasks

If you go to an automobile repair shop to have some work done on your car, the estimator will first list all of the tasks to be performed. Then he will take out a book which has all of those tasks listed together with the standard time allowance to be made for each task. This does not mean that performing a certain physical operation, listed in the book at two hours, will actually take that amount of time on *your* car. It probably will take less although it might also take a little more. Depending upon the honesty of the estimates and the standard times, it is assumed that with competent mechanics, these should be fair charges *in the long run.* That may not help your feelings, however, for if you have only a little bit of work to be done, you undoubtedly will feel that you should be charged accordingly—on the basis of the actual time rather than on some theoretical average.

When you are estimating time for a new task, you can't work on averages. You might use them as starting points in making your estimates, but you need to know specifically how long it will take before you will compile all the data, analyze it, draw your conclusions, and whip them together into the form of the report which will be due next Monday.

The key to making a realistic time estimate is to individualize it. You must take into account your personal working characteristics and you must also make allowances for the situation in which you will need to operate.

On the personal side, two things, at least, for which you must account, are your personal capabilities and your personal slippages. If you have had actual experience with the kind of task you are to perform, you should be able to estimate with a fair amount of accuracy, provided the new task is almost the same. About the only allowance you need to make, then, is for personal slippage. That is, if you know that you tend to underestimate by about 25 per cent, you should add this much in as a protection factor.

Where you have not had prior experience, your first effort should be to make an estimate based upon analogous experience. That is, you may have performed tasks having similar elements in them. You might draw a little here and a little there, by comparison. As a rough base of departure, you might go to others who have had actual experience in order to obtain their estimates of time. Remember, however, that you will not know how accurately they estimate and you cannot necessarily use their rate of performance as a basis for determining what yours will be.

If you must acquire new skills or if you must learn new information or ways of doing things or how others think, you must then estimate how long it will take you to acquire the new knowledges, skills, and abilities.

Even more important, in many respects, than your own prior experience, is the comparability of situations. What may have been a "breeze" under prior conditions may not be quite so easy to do under the new conditions. If you are looking for comparable experience, you must compare conditions then or there with conditions here and now. Then, having a base of comparability, you must project the situation forward. Will conditions be any different in the future? Will the resources available to me be any greater or will they be any less? Will the people with whom I used to work be available? How will events shape up over the period of this task and what effect will they have on my performance? Remember that nothing continues without change.

Fitting In the New Task

Now that you have an estimate of the "time dimensions" of the task, you can face the problem of how and when to fit the task in, if at all.

The simplest solution is to fit the new task in as a replacement for something going out of phase. If you cannot drop anything but must take on the work, another alternative is to plan to put in overtime or to defer another task which is either less timely or not as important.

This brings us to a very critical question of whether you are planning for growth or for more of the same. If you feel that you are on the move upward and are planning to achieve higher responsibilities or more selective clientele or accounts, you will find yourself continuously preoccupied with the problem of what to drop in order to move forward.

Some current tasks you may want to drop completely, some you might retain with modifications, and some you might want to upgrade. To make your judgment as to any of these, you must have personal plans for your own future. Only in this way can you assign suitable values to potential new tasks as they come along.

Of course, the decision as to whether to take on a new task may not really be your problem; you may have no discretion as to this. Your only problem will be how to take it on. This is often the case with people who work in organizations. While they can influence their own task selection substantially, they cannot usually determine this entirely.

One solution to the situation where you cannot take on a new task because of the amount of time it will consume is to make a monitoring commitment. That is, you decline to take on the new task for lack of sufficient time, but you agree to keep an eye on the problem, keeping informed about it, so that if conditions change you can move into it.

HOW TO LIMIT YOUR OUTSIDE ACTIVITIES

There are many reasons why you should give of yourself to your community and to your church. We don't really need to go into the reasons in depth because if you are a man on the rise, you will find the reasons coming to you in greater numbers through the medium of claimants for your time. There can be no end to your involvement in outside activities. If you are not careful, they can easily take over your business or professional life and they can replace the few hours you try to keep for family activity.

On the other hand, you cannot completely divorce yourself from community activities. In smaller communities especially, professional and business men are almost without choice. This is a kind of tithe which the community expects of you in return for the support which it gives to you. We cannot be unmindful, also, of the side benefits which may be derived through participation in community activities. The growing young businessman or professional recognizes the importance of exposing himself to as many people as possible in order to build an awareness in them of what he can offer.

As with all things, it gets down to the question of moderation. You can plan for your outside or extracurricular activities just as you can for those which you take on as part of your regular business life.

The Outside Budget

A typical time trap is the request for you to participate two or three months hence. The program chairman insists that the program will be worthless without you making a speech or that you should be chairman of the refreshment committee or the social committee because only you have the touch that will make a howling success out of the affair. Since nothing is to take place for a few months, the remoteness of the occasion and the persuasiveness of the claimant for your time combine to win your agreement.

When the time rolls around for you to make good on your generous commitment of self, the utter desperation of your situation dawns upon you one morning when you open your mail to find a reminder of your participation. How you wish then that you had never committed yourself! Never again—at least, until the next time you try to be nice, perhaps just to get someone off your neck. The secretary to one prominent man told me that he has made as many as three commitments for luncheon discussions on the same day. It is all she can do just to get him to tell her about them.

Elmo Roper, the public-opinion expert, told me: "In my case the main difficulty is that I am prone to say 'Yes' when some friend asks me if I will speak several months hence. Then I lose track of that acceptance and go on saying 'Yes' for several more speeches or out-of-town trips for one purpose or another, and then inevitably the month in which I have scheduled all of these things rolls around, and I am faced with the very difficult job of keeping up with my daily and weekly work and at the same time working in rather more out-of-town trips or speeches than should have been scheduled for that period of time."

In the long run the only rational way for judging whether or not to take on a new commitment is to do so in the light of a time budget for total living. Out of the twenty-four hours in each workday, your minimum time commitments will be somewhat as follows: sleep—about 8 hours; dressing and personal hygiene, morning and night—about 1 hour; eating—2 to 3 hours; working hours—about 8; and going to and from work—about 1 or 2. This adds up to 20 to 22 hours each weekday. This leaves 2 to 4 hours for the business of living itself, self-improvement and professional activities, time for family and friends, relaxation and recreation. It's not really very much. So far as your weekday activities are concerned, therefore, unless you control them carefully, you will find them pre-empted by outside demands.

Of the 2 to 4 hours available to you during the weekdays and of your weekend time, which you should allocate in accordance with your own pattern of living, you should assign so many hours per month for family, recreation, leisure, and friends, so many hours for self-improvement and professional activities, and the remainder for community activities.

The time budget for outside activity has two advantages: One is that you force yourself to think more critically of the ways in which you should spend your time away from work and the other is that when a new demand is made upon you, you have a basis for considering it and for turning it down, if necessary.

The Technique of Accepting

To be safe in estimating how much time a new commitment will take, don't accept the estimate of the man who asks you. He's likely to underestimate, even though he tries to be as honest as possible about the matter. In actual practice, voluntary activities are rarely consummated with the same precision you might expect in an office that has lots of procedural experience. The facilities, information, equipment, or personal assistance which was promised to you may not be forthcoming without personal follow-up on your part. Also, because of your commitment, you may find it necessary to do many of the things yourself for which you had depended upon others. At the very least, the safe thing to do is to double your preliminary estimates.

Pin down exactly what is expected of you and what type of assistance or co-operation you may expect. If the program organizer cannot tell you and if this is important information for you in order to make your decision, it is only fair that you should tell him to obtain the information before you commit yourself.

Avoid taking on too many different outside activities simultaneously. If you do, you risk having multiple crises simultaneously. Your outside activities may intrude upon your regular business hours. You'll be having these intrusions anyway, because of the daytime meetings you'll be asked to attend, the telephone inquiries, and the burdens of additional correspondence.

If the activity is something you have not undertaken before, such as heading a drive, you should play it safer by doubling all previous estimates, because you will be surprised at the number of time-consuming details you have not anticipated. Moreover, if it is a new experience, you will have a great deal of inquiring and learning to do. Hence, you should be very cautious and slow about loading yourself with new kinds of activities.

Finally, make some effort to cut back on your responsibility as a condition of acceptance. Offer to do a little less. Ask for helpers to whom you might delegate part of your responsibilities.

If you have a choice, be a little selfish about the kinds of things into which you enter. Choose those activities which give you the most personal satisfaction and those which may contribute to your own personal and professional development.

HOW TO PLAN A PROJECT

Another specialized type of planning is the laying out of a major developmental work project which you will carry out yourself or which you will accomplish through group activity. In a later chapter we will note that one of the typical faults in undertaking the writing of a long paper is the inclination to start writing before all of one's ideas have been worked out and before the general plan of the paper has been developed. If you devote the necessary time to thinking through and planning the composition, you can do a much better job in much less time than if you plunge into the work directly.

It is much the same in the planning of a project. In fact, in creative-engineering situations one frequently encounters the argument that you cannot plan the steps through which you will go and the difficulties you will encounter when you are working on tasks that require developmental break-through. To the contrary, the more intangible the problem, the less precedent and the less background for what you are trying to do, the more essential is it that you block out in advance at least the tentative course of activity. Otherwise, your time will slip away without your realizing it until the situation is almost beyond repair.

"On one day a project engineer would tell me that he is within 90 per cent of achievement of his goals and deadlines; the next day, he would report, tremulously, that he has run into trouble, that tests did not work out as he had hoped, and that he finds now that he has 90 per cent of the work yet to be done with only 10 per cent of the project money left with the deadline almost upon him, if not behind him," said Dr. Harold Goldberg, executive vice-president of Emertron, Inc., an electronic research and development organization.

It is just as wasteful to try to start a new project without some planning (in proportion to the complexity of the project) as it would be for a custom builder to try to put up an original house without detailed blueprints.

On an individual project the failure to plan in advance may result in poor allocation of time to the different stages as well as a wrong sequencing of activity. The latter can be even more wasteful because it might result in the performance of unnecessary activity or the redoing of work in the light of subsequent developments.

The group project presents these additional pitfalls in the absence of advance planning: confusion and overlapping of effort, things not being covered by anyone, and contradictions in approaches.

For both the individual and the group, the unplanned activity is usually characterized by a lack of control. Not having thought it through in advance, you are not quite clear as to the points at which you should check upon yourself. Consequently, there is generally a tendency to lag, with a feverish uptake in activity as the deadline approaches. When that happens, the lights may be burning most of the night and mistakes of all kinds are made under the hectic conditions of chasing deadlines.

The Stages of a Project

There is a logical way of approaching a new project in order to be most assured of success at least cost within the time limits. The properly planned project will usually proceed in accordance with the following sequence:

1. Recognition and clarification of the project requirements.

2. Fact-gathering: prior experience, research into the "state of the art," solicitation of qualified sources of opinion, etc.

3. Tentative decision as to the basic approach to be followed, including identification of main assumptions, limitations, and unknowns.

4. Laying out of the basic plan of action, including those things to be done in sequence and those things to be done in parallel; summation of requirements for each phase together with criteria for accomplishment.

5. Review of project plan, either by self after a brief "cooling off" for purposes of detachment, or by others who can make critical contributions.

6. Assignment, discussion, and "kickoff," if a group project.

7. Monitoring of project at predetermined control stages, in accordance with previously established criteria of performance; decisions as to revision in approach, if necessary, in order to accomplish goals within limits of time and funds.

8. The manner of completion and delivery of the project, with special attention to buttoning up all necessary details.

In a small or limited project you might not identify all of these steps, but if you were to take the trouble to look for them, you would find them present. In a project of great scale the foregoing list would constitute a great oversimplification. In either case, the key to successful project management is the skill with which you subdivide the task into its separate stages of activity. "A task too long to be accomplished at one stretch," wrote André Maurois, "may be legitimately divided into stages; then each stage should be given one's entire attention. One must not look further than each stage, thereby following the example of the mountaineer who cut steps in the ice, refusing to look up at the heights or down into the depths because the sight of either would terrify him."

How to Watch a Project

The division of a project into separate and successive stages of activity serves both as a basis for operation and a basis for control. Certainly, the effort is procedural but the effect of the control technique is psychological.

What we are getting into now is not one of the happier phases of self-management or of control by others. Especially as to the latter, nobody really likes a reader over his shoulder. Nevertheless, when a project is in the making, adherence to a time schedule may mean the difference between profit and loss, success or failure. Doing the job right but doing it on time are both very, very important. Specifically, in monitoring a project, you aim to accomplish the following:

1. Satisfactory achievement of the agreed goals.

2. Early detection of the need for revisions in the goals themselves as well as in the approaches being followed to reach them.

3. Determination that the criteria of performance are being met satisfactorily.

4. Determination as to whether all separate elements of the project are in balance and in harmony with each other.

5. Checking of time schedules, not merely to verify that they are being met, but to act also as a prod upon performance.

One might ask—and, indeed, many creative people do—why it is necessary that there be any special effort to make follow-ups of this kind. One need not go too deeply into the pathology of slippages. Anyone who has watched the development of any number of projects knows that the normal tendency is for progress to lag until consciousness of the approaching deadline triggers off a frantic endeavor to meet it. This is just plain normal.

In some kinds of work, such as creative engineering, this normalcy is compounded with professional self-defense. If the solutions are not forthcoming, the engineer may beseech the coming of a miracle. Somehow there will be a breaking apart of the dark clouds to let the bright light of realization shine down on the project. Whether it be his professional pride or his personal insecurity, the engineer does not want to have to admit that he is blocked. When, eventually, this is ascertained by one means or another, it may then be too late to bring the project through on time. For this reason, some routine method of checking on progress is expected to anticipate difficulties before they become catastrophes.

The basic approach is to take the key stages of completion— especially where there is something demonstrable, such as a written report, a physical product, a compilation of information, or the results of a test or analysis—and to set these up in a schedule for checking.

If you are doing the project under your own self-control, by yourself, a simple calendar notation of when to check on yourself might be sufficient. A visible schedule control board on the wall near your desk would serve as a ready prompter if you are disinclined to look at the calendar pages. You can also try to commit yourself to others, thereby building up a counterpressure against yourself.

Group project control tends to be more formalized. Some member of the group or some central control point calls for reports of progress. This is where some artistry must be brought into play. If you're not careful, you can become mired in a lot of paper work which will become so cumbersome that no one can do anything with it. The artistry lies in being able to operate on exceptions. If a project is running according to schedule, you don't need to have an abundance of reporting that says so. What you really need is a report of any deviation from an originally agreed-upon approach as well as any deviation from the agreed timetable. Project reporting can be simplified, then, by asking project personnel to report in detail only when there is such deviation. Furthermore, all items should not be reported upon regularly. It should be sufficient to call for reports only as the due dates for intermediate achievements come up on the schedule.

Finally, success in adhering to a timetable is most likely to be achieved when you run scared. There can be no easy build-up. From the very beginning you must operate on the assumption that every minute counts. Chances are that every minute will.

SUMMARY

Planning is the blueprinting of a course of action which will take us from a starting point to some other point in the future. Through anticipating the conditions and crises that might be met along the way, we can be prepared with the necessary resources, the courses of action, and even alternatives of action that might be required by actual events.

Just as each of us may have a multiplicity of subsidiary goals which are designed to help us achieve larger goals and ends, so must we also have a multiplicity of supporting plans for achieving those goals and ends. We may plan our individual professional and economic goals. We may also plan our work loads, using the plan as a basis for taking on new work commitments. This approach is singularly applicable to a very sensitive area of time consumption—the pressures upon us to engage in a variety of extracurricular and community-service activities, however deserving they may be of a fair share of your time.

In yet another sense the techniques of planning will carry you safely through a specific project, from start to finish. You will be more likely to achieve your goals with a minimum of slippages and with maximum economy in your utilization of working resources.

V

The Basic Time Budget

"Never ask a politician how he manages time," said United States Senator Barry Goldwater in reply to my question. "There is no easy way of doing this; it is our constant challenge and I see no chance of it changing—in fact, it will get worse.

"The fact that the overriding responsibility is our duty to our job precludes any long-range commitments with any assurance of adherence. In fact, if you were to call me today for an appointment tomorrow, I would probably tell you to call again in the morning and see what we were up to. That is how tight a schedule we work on."

This is about the only way *some* people can plan their time ahead. They know that they have a great many fixed commitments which they must honor, as part of their way of life, somehow fitting in other things in between on a play-it-by-ear basis. It is probably like the personal budget management that most of us do: we have very little to play with after taking care of the fixed overhead, the regular payments, and the unexpected, unavoidable emergencies.

Now, being a senator in Washington is a special case. It is not at all typical of most jobs. For most of us, some rational choice of activity is essential to carrying on an economically productive business life.

I put this problem to an attorney friend of mine, Ellsworth C. Alvord, whose corporate affiliations and interests are both national and international in their scope. I asked him how he keeps ahead of his extremely busy schedule.

"To manage my time," he said, "I first prepare a schedule looking ahead as far as possible and setting down the known appointments—such as hearings, meetings of boards of directors, meetings of committees, etc. This schedule I keep in front of me at all times. As time passes, the schedule for the immediate future becomes more detailed. However, I attempt to save at this juncture an occasional day or two with nothing scheduled. Then, as more time passes, the schedule for the forthcoming week or ten days becomes rather well-filled. But I find I must still save a couple of hours a day, if possible, and perhaps a day a week, if possible, for unexpected and unscheduled matters. In this way I usually find adequate time for the matters which I am called upon to do."

Thus, we are back to the basic principle that to be able to organize your time in the present, you must have prepared for it when it was part of your future. In the preceding chapter we covered specific techniques for planning sequences of action in order to achieve our goals with an economy of effort. Our present problem is to take a variety of activities and fit them into a limited time period. This divides into two parts: (1) to achieve flexibility on a day-to-day basis, you need to see your work picture over a period of a week or so; (2) within the context of a weekly time budget, each day then becomes a challenge to your immediate productivity.

The weekly—or even monthly—time budget with which this chapter is concerned, is a basic unit for work scheduling for those who have no typical day or for those who have open-ended targets with unpredictable interruptions and emergencies. The weekly budget, also, affords you the flexibility for allocating sufficient time for all of your activities, other than the immediate crises, including your creative, preparatory, and overhead tasks.

ESTIMATING THE WEEKLY LOAD

One of the values of making a weekly time budget is that it obliges you, periodically, to take stock of yourself—to see how far you have come on some things and how much further you have yet to go. Because of the tendency for time to slip away from us without our being conscious of the extent to which this may be happening, the weekly inventory will provide the sharp awakening we need and serve as a spur to action and to the avoidance of interruptions and diversions.

How Long Is a Week?

If the hours in your work week are fixed, say from nine to five, you are fortunate in at least having a firm basis on which to allocate them. What is more likely is that your week may be longer and often quite irregular from day to day. It is probable that few of the readers of this book will have the theoretical 40-hour week of five days. For example, a survey by *Fortune* magazine showed that the typical work week for executives ran from 45 to 48 hours. When you add the outside demands on their time which accompanied their status as executives, the total ran to a range of 57 to 60 hours a week. Under some emergency conditions executives found themselves working 70 to 80 hours a week.

Salesmen may work about 54 hours a week on the average, according to a survey by *The American Salesman* magazine. Of this, only about 14.5 hours a week are devoted to face-to-face contacts with customers and prospects, 20 are devoted to travel time, 12 to work in the office, and 7.5 to work at home. Eleven per cent of the salesmen surveyed work as long as 70 hours a week. This survey was taken during a period when salesmen had to work a little harder to sell. Under easier selling conditions the work week might be closer to 50 hours, with as little as 2 hours a day spent in face-to-face contacts or only 10 hours a week!

The physician's work week averages about 55 hours according

to Joseph M. McElligott, a New York City medical management consultant. He found that the average physician worked 30 hours in his office, 15 at the hospital and on house calls, and about 10 hours a week doing charity work or attending meetings of all kinds.

Thus, each of us must decide how much of his own week he will try to bring under budgetary control. Is it only the time spent on productive work or does it also include all the other auxiliary activity at home and in the community?

The Total Time Budget

The weekly load can be almost anything you want it to be if your work aims toward a variety of intermediate and long-range goals. The same open-endedness applies to people in selling, engineering, writing, supervision, and many other nonroutine kinds of work.

Accordingly, you must start with a self-imposed limit on your typical work week. To accommodate emergencies, this may need to be lengthened, but at least you will have a base of departure.

With the total time availability which you have budgeted, you then can refer to your goals, plans, and commitments in order to identify those things which must or should be done, if at all possible, in the ensuing week. You would consult, obviously, your desk calendar and appointment book, your accumulated paper work and correspondence, and the various pending demands by others who spend time with you. As you begin to fit these into place over the period of a week on some rational basis, you may find that some things must be sacrificed or deferred and that other things must be given priority. You will find, also, that unless you allow sufficient time for creative, preparatory, and overhead activities, these will tend to be put aside time after time until you fall horribly into arrears, with resulting inefficiencies and the emergence of new time problems for you.

You will need to follow some pattern for allocating blocks of activity time to your schedule. Here are a few of the points to keep in mind as you do this:

1. Assign substantially long periods of continuous time, without interruption, to major tasks. If they involve deadline re-

quirements, try to schedule them for completion before deadline delivery. This will allow for emergencies and slippages.

2. Arbitrarily block out average percentages or amounts of time for the creative, preparatory, and overhead aspects of your work. If you curtail on any of these *averages,* you must make up for them in subsequent weeks. If you spend more time on any of them than the average calls for, you must try to economize on them to the same extent in subsequent weeks.

3. Group related kinds of problems or work for attention in sequence in order to save on the starting and stopping of a miscellany of unrelated tasks.

4. Assign to the early part of the week those tasks which are top-priority, those on which some kind of return effort from others is needed during the same week, and those things whose time requirements are indeterminate but must be completed at some time in the week. In the case of the latter, these are things you can afford to keep slipping somewhat as you approach the end of the week, provided you are careful not to slip them off the schedule entirely.

5. Keep in reserve some average percentage of time for the unexpected visitors, telephone calls, crises, or underestimates of time. You will always have available a number of reserve tasks which you can perform if any of this contingency time should not be used completely.

TIME BUDGETS
FOR EXECUTIVES AND SUPERVISORS

The terms *executive* and *supervisor* cover almost every kind of work as well as a fairly long range of levels of responsibility. There will be considerable overlapping with some of the categories described below. For example, if a salesman has others under his supervision, as in the case of a crew manager, he both sells and supervises. If he becomes a district sales manager, he may spend less time in direct selling and more in office work and supervision. If he becomes the national sales manager or sales vice-president, the selling is accomplished almost entirely through tiers of subordinates. Moreover, much of his time will be spent in corporate activities not directly related to selling, as he co-ordinates with his corporate colleagues to bring his selling problems to bear on their planning and execution of their responsibilities.

Accordingly, because of the many different situations we must encompass here, I will list first a general outline of procedure. This will be followed by special notes for staff assistants and production supervisors.

How to Allocate Your Time

In the preceding section we listed some general rules you might follow in allocating your time throughout the week. These should be kept in mind as you read through the following specific suggestions.

First, block out the committed time over which you have no control. This would include participation in conferences and staff meetings, out-of-town engagements, important visitors, and unavoidable personal engagements, such as visits to the doctor or dentist. Next, spot the important deadlines which must be met during the week (or at some time in the future if the required work will take more than a week). Now, estimate the amount of time you will need to spend on each deadlined task and work back from the deadline (allowing for an intermediate cushion) in order to find the latest point in your schedule at which you can safely begin work. Finally, take all matters which *must* be done during the week, as priorities, and estimate the time required for each of these.

You are ready now to block in all the must items. If, at this point, you have more than enough work to do in the week, without having even allowed time for the inevitable interruptions and for your other tasks, you must go back and re-examine the legitimacy of each deadline and priority. You may need to negotiate with those to whom you are committed for a revision in delivery or, if your priorities are self-imposed, you may need to make your own frank reappraisals and judgments. After all, you can do only so much in any one week. While you can exert an unusual effort in a given week, in the long run you will need to come back to normal proportions—*whatever normal may be for you.* Don't forget, however, that in spite of your priorities and crises, you must somehow take care of your creative, preparatory, and overhead activities, whether you do these at night, carry them over into the next week, or get special help on these matters. I can't overemphasize that while you may defer these for the moment, you cannot keep doing this week after week without inevitably impairing your personal effectiveness.

Into your schedule now you must block out time for the following:

1. Secondary priorities.
2. Odd-moment work.
3. Additional telephone work.
4. Additional personal discussions with your colleagues, superiors, visitors, subordinates, important clients, etc.
5. Additional out-of-office work.
6. Additional time for creative, preparatory, and overhead activities.

If, chronically, you have things left over at the end of each week which are of a priority nature and if, over any reasonably long period of time, you are not able to give adequate attention to *all* phases of your work, the chances are that you should go back to an analysis of your work, as suggested in the preceding chapters.

Staff Assistants

Staff assistants characteristically must adjust their work and schedules to the requirements of the principals whom they serve. Naturally, their duties may vary widely in accordance with the needs and personalities of their superiors. They may sit at desks, merely monitoring the flow of paper and information and sending out follow-ups. They may, also, undertake a variety of specific projects. Their work may take them away from their desks for attendance at meetings and conferences with others both in and out of the organization. They may be expected to prepare briefings, reports, analyses, etc. Whatever they do must be responsive to the priority interests of their superiors, calling for "crash" activity on short notice. Additionally, a staff assistant may, himself, be responsible for the supervision of a few or many other employees.

The priorities of the staff assistant, as he devises his own schedule, may be taken first from the known or anticipated needs of his principal. He must anticipate the informational, analytical, representational, and service needs of his superior, in relation to specific activities coming up on the calendar. In working out lead-time requirements for these, the staff assistant may need to begin his actual work in the preceding week or before that, if necessary.

In his remaining time, then, the staff assistant can plan for such independent activities as he performs generally in accordance with the over-all procedures set forth above.

Production Supervisors

The production supervisor occupies a man-in-the-middle role. He is pressed by others to get the work out, whether it is a physical or paper product, whether to meet production quotas or to meet time schedules. While being so pressed, he in turn looks toward those whom he supervises to deliver the output for which he is held responsible. In achieving the desired productivity, he is constantly reconciling matters of quality, speed, and cost. On top of all this he has many auxiliary responsibilities, including personnel development and training, preparation of reports and paper work, work scheduling, and participation in meetings, among others. He, like all others, has his share of creative, preparatory, and overhead work.

His work week is characterized by unanticipated crises and trouble-shooting, interlarded with the endless stream of questions and problems presented by employees. In spite of all, he must keep the line moving or, if his output is less visible, he must avoid the creation of paper backlogs.

Since his overriding function is to keep the work moving, he must give primacy to anything that would jeopardize his production goals. Obviously, a work stoppage would take top priority. Next in order (if not higher in importance) is the anticipation and prevention of emergencies. In his case, then, attention to the creative, preparatory, and overhead activities is highly important because abandonment of any of these could cause some deterioration or breakdown which would interfere with production. For example, inattention to recruiting work might leave him with a manpower shortage. Inattention to materials procurement might lead to his having idle employees on his hands with a mounting backlog. Similarly, work stoppages can be averted by preventive maintenance of equipment.

Although outside demands upon his time should be blocked out in his work schedule for the week, the production supervisor would be expected to have some license in disregarding these when a serious work crisis arises to command his attention. (Naturally, he would confirm each situation with his superior.)

In order to keep his own desk work moving he must aim at reserve periods during which his own employees, at least, would not interrupt him, except in emergencies. These reserve periods would be scheduled at times when he would expect the productivity of his group to be well under way.

TIME BUDGETS FOR CLIENTELE MANAGERS

Here we will discuss four different occupations distinguished by one feature which they hold in common: their earnings are derived from a personal clientele. Also in common, those who practice these occupations seek to derive as much return as possible from the time spent with their clientele.

A difficulty under which they all operate is that some portion of their clientele may cause more of a time-management problem than the overwhelming majority. One cause for this may be found in the insecurity of the clients who use up time as they seek additional information and assurance. Another reason is that some people are more demanding than others when they pay for personal service. These are background considerations which should be kept in mind because they require preventive measures by busy people.

Physicians

The tremendous amount of specialization that characterizes the practice of medicine today makes it difficult to suggest any standard situation or remedy. Some physicians keep regular office hours and rarely, if ever, make a house call. At least in larger cities and metropolitan centers, general practitioners will have many house calls but little—sometimes no—hospital work. In some kinds of practice the physician has neither house calls nor hospital work. In spite of a number of shining examples, quoted elsewhere in this book, of physician-managers who are highly efficient in their practices, a skeptical view is worth noting. One physician, Dr. Lou Fettig of Philadelphia, insisted to me that time generally is not in the consciousness of the average physician. He asserts that most men dedicated to the practice of medicine would not have entered this field if they were predisposed as good managers.

The comments which follow are based on discussions with a number of physicians as well as on a reading of many interesting articles on the business side of medical practice, found in the attractively edited pages of *Medical Economics* magazine.

The well-organized physician attempts to accommodate as many patients as possible within the working day or that part of it set aside for visiting hours. He limits the number of patients he will see consistent with his ability to practice good medicine and, incidentally, to convey to his patient the feeling that he has received adequate attention.

If the physician does hospital work or makes house calls, some of this may be on an unscheduled, emergency basis, but the main body of it may be accommodated by setting aside certain days or certain times of the day for these outside activities. Additionally, time must be provided for an astonishing amount of paper work, which may be done in the office or at home but preferably in the office to avoid such incursions into the physician's home life. Assuming a busy practice, the physician should be able to afford aides who will relieve him of the paper work and other nonprofessional activities. He will find, in fact, that this is an economy, because it will free additional hours for income-producing medical practice.

The efforts of the physician to plan his schedule are constantly under attack by patients with real or imagined emergencies as well as by patients whose interest in their own bodily preoccupations, even of minor account, prevents them from recognizing the need for and right of the physician to have a well-regulated practice. They disregard, also, the rights of patients who take the trouble to schedule their appointments beforehand. The hazards of the physician's office include telephone interruption, unscheduled appointments, missed appointments, and unnecessarily prolonged appointments. For those who must make house calls, the avoidable or totally unnecessary house call is one of the most frustrating annoyances. Such problems as telephone interruptions and excessively long visits are covered in other chapters dealing with these topics. In the material which follows, we will cover some of the more unique problems of the physician.

The house call is monetarily a losing proposition. Considering the time spent in transit, the physician can scarcely charge enough. In effect, the physician charges what amounts to a subsidy rate. It behooves him, then, to limit these house calls to the truly deserving cases and to insist that the others come to the office during regular hours. Admittedly, this is more easily said than done. The physician must be well established, usually, before he feels that he can assert the independence that is needed to tell little Johnny's mother that billions of babies have had colic pains and that billions more in the future will have them. For her apart, the mother couldn't care less; in her mind there are no other patients and there are no other babies as important as Johnny. This feeling on the part of the mother is readily understandable, but there are people who are not genuinely frightened; they are merely indifferent to the comfort or convenience of the physician.

The experienced physician may be skeptical of "urgent" calls. Before committing himself to a house call he will review carefully over the telephone the symptoms of the patient, mindful of the possibility of an actual emergency.

The unscheduled appointment may be an actual emergency or an imagined one. Some patients who have no emergency complaint may drop in without even trying to ascertain over the telephone whether the doctor has any free time, perhaps a cancellation. At best the unscheduled appointment which does not make up a cancellation is one of the gremlins in the doctor's time budget. Here again one must bear in mind the need for distinguishing between the true emergency and the imagined or feigned one. The imagined problem may loom very large in the patient's mind. Some physicians accept unscheduled appointments by leaving a certain amount of slippage time in their preplanned schedules. Others work them in as best they can. For the telephone call where the emergency is doubtful, the patient may be told that he will be called on the first available cancellation.

The missed appointment may be a double nuisance in depriving the physician of income as well as in preventing another patient from having an earlier appointment. Some doctors with busy practices will overcommit their appointment books in accordance with their experience on the probable number of misses.

Whether or not they actually charge for missed appointments, some physicians post warning signs or tell new patients that a charge will be made for a missed appointment. This can be very effective as a deterrent.

The interval of time scheduled for each patient will vary according to the nature of the problem or complaint and whether or not it is a new patient. Even as to old patients, a new complaint may require more time than a revisit on the same complaint. Some physicians find that if they take only certain kinds of cases on certain days or parts of days, they can develop a momentum and rhythm for handling them in fairly rapid sequence. This is especially advantageous for matters that require only a few minutes for diagnosis and prescription. The same principle applies, however, to hospital work. Whenever there is any latitude in scheduling and admission of a patient to the hospital, the doctor can save a great deal of time by operating on or treating two or more patients in sequence. He saves time also by being able to visit all the same patients during one journey to the hospital.

Professional aides can be of considerable help in relieving the doctor of just about everything except the most professional part of his work, which is the making of a diagnosis and a prescription. An efficient secretary or nurse can relieve the doctor of many of the time-consuming preliminaries that precede his actual examination of the patient. She can obtain from the patient whatever information is needed for his medical-history card and she can guide him to an examination room where, if necessary, he can disrobe. Multiple examining rooms are indispensable to a growing practice. The physician loses no time by having to wait until the patient has completed disrobing and then dressed again before another patient can be admitted to the examining room.

Lawyers

Lawyers, also, are not a single breed. They specialize in many different aspects of the law. A tremendous number of them are not engaged in private practice as commonly visualized; rather, they are on the payrolls of government agencies and private industry. Such lawyers have the problems of most professional office employees in the management of their time. We will be concerned here with the problems of attorneys who manage their own private practices. Even this gives us a fairly wide range within which to manage some constructive comments, because of the diversity in the make-up of private legal practices.

Within a single field of specialization a lawyer's work may be characterized by a variety of problems and assignments. He may spend a lot of time in court or very little. He may work with corporate clients or with private clients or both. If he has an instinct for making money, his exposure to many different business situations may involve him in them beyond ordinary requirements of legal counsel. Attorneys who practice corporate law may be called into executive conferences and they may also become part of the management through election to the board of directors.

Ethical standards prevent the lawyer from directly advertising for a clientele. His advertisement of self is accomplished indirectly through personal exposure and through referrals by friends and satisfied clients. While he will be most preoccupied with the business of getting business in the early days of his practice, he might never lose this preoccupation, whether it be directly or indirectly manifested, because one always needs new clients to replace those who fall aside. For this reason, the lawyer may find himself giving some substantial amounts of time to community, professional, and even political affairs.

Operationally, the busy lawyer finds inroads on his time from clients who may want to talk too much, and then there are those who call for free advice. Each case must be evaluated on its own as to the time it will take in research and fact-finding, documentation, correspondence, meetings with other parties or lawyers, depositions, pretrial testimony, courtroom work, etc. The client may want to know what the legal service will cost him but, aside from this, in a busy office where the lawyer has partners or assistants or both, a subdivision of the work into its different task elements is necessary for billing purposes.

One of the real problems is the conflict of deadlines. These may need to be worked out with opposing counsel (who are accustomed to agreeing to reasonable arrangements since they frequently have the same problem themselves), court clerks, and the clients themselves. In the long view of time, looking backward, many urgencies prove not to have been so urgent.

Deadlines, once established, govern much of the schedule-making of the lawyer. The work plan for the current week and for ensuing weeks must start with the posting of deadlines so that the time for the necessary work can be computed backward, with a safety factor, in order to know when to start.

His skill in using time covers such abilities as knowing where and how to obtain research data, knowing how to estimate time on various tasks, and knowing how to monitor his accomplishments against self-imposed targets as well as those imposed by others. Reminder systems, general defense against telephone interruptions, and skill in handling visitors are essential.

Multiple-Account Managers (Especially Stockbrokers)

In common, people who sell personal service to many clients have a sensitive relationship problem in that each client wants the best and most prompt of service for himself. He is preoccupied with his own problems and may not be able to appreciate those of the person to whom he gives his patronage, for the simple reason that he does not see the other side. The client may feel, often with good cause, that he is not getting the service he desires because his account is not as big as others.

The stock-brokerage business is a good example because of the growing interest which it holds in the public view and because the timeliness factor points up the need for careful work organization. In the nature of the work it also brings out the importance of creative, preparatory, and overhead work. Whether he buys ten shares or a thousand, the customer demands timely service and reporting. To him, his investment is an important one. It may be all that he has and it may represent the highest of hopes. The number of small investors is many, many times greater than those comparatively few with bulging portfolios.

The Number One priority is to execute orders to buy and sell. These must be given to the trading department with least delay. When prices are changing upward or downward, a moment lost can mean few or many dollars lost or not gained. It might seem to the casual observer that this is the essence of the broker's work, but to the customer's broker (or customer's man or account executive) it is merely the tip of the iceberg, so far as actual work is concerned, even though actual buy-and-sell transactions are the source of earnings from clients.

Irving Rudd, managing partner in charge of the Washington branch of Sutro Brothers and Company, commented to me about what lies beneath the tip of the iceberg. "Of course, many of our client relationships are limited to the execution of buys and sells," he said, "but the more professional contribution of the customer's broker is to be found in the investment guidance which he gives his clients. In this business, so very much depends upon your ability to anticipate market trends in general as well as the probable performance of individual securities. With the thousands and thousands of them which are traded through the listed exchanges as well as over the counter, any single person is not going to be able to do very much original research on any number of companies. In the main, he will need to depend upon his own reading.

"Just to give you an idea of the reading load, I read four daily papers: the *Wall Street Journal,* Washington *Post,* New York *Times,* and *Journal of Commerce.* Besides these, I read *Barron's* and *The Commercial & Financial Chronicle.* Also, I try to keep abreast of general publications, such as *Fortune, Business Week,* and the general news magazines. Then there are the various investment services which give you a great deal of predigested material and, of course, there are the special reports I get out of Sutro's own research department."

"Surely, you can't read all of this during the day?" I remarked.

"No, indeed! When I get out of here each night, I take with me a bulging briefcase."

Getting a little closer to the firing line, I approached a customer's broker at Sutro, Mrs. Miriam Baller. Knowing that she puts a great deal of time into servicing her accounts, I asked her how she is able to keep abreast of her other activities.

Her reading, also, is done mainly at home, where she must also catch up with much of her paper work.

The customer's broker must keep track of the finances and the delivery of securities of each of his accounts. The buying and selling of securities is handled almost entirely on a verbal basis. Responsibility for each transaction rests with the customer's broker who handled it. If there is no money in an account to cover a buy, he must follow up with the client to get a check. He must make sure that the customer makes actual delivery on securities that have been sold for his account.

"On top of all this—and a lot of other paper work—I need to keep my customers informed, as well as myself, of quotations on their securities holdings," said Mrs. Baller. "I try to sense how closely each of my customers wants to keep track of his holdings and I obtain quotations which I telephone to them or, if they prefer, I have them available when they call.

"I also try to keep on hand the different reference materials which will help me answer telephone questions without having to leave my desk. Naturally, I can't have everything."

I discussed the service aspect of individual customer's brokers with Mr. Rudd, and he commented, "It's true that individual account executives, as I like to call them, differ in how effective they are in providing individualized service. The best of them, however, as good as they might be, would not be able to do as well if they didn't have good organization behind them."

During trading hours, when the market is active, the busy stockbroker tries to give his attention to many things simultaneously, such as watching the ticker, answering and making telephone calls, talking to fellow brokers, obtaining quotations, and executing orders. Obviously, the work schedule must be organized for paper work to be done at other times. On top of all this, the broker cultivates new prospects. Mr. Rudd urges his people to call a certain number of prospects or customers each day. In accordance with the law of averages some of them will become new customers, while some of the old customers will turn in new orders.

Outside Salesmen

For the outside salesman, the big effort is to have as much time as possible in face-to-face productive contact with the prospective buyer. The estimates as to how much time he actually spends in this way vary from about two hours a day to as much as four hours with the probable average being closer to three. These hours are not necessarily uniformly productive, whether or not they result in actual purchase orders. Time is lost due to interruptions during interviews and to nonproductive talking. The other hours that go into the salesman's day include travel time, waiting time, broken appointments, and creative, preparatory, and overhead work performed at the office, on the road, and at home.

To enhance his potential earnings, the outside salesman must take a creative approach toward his task. This applies to the things he tries to sell and the manner in which he tries to sell them, as well as to his selection of prospects and the order in which he tries to see them. The last item calls for careful routing and scheduling of his calls upon prospects.

The schedule of the outside salesman, as he plans it ahead, might embrace more than a single week. The salesman might plan a routing that will take him into the field and back to his home base over a much longer period. For him, the time budget should be the planned duration of that trip, covering whatever he aims to accomplish.

More so than the other occupational personalities we discuss in this book, the salesman is stimulated by incentives. He is also a man driven by the management to produce the orders that feed the enterprise. Sometimes he is spurred on by the carrot and sometimes by the driver. It is natural, then, for him to work in pursuit of a variety of achievement targets against which his performance is currently evaluated by himself and by those who watch the sales indices. The achievement targets are quite tangible. For example, Dr. Charles L. "Chuck" Lapp, professor of marketing at Washington University, St. Louis, suggested to dental salesmen that they assign the following quotas to themselves on a weekly or monthly basis:

"1. Certain number of calls on present customers.

"2. Certain number of telephone calls on customers.

"3. Certain number of prospect calls on dentists not sold.

"4. Certain number of attempts to sell supply or equipment items.

"5. Certain number of sales letters written to prospects and present customers."

The time budget could be devised to cover specific targets, such as those just cited. The salesman might also aim to cover a certain territorial area.

Most salesmen do their planning and paper work at home or in their hotel rooms in order to keep their days as free as possible for calls on prospects. While they are on the road, many salesmen try to schedule their traveling during the evening hours, also to keep their days free. This calls for advance planning of schedules with due regard to highway conditions and mileages or to available public transportation.

Because of the high incidence of broken appointments or other frustrated efforts to see prospects, the salesman may be inclined to build his routing schedule around the most likely calls —those on which he can most depend. He might also try to schedule his calls so that if one should not materialize, he would still have sufficient time to make another call or do something else constructive in the remaining time that day.

All personal chores should normally be scheduled for non-business hours, unless absolutely unavoidable. As unnecessary as it may seem to emphasize this, salesmen themselves know how easy it is to let time slip by with personal telephone calls, shopping, paying bills, "dropping in" while in the neighborhood, grooming oneself and one's car, taking long lunches, and engaging in fraternal post-mortems with other salesmen whom they meet while making their calls.

TIME BUDGETS FOR CREATIVE PEOPLE

More than with others, creative workers are ruled by mood and temperament. They may be the worst of deadline-chasers. Sometimes they are optimists, delaying the inevitable reckoning when they are unable to deliver, hoping for some heaven-sent miracle to pull them through. Creative people will assert that their work cannot be organized and some of them will insist that they work without plan. To the contrary, I insist that no elaborate effort can be undertaken without a plan if it is to be executed effectively and economically. Those who insist that they feel their way as they go, in reality do their planning in the mind, relying upon elaborate mental imagery for the structuring of their plans.

The remainder of this section will be devoted to the time I've spent on the budgeting problems of two types of creative people with whom I have had substantial contact: creative engineers and writers.

Creative Engineers

The creative engineer with whom we are concerned here is a project engineer. He might have a research objective or he might be given an assignment to develop a proposed solution to a problem or he might be given the task of developing a piece of equipment that will perform certain functions—a "hardware" assignment as opposed to a "study" assignment. We will assume that he is pursuing one project objective, although, if he is a supervisory engineer, he might be pursuing one or more task objectives simultaneously.

Some element of his work involves the unknown or the un- tried. To fill this void, he will make assumptions which he will try to prove or disprove. He may make extensive tests or con- duct a variety of experiments. Working under pressure, he may experience creative blockages. Vast amounts of effort and ex- pense in time, personnel, and material may be incurred in ex- perimental development only to be lost entirely through a test failure. When this happens, work may need to be rescheduled and costs may mount and mount and mount.

As deadlines approach, the earlier pace of optimism begins to quicken. Minor disappointments along the way and a cumulative slipping of intermediate target dates will bring on a more anxious pace which will yield, in turn, to frantic efforts toward the last. The days will grow longer and the nights will be brightened by the glare of industrial illumination. At this point one might well conjecture whether the around-the-clock pace is really productive of worthwhile returns. My own feeling is that creativity cannot be pressured to that extent while yet retaining anything approaching economy. Mistakes of the mind and the hand will be made, and their costs will be insufferable unless they are covered by military defense contracts!

While many engineers believe that project planning is not feasible for creative work, there are many others who insist that it is. Conceding that the plan will be subject to constant revision as one moves along, the plan that is to be revised is still very much better than no plan at all. At least, the first cut of a project plan forces the project engineer to approach the task in some logical manner. He is obliged to clarify his goals, limitations, and resources. This, in itself, gives him a sense of tangible achievement. Moving beyond this, he lays out a tentative lifeline for the project with intermediate points at which he should take pause to evaluate progress and plan anew. This, too, is an achievement, because otherwise his optimism or his quickening of pace might cause him to overlook the taking of intermediate readings as to his actual satisfaction of project criteria.

If he plans ahead, he will identify the critical points of achievement and the alternative courses of action or lines of inquiry in case he should encounter blockage or failure.

His time budget is coextensive with his project plan. Necessarily, it overlaps the plan of the administrative work week with which he must also reconcile himself. We must not forget—for he cannot—that he has a goodly share of project paper work. There will be reports to write, meetings to attend, correspondence to read and write, telephones to answer, and other engineers to supervise. The project plan is not a realistic one if it does not provide for these time demands. They must be anticipated and averaged out in advance as part of the noncreative work to be accomplished during the work week.

As to the arrangement of effort within the week, the personal preferences of the engineer may govern. As to creative work generally, I am inclined to believe that it should not be sustained for long periods. Rather, there should be an alternating of creative involvement and detachment. During the periods of detachment one can busy himself with administrative tasks or with miscellaneous tasks of the hand or with passive kinds of mental activity. During these periods of detachment from creative work one has an opportunity to reflect with some perspective on what he has done and the creative problems that lie ahead. Even if he does not do this, the rest from his sustained creative pressures will enable him to return to them somewhat refreshed.

Creative Writers

Most creative writers do not live up to the "beatnik" image. They do not subsist on absinthe or other more readily obtainable spirits. They are, in fact, rather normal human beings. They wear the same kind of clothes and eat much the same kind of food, consistent with their incomes.

While independent writers may work at odd hours to suit their own situations and temperaments, few of them, like the now-mythical Thomas Wolfe, will write while standing up, using the top of a refrigerator as a desk, and none, like Wolfe, have been known to march up a Manhattan avenue in the dead of night chanting aloud, "I wrote ten thousand words today."

Writers fall into two categories: staff writers and independents, the latter including both full-time and part-time. The staff writers may work under varying kinds of pressure but, in the main, their problems of work planning and scheduling embody aspects of the lawyer, the project engineer, and the staff assistant.

The independent, frequently, has other employment; he does most of his writing in the evening or on weekends. Occasionally, he might take some time off from work for a sustained effort. Not the least of his problems is trying to do creative work at the fag ends of his energies and trying to get materials from people or facilities by remote control. One of the greatest of the part-timer's problems is to work out a formula for working at home in spite of the distractions of visitors, telephone calls, family, and the lure of the TV set.

For the writer, as for the engineer, the project-planning approach seems to be the most rational way of accounting for his time. If he lays out his total plan of research and writing, he will identify those informational items which will take the longest to procure or which will require the most effort. He can schedule these the earliest so that when he needs the information, he will have it on hand. Scheduling of time must include the effort which will be required to procure information, to sift through it and analyze it, to organize it, and to revise it after it is once written.

Paul R. Reynolds, a well-known literary agent, said, ". . . Some writers, while they are working at one book, spend a half an hour a day making notes, doing research work, and outlining their next book. They are then ready to start their new project immediately after completion of the previous one. Permanent success as a writer requires concentrated and continuous effort over a long period of time, just as in any other field of endeavor."*

Because of the highly intangible nature of the effort, because of the attractive distractions that abound, and because writing is difficult, the writer is in constant need of imposing deadlines and rewards for completion upon himself. Herein the schedule may be of use because desired nonwriting activities can be included on a provisional basis—provisional upon completion of a predetermined amount of work.

MAINTAINING THE TIME BUDGET

The time budget is a point of departure. It is rarely a fixity to which you must adhere resolutely. When you first conceive your current time budget, you make various assumptions as to the conditions you may encounter and the length of time it may take you to perform tasks. As you approach reality, you find that you must make adjustments in your schedule in consequence of actual conditions as they develop or to remedy slippages in your time.

New Commitments

The unanticipated visitor, project, or crisis is the most frequent cause of the disorganized schedule. When you take on an additional time commitment within the period of your time budget, you must drop something else entirely or defer it unless you provided for contingencies in your budget. Otherwise, you will have to work longer hours or somehow steal time from each of the remaining commitments during the week.

* *The Writer and His Markets* (Garden City, N.Y.: Doubleday and Company, 1959).

There are times, however, when just the opposite will occur. Something which had been planned for the schedule must be postponed or is canceled entirely. Then, you must be ready with some reserve activity held in readiness for just such an occasion. You can also take on a new appointment or a new commitment to fill the released time.

Wrong Estimates

An underestimate of time should be treated like a new commitment: something else must be set aside or deferred or you will have to find the time in some other way as indicated above.

You might, however, consider dropping the effort entirely if you find that the additional expenditure of time is not worth the return you expect from it. This is a more difficult judgment to make because you have already invested some time.

Overestimates are a more happy situation because they release time for additional activity. Nevertheless, they are to be avoided because you might have deferred something from your schedule or excluded it—something important—because of the overestimate.

If you have made either an underestimate or an overestimate, take the little extra time to find out why, so that the next time you will be able to profit from the error.

SUMMARY

Time-budgeting begins with a realistic estimate of the time available within the normal work week. Depending upon your work circumstances, this might include your hours at the office, your hours in contact with outside clientele, and your hours at home. Against this time availability you must array all of the tasks which are tentatively scheduled for performance within the week or other time period that constitutes your budget.

While you will first schedule those things over which you have no control and those things which should be your work priorities, you must also provide for performance of a full measure of creative, preparatory, and overhead work. If these are not performed in the current week, they must be provided for, in added measure, in subsequent weeks. That is, in the long run, unless you accommodate all of your responsibilities in balance, your work inevitably must suffer.

Having determined just what you expect to get done within the week, you must then arrange the tasks in some flexible order with due regard to the intervening vicissitudes. Some tasks should be scheduled for the earlier part of the week to assure that they will be completed at least by the end of the week. Series of related small tasks should be grouped in continuous effort in order to have an economical momentum. Reserve and alternative work should be provided for in case of unanticipated changes in the schedule.

For people who work on a project basis, the single week may not be a sufficient period of time. For them, the time budget should be geared to the project plan with due allowances for auxiliary and indirect work which occur in average proportions throughout the administrative work week.

As you proceed under a time budget, you will encounter frequent changes in conditions which necessitate corresponding changes in the budget. If this adds up to additional work load, something must be canceled or deferred or, as an undesirable alternative, the day must be lengthened. While squeezing new commitments in may seem to work, it is at the risk of impairing one's effectiveness in disposing of the other tasks. Something might be rushed unduly. Canceled commitments or activities provide an opportunity to dispose of other activities held in reserve. Underestimates and overestimates should provide a lesson in time-estimating for the future. Meanwhile, they should be handled as released time permitting new activities to be undertaken or as a new commitment calling for curtailment elsewhere.

VI

How to Get through a Day

"In my own modest administrative job," wrote Melvin T. Copeland in his book *The Executive at Work,* "I often go to work in the morning with a light schedule in prospect, but about this time the mail arrives, numerous other problems begin to appear, presented personally, or over the telephone, or by memorandum. Thus it goes, hammer and tongs, all day. At night I go home with ample realization that it has been a busy period even though there may be some difficulty in pointing to specific things accomplished."

This is a typical expression of a typical day. It would be wonderful if we could anticipate the specific interruptions and distractions which we may encounter during the day so that we could be on guard for them. The specifics themselves we are not likely to anticipate but our experience will tell us that there are certain *kinds* of things to avoid. Anticipating these, we can organize against them. But getting through a day is not entirely a matter of avoidance; it is also the judicious sequencing of our activities and actions. Thus, our approach toward coursing successfully through a day should be both negative and positive, or, as one friend put it to me, "You must learn the arts of omission and commission."

The topic of managing a day brings into focus all that we have covered up till now and much of what will follow in succeeding chapters. It is in the day that you can find the fruits of good work organization and good personal methods. Fortunately, I was able to obtain an example of a typical day in the life of one of the most dynamic businessmen of our time, Mr. Charles H. Percy, chairman of the board of Bell and Howell Company, written at the time that he was president of the same company.

MANAGEMENT PRINCIPLES
FOR THE SINGLE DAY

In Mr. Percy's description of how he manages a day, he does three things: first, he tells how his day used to go, quite frustratingly, before he did something about it; (2) then, he tells what he did to achieve better organization of his time; and (3) finally, he tells us how he operated under his new arrangements. The words which follow now are Mr. Percy's.

"There's a rhyme by Robert Louis Stevenson that might have been written especially for the corporate president. It reads, 'The world is so full of a number of things, I'm sure we should all be as happy as kings.' Unfortunately, sometimes our world and our days are all too full.

"A typical day used to go like this. Perhaps it will sound familiar to your readers. The morning mail includes a request from the Chamber of Commerce for a speech on foreign trade, from a public-service television program for a talk on aid to education, from a service club for a talk on 'The Social Responsibilities of the Industrialist.'

"A major share-owner writes for information on dividend policy; a security analyst asks about anticipated earnings. A group of teachers is taking a plant tour and wants to meet the president of the company.

"The phone rings steadily. A distributor in Holland calls about a new trade fair. An irate customer can't get service in Muleshoe, Texas, and insists on talking directly with the president.

"More mail: A distributor from Thailand announces an impending visit. A key division manager outlines a proposal for reorganizing his area of the business and requests my advice. An aggrieved employee wants to discuss his problems.

"Meetings: A civic lunch for Project B (the host has come to your luncheon for Project A). A directors meeting the next morning in Detroit. Turn down gracefully (impossible!) a request to introduce a friend to the Director of Purchases; discuss two new appointments in our electronics subsidiary and a major capital equipment acquisition. Write a column due yesterday for the employee newspaper.

"Into the briefcase, at the end of the day, goes the balance of the mail along with reading matter marked 'must.' Before turning off the office lights, I take a look at the sign over my desk which reads, 'MY JOB IS TO BUILD OUR COMPANY'S FUTURE!'

"Such days were standard procedure for far too long. But eventually came the realization that the man should run the job rather than the reverse. Through a gradual and cautious program of trial and error, I began to evolve a more intelligent mode of operation.

"Few chief executives would quarrel with the concept that their principal responsibility lies in planning the future of their business. Most would admit, however, that the responsibilities of their offices all too often combine to prevent their fulfilling this principal responsibility.

"The technique of diverting time from the immediately urgent to the ultimately important is a subject in itself. The strategy involves both organization and delegation. To some extent it *must* be learned by the president of any growing organization.

"First, the mail. A competent secretary and executive assistant handle most of it, drafting a letter for my signature when necessary, or routing it to the officer or division manager directly involved. All letters are answered informatively. This permits me to deal thoughtfully with those letters I must answer myself.

"Many phone calls to the president of a corporation concern an area of the business which is the direct responsibility of another officer or executive. Such calls are handled by having the person involved call back and ask if he can be of service. To answer such calls myself, I have found, not only unnecessarily erodes my day, but abrogates someone else's responsibility.

"Having delegated as much responsibility as possible, it remains to organize my days so as to include the three functions which I consider most important to my job: (1) future planning for the company, (2) the co-ordination of the various divisions and functions of the company, and (3) participation in civic activities, which I believe to be the duty of every citizen.

"A typical day, although no day is entirely typical, would then go as follows:

"I arrive at the office around eight-thirty and leave about six. During the short drive to the office I try to think through some of the business of the day ahead.

"Arriving at the office, the first hour is often devoted to a conference with my business associates, following an informal agenda previously prepared by my staff. Usually during the morning I also have about an hour's meeting with someone outside the company in connection with company objectives. This often involves other officers of the company or members of my staff. The remainder of the morning would be spent on mail which arrived that morning and at the end of the previous afternoon.

"The lunch period, usually in our company dining room, is used to bring me up to date on current developments, or with company guests. Ordinarily, I try to lunch with a different officer or executive each day to keep abreast of developments in all areas of the company.

"During the morning a number of phone calls have come in. Rather than taking calls while holding a discussion with someone else, thus delaying them, I prefer to make as many of these calls as possible immediately after lunch. While talking on the phone, I often read and sign letters which have been typed during the morning.

"Following this period, I am often out of the office for a meeting—either company business or civic. Usually, I also try to include one other outside appointment the same afternoon. Returning to the office, I spend about an hour handling any problems that have come up during the day, reading mail and staff reports. The last hour of the day is usually spent in dictating memorandums and letters. Mail dictated the previous day is signed before leaving for home.

"Such a typical day still leaves little time for long-range, thoughtful planning. In fact, I have learned that even with the best planning, organization, and delegation a typical day will never permit the time and detachment necessary for the important planning function. Thus it has become our custom at Bell and Howell to hold periodic day-long sessions with top officers of the company away from the plant and out-of-reach of telephones.

"In addition, with Bell and Howell's electronic subsidiaries in California, with a photographic subsidiary in Canada, a film plant in Rochester, New York, and a world-wide organization, I necessarily spend much time in traveling.

"Therefore, no single day is entirely typical, yet the principles of organization, delegation, and planning are essential if time is to be stretched to embrace the world's 'number of things' which it is a corporate president's duty and privilege to handle."

TECHNIQUES OF SCHEDULING

Do you ever go home at day's end, feeling as limp as some wilted lettuce, ready to pour yourself into a drink, rather than vice versa, as you wonder where the day went? The chances are that if you had a satisfying day—one which went according to schedule, one which produced tangible accomplishments—you would not have that depleted feeling. Just getting through a day according to schedule would, in itself, produce a feeling of exhilaration.

How you manage your schedule must depend a great deal on your own working environment and your own temperament and habits.

Throughout this book, frequent references are made to the avoidance of interruptions, whether by telephone or by visitors. This does not mean that all visitors and all telephone calls are to be excluded. There are some which you may wish to accommodate as a matter of public relations. Thus, James Lutz, president of the McCrory Corporation, told me:

"We attempt to practice an 'open-door' policy in our company. Anyone with a problem—real or imaginary—has the privilege of walking into my office, or that of any other executive, to discuss it. It is true that each of these visits does not contribute something toward the solution of a problem, and does something less than assure a continuous practical control of time, but some do help the organization to make sounder decisions. Of necessity, the time devoted to these exchanges differs daily and must be regulated according to the work load to be handled in my office."

Even an open-door policy, then, must be brought under some orderly control if the day's work is to be done. The visitor cannot just drop in without notice and without regard to any other priorities. I asked Maurice H. Stans, president of Western Bancorporation, about his management of time, mindful of the fact that he is one of the most well-ordered personalities I have ever known. He replied:

"You asked what is the greatest difficulty that I experience in the management of my own time. I think without a doubt that it is the unexpected visitor, the intruder who just drops in. Like most people, I try to plan each day's work at the beginning of the day. Usually it is a full calendar because there are always things that one would like to do, and many times some of them are on a timetable which should be observed. An unexpected casual visitor, an out-of-town friend, someone with time to kill between calls, can destroy all of the planning.

"It is difficult to find a good solution. In government service one cannot very well ignore callers because it is not possible to know in advance which one has an important message. In banking and in many professional services the same difficulty of distinction may exist. My solution is a two-way one. First, never schedule the full day in advance—allow part of the day for contingencies which can then be devoted either to unexpected visitors, to new matters, or to anticipating some of the next day's work. Then, if an accumulation of the unexpected still threatens to prevent necessary work being done, I close the door of my office and announce that I am 'out.' This may be slightly dishonest, but it is very practical."

Hence, one sees that the realities of life are that you are not the complete master of your schedule. You may be making appointments in advance with people without really knowing whether their business with you is worthwhile or legitimate. You will also, somehow, squeeze in a few minutes for an old friend whom you have not seen in fourteen years. How can you do otherwise and still keep him as your friend?

In other words, in the interest of good public relations you plan for a less-than-perfect schedule of activities. The interesting thing is that you even schedule the unscheduled demands upon your time!

As I mentioned earlier, your own situation and temperament will be largely governing in the way in which you set up your schedule for most effective performance of your work. In the remainder of this section I shall comment on ten useful techniques. They are:

1. Schedule the day around key events.
2. Schedule actions which require early-day attention.
3. Perform related small duties in continuous time periods.
4. Match your work to your energy peaks and valleys.
5. Allow enough time for each task.
6. Use your secretary or aide to control your calendar.
7. Don't bring up unscheduled business in a meeting.
8. Restrain your unscheduled action impulses.
9. Confirm your appointments.
10. Watch your time.

Schedule around Key Events

These are fixed, committed, critical, or strategically important activities. Also, the timing may be governed by the availability of others or by situations over which you have no control.

When traveling, you may give yourself a list of many things to do or people to see. Hit the key ones first or allow enough latitude in your schedule before them, just in case you are caught up in traffic or transportation delays as well as in unforeseen difficulties with your earlier engagements. Make all other plans subsidiary to the key events.

Schedule Early-Day Actions

Everything can't be done first but consider giving priority to:

1. Getting others started.
2. Doing work that you need returned to you before the day is out, such as dictation. (You might save a whole day in mailing time.)
3. Doing creative tasks for which you need your best mental and physical energies.

4. Starting work that must be completed during the day but whose work duration is indeterminate because of the likelihood of interruptions.

Group Related Activities

Group your small tasks for attention one after the other. You develop a working rhythm and momentum. Your work make-ready may carry over from one to the other. It will save time in and out for anyone else who must work with you on most of these items. You have continuous use of the same equipment or supporting service or other facilities.

Thus, a physician might take new appointments in the morning, repeat appointments in the afternoon, and difficult ones later in the day.

Other examples: Batch up your correspondence for continuous dictation. Except for emergencies, handle your in-and-out telephone calls in batches. Allocate a time for visitors to be seen in rotation, when their business is brief. Accumulate reading matter for quick scanning.

Match Work to Energy Curves

Most people are said to have energy peaks from about 10 to 11 A.M. and from about 2:30 to 3:30 P.M. Check this against your own cycle. These are times for tasks which are the most challenging or creative. Schedule conferences or interviews at these times when you want to be mentally at your sharpest.

Conversely, don't schedule routine or unimportant activities for those prime periods during the day—if you have any choice.

If your energies are down, mentally or physically, switch to work that is of a more passive nature. Pick up routines. Try to take a restorative break.

Allow Enough Time for Each Task

When you consider the make-ready and the windup or close-out phases of each task you undertake, you must have enough productive effort in between to make the total undertaking worthwhile. Where results count, avoid trying to crowd too much into the day. "As a general rule," said Dr. James H. Davis, in his book *Increasing Wholesale Drug Salesmen's Effectiveness*, "the more calls a salesman makes in a given period, the less time he can have for selling." He backed this up with statistics from his surveys which showed that the most efficient wholesale drug salesman spent 14.1 minutes per call while the least efficient spent only 9.6 minutes in promotional selling.

Also, when the work itself will require a great deal of attention over a period of time, try not to break it up into too many small pieces because, in the aggregate, too big a percentage of time will be spent on stop and start.

Use Your Secretary

If you make time commitments or cancellations of prior engagements, tell your secretary. Do so immediately after making the commitment. If you have been away on a trip, tell her about all the promises you made as soon as you come back.

Avoid casual invitations to "call up tomorrow" or "drop in sometime" or "come back in a week." Professional men, particularly, run into this at club and community affairs. Get into the habit of telling people that you must check with your secretary. Do so in the presence of visitors or while talking to someone on the telephone.

Rely upon your secretary to keep your appointments moving. Acquaint her with your priorities and deadlines and encourage her to prompt you when necessary.

Don't Bring Up Unscheduled Business in a Meeting

If someone calls upon you on a matter whose nature he has previously discussed, discourage him from bringing up new business that might unduly prolong the interview. If necessary, tell him this is something that will require more time than the two of you will have and suggest that you set up another appointment. Likewise, avoid doing this to others when you call upon them.

Of course, there will be emergencies and there will be times, as suggested above, when you will not know the business of your caller. For the true emergency, you may need to adjust your schedule. For the unexpected business which will command more of your time than you can afford, unless it is an emergency, you should beg off with a request that the two of you resume at some other time when you both will be able to devote more time to it.

Restrain Your Unscheduled Action Impulses

While at work on something else, you may suddenly feel impelled to make a telephone call or call someone in. If you do this, it should be germane to the business at hand and it should be necessary. Avoid yielding to your impulses, particularly when you have a visitor present. Besides interrupting the continuity of the interview, you will prolong his stay unduly.

Governor Michael V. DiSalle of Ohio told me: "I have not liked sitting in an office talking to an executive while he spent his time on the telephone. No more would we again begin our conversation than the telephone would ring and, again, he would be on another important call. The business that I had that would have taken possibly ten minutes consumed an hour, and I am sure that he got very little out of our conversation since it was interspersed with so many other conversations."

When working by yourself, you may come across interesting ideas or you may be reminded of information you would like to obtain. If it is pertinent to your present work, you should yield to your impulse. If it is something which you need not attend to at the moment, make a note of it for attention at a more appropriate time.

Confirm Your Appointments

The appointment for your schedule today may have been made yesterday, the week before, or many weeks before that. If you think it important enough to ask for confirmation of a hotel reservation, because of the possibility of an occasional error on the part of the hotel, you should also think it important enough to confirm other engagements.

Doctors and dentists have their secretaries give appointment cards to their patients when they stop by the desk on their way out. Some of them will send out reminders if the appointments are scheduled so far ahead that they might be forgotten in spite of the appointment card.

In ordinary business relationships you can't ask for a letter of confirmation of a business engagement. You might have it if the arrangements were initially made by mail, and sometimes people will write you letters of confirmation of a telephone call. Within your own organization, however, you will not ordinarily ask for memoranda or other written confirmations. When in doubt, then, call up the day before or in the morning of the day of your engagement and confirm the time. If you have a secretary, it is easiest for all concerned if she does this for you.

Watch Your Time

Conversations, like projects, tend to get off on an easy pace and then, when about 10 per cent of the business has been completed, with only 10 per cent of the time remaining the visitor tries to crash ahead to squeeze in the remaining 90 per cent. At this point the cause is probably lost.

For the benefit of your visitor as well as yourself, monitor your pace against a clock on the wall or on your desk or against the watch on your wrist. Don't contribute to nonessential talk, and do whatever you can to get the topic back on the main thread.

Set up a system for using your secretary or aide to put pressure on you and the visitor when you start running toward the end of your time.

HOW TO GET THE MOST OUT OF A DAY

Next we come to a number of suggestions for making time count. Some apply to all types of work while others may be a bit more limited.

1. Make an early start.
2. Don't generate unnecessary feedback.
3. Don't take on marginal emergencies.

4. Work at a controlled pace.
5. Finish what you start.
6. Finish fully.
7. Plan the next day.

Make an Early Start

At home, try to pick up at least a fifteen-minute head start by abbreviating the nonessentials. Scan more briefly through the morning newspaper and curtail your morning reverie on the pillow or over the cup of coffee.

At the office, save the morning warm-up. While it's nice to exchange greetings and brief pleasantries, stop there. Avoid inventorying the news and rehashing last night's poker game and other sporting events. Get a head start on interruptions and the day's unavoidable crises.

The same applies to the way you move in on individual tasks and conferences. Shorten the warm-up.

Don't Generate Unnecessary Feedback

Active personalities tend to create counterpressures on themselves. They are constantly starting new things or solving problems and they are anxious to learn what has happened. Such a personality can be very good for an organization, but he needs to protect himself from his own dynamics. If you're that type of person, here are some suggestions for you:

1. Don't provoke new activity which will involve you unless you're prepared to handle your part.

2. Don't request information or action reports unless they will really be useful to you.

3. Be explicit in giving out any instructions; anticipate the clarifications that will be asked and dispose of them in the first instance.

4. Don't press marginal points unless they are very important; they frequently require more time than major items.

5. Avoid giving assignments to people who require excessive monitoring or hand-holding. They will become burdensome.

Don't Take On Marginal Emergencies

In the best-run organizations there is always some new crisis or unexpected development. When the big things are disposed of, the little crises move up in apparent significance. There can be no end to them. Remember that when you move in on a crisis, you must set aside other activities permanently or temporarily. Remember also that a crash effort is always more expensive in time and resources than one which is preplanned and prescheduled.

Therefore, place a value on your emergency tasks. Ask yourself these questions:

1. What loss would you have if you took no action or if you deferred action?

2. Stated otherwise, is the effort worth the gain?

3. Is action on the crisis unavoidable, regardless of your estimate of loss or gain? Is it essential to well-being or to continued operation?

4. Is there some other way of disposing of the crisis by buying outside help?

Work at a Controlled Pace

In my friend Chuck Woods' office at the U. S. Bureau of the Budget there is a plaque which reads: "The hurrier I go, the behinder I get."

In the long run, rush activity costs more than that worked on under a moderately brisk pace. The first step in accomplishing this is to cut off the nonessential steps and conversations. Next, if you think you have found a comfortable pace, squeeze in just one thing more to be done that day. Get accustomed to this and then squeeze in just a little more. Stop doing this when the pace gets just a little uncomfortable and you find yourself tiring more readily and recognizably.

Finish What You Start

If you don't finish, you'll need to put the work away and retrieve it later. When you pick it up again, you will need to reacquaint yourself with the task, retracing your last efforts. Here are some suggestions for avoiding such time losses:

1. If you need some fill-in work or something to work on during the last minutes of the day, give preference to things which you can complete once you pick them up.

2. On work which *will* need to be carried forward to another time, try to wind up at a natural stopping-point.

3. When you have to carry unfinished work over, make some notes on your undeveloped thoughts, what you would have done if you continued, and anything else that will enable you to get off to a brisk start when you pick the work up again.

Finish Fully

As the end of the morning or the afternoon approaches, don't anticipate it. Use every moment of time constructively. Come to a full finish. The amount of time you will pick up in this way over a period of a week will amaze you.

Paper work growing out of today's activities should be done today. Deferring it until the next day will create a double load. If you do this for several days running, you will soon be heard to complain that you are bogged down in paper. Others may observe and say the same thing.

Plan the Next Day

If you operate under a time budget, the next day should be planned long before you reach it. Still, there will be many details which you will want to fill in, including any action carry-overs from what you did the day before.

Make a note of items for tomorrow (growing out of today's work) immediately, because if you wait until the next day, you will probably have forgotten the fine points. Whatever you do now in anticipation of tomorrow will enable you to get off to a much cleaner start. The next day, when you take a new look at things, you may make further modifications but at least you will have something with which to work.

If the next day starts off with a conference or an important presentation, or if a series of outside calls is to be made, you should prepare the day before with any papers, presentation materials, sales aids, equipment, and other materials and supplies which you might need. Check everything out so that you will be able to rest easily in the knowledge that the next day is already well-prepared.

SUMMARY

To get through a day successfully and satisfyingly, you cannot approach it as though it were a period of time of and by itself. The day is an action period in the stream of your total time budget. How effectively you get your day's work done will depend partly on the institutional resources which support your efforts, your own self-organization, and your own working habits. All of these things, in combination, are the basis for coursing successfully through each day.

If you operate in this way, then you can say, as the president of the American Telephone and Telegraph Company, Mr. F. R. Kappel, said to me: "I don't think I really experience great difficulty in managing my time. This is not because of any special virtue on my part, but is due mainly to the consideration extended by my family and business associates. It seems to me that if a person will just go ahead and schedule the things he needs and wants to do, and make liberal use of the things that are available to help him use his time efficiently, such as the telephone and the airplane, he ought not to run into much trouble. This means using your mind and your eyes and ears all the time while you are awake, but if you don't do that you have no cause to complain anyway."

VII

How to Multiply Yourself

I have an attorney friend, Ellsworth C. Alvord, whose interests are so widespread that I am not at all surprised to call his Washington office and find that he has just left New York for business in Los Angeles. My own business with him is to have lunch, so I inquire as to his return.

"Next Monday, but he'll only be in the office long enough to go over some papers and then he'll be off to New York."

"When will he be free after that?"

"Well, he's leaving New York for Paris. . . ."

Occasionally, we do manage to get together for lunch, although this has been the pattern of his practice throughout all the years I've known him. In telling me about how he manages his schedule he paused and said, "I assume it is not necessary for me to add that good associates and good organization of my office are essential."

William Zeckendorf is one of the most important builders in America. As president of the New York firm of Webb and Knapp, Inc., he may be engaged simultaneously in shaping the decisions on scores of projects. He, too, may be in New York one day, in Vancouver, B.C., the next, and in Chicago the day after.

His vice-president for public relations, Stephen G. Thompson, told me: "On occasion, it has taken me literally more than one-half hour in his office to complete a two-minute conversation with Mr. Zeckendorf, while he has fielded a score of telephone calls and other interruptions."

In that case, one naturally asks, how does Mr. Zeckendorf use a personal staff to help him get things done?

Apparently, Mr. Zeckendorf spends his own personal time on those things which he feels he alone should handle. There are many details of preparation and execution for which he looks to his immediate staff. "To conserve as much time as possible," said Mr. Thompson, "Mr. Zeckendorf delegates to responsible assistants and secretaries virtually all matters that do not require his personal attention."

This is a necessary way of life for the busiest people. They use every resource available to multiply the impact of their best efforts. It is true of heads of governments, heads of corporations, lawyers, physicians, engineers, supervisors, production managers, and even successful writers. The lone salesman, too, operating out of his own home, can multiply his effectiveness by delegating some things to his wife, if she is able and co-operative, and to the sales service staff in the home office.

Of course, there are some dangers in not doing *everything* yourself. Something might be done in a way that you wouldn't approve. You would have done it differently. True, but then you would not have got as much done in the aggregate.

In the typical small business which might consist of little more than the proprietor and a single secretary, bookkeeper, and telephone receptionist all rolled into one, plus a few additional employees, the proprietor may be the one who grabs for the morning mail. There might be an order or a check in the mail. His dream might be to grow into a great enterprise and sometimes this does happen from the lowliest of beginnings. Now, as he moves up the line, he must shuck off duties and responsibilities on his assistants, including the reading of the mail. He cannot take care of everything by himself, even though he thinks he can do it best. In fact, he might find that others can do it better.

With increased scope and organization, you discover another risk—a risk that you won't know what is going on in your own bailiwick.

To illustrate the point, let's move up to the very summit of national affairs, to a story of how a breakdown in staff procedures almost caused a rift between the President of the United States and the President of Ghana as well as between the two countries. What follows is based on a story by Drew Pearson, the national columnist.

It seems that President Kwame Nkrumah of Ghana was disturbed by a report that former Secretary of State Christian Herter had indicated that Ghana was leaning toward the Soviet bloc. Disturbed by this, as reported by Pearson, President Nkrumah indicated a desire to talk to Secretary of State Herter. An approach was made to State Department officials, but a call from the Secretary of State never materialized.

Five months later, in Ghana, the considerably miffed President Nkrumah explained to Chad Calhoun of Kaiser Industries that he had subsequently written a letter to President Kennedy but had never received a reply. Later that afternoon Calhoun learned from the American Ambassador in Ghana, Francis Russell, that he had delivered a letter from President Kennedy to Nkrumah's Foreign Minister. Nkrumah told Calhoun, "I never heard of the letter."

Looking into the matter, he found that his Foreign Minister had not bothered to deliver the letter from the President of the United States. That letter, when finally read by President Nkrumah, so pleased him that he wrote a twelve-page reply to President Kennedy.

Once again, in those early weeks after the new President had taken office and staff procedures had not yet been well established, President Nkrumah's letter failed to receive attention. When it was finally located and delivered to President Kennedy, it resulted in immediate action leading to a friendly visit between the two heads of state.

Now, if these two men were to have received and read all their own mail, without intermediate staff, the mishaps never would have occurred. But then, they would have accomplished nothing else and many more important mishaps would have occurred.

This chapter, then, is devoted to the techniques of getting things done through others within your own establishment, people who in one way or another are responsible to you. We will cover, first, the general techniques of delegation. Then we will apply the principles more specifically to the use of a secretary and to the use of service and staff aides.

THE ART OF DELEGATING

Personal success in business has been correlated with effectiveness in delegating tasks. On the other hand, failure to delegate has been correlated with failure to move ahead. "The trouble with John," who works long hours overtime and never has time for his family, you hear people say, "is that he cannot delegate. He must do everything himself." Another oft-heard remark about Ken, who has not moved up the line as fast as some of his friends, is "He keeps himself mired in details because he won't let go of them, while the others have learned how to work on the most important things, delegating details to their subordinates."

Among the fads of management, the idea of delegation has been assuming greater prominence in recent years. It is held forth almost as a panacea. There has been a great proliferation of writings on the techniques of delegation. What bothers one about most of the things in print is their oversimplification. When you consider the ramifications of delegating, it is apparent that it is a topic not lightly to be treated. Delegation, to be effective, must be preceded by a fairly high order of work organization. It requires goal-setting, policy formulation, program planning, employee evaluation, employee training, effective communication, performance review, and performance control. In short, you cannot merely tell people to do something and expect good performance if they don't have a pretty fair idea of what you want done and why.

Delegation can be overdone. In some situations you must give preference to the practical aspects of your dealings with the people who demand your time, quite apart from the theory of relying upon your subordinates. For example, "In politics, there are many more things, than in business, that have to be tended to personally and that cannot be delegated to someone else." So said James C. Worthy, who has faced the problems of managing time in business as a vice-president of Sears, Roebuck and Company, in government as Assistant Secretary of Commerce, and in politics as head of the Republican Citizens League of Illinois.

Effectiveness in delegation does not mean that you relieve yourself of all your tasks or that you rely entirely upon assistants to decide what it is that you should do. It is a reciprocal process of you telling them and their advising you and out of this interaction comes a constructive balance. "Where an exaggerated emphasis is placed upon delegation," said Dean Acheson, "responsibility, like sediment, sinks to the bottom."

We often hear, with sound basis, that people occupying the highest posts must reserve a big part of their time to think. The development of original thought or of constructive solutions to problems of the highest importance is regarded as one of the prime responsibilities of top management. The panacea that is so often offered as the way to obtain more time for thought is delegation. His visitors, his telephone calls, his incoming correspondence, and his reading matter are screened ruthlessly and rechanneled to others for attention. This may be carried to such an extent that the top man finds himself completely divorced from reality. He becomes the captive of his staff, doing their bidding.

"One may predict with some assurance," said Mr. Acheson, "that any attempt to reorganize the highest echelons to give them more time for thought will inevitably have two characteristics. It will cut the chief off from his principal officers, and, in accordance with Parkinson's law, it will interpose new personnel, or 'coordinating' staff, between the chief and his principal officers.

"The result will be that he will have to see just as many people, but they will be the wrong people. His reading may be reduced, but it will be predigested and both the protein of facts and the fermenting bacteria of conflict and criticism will be minimized in the bland passage through an insulating special staff."*

Thus, there is a middle ground which enables you to remain the master of the situation. How much you can delegate, to whom, and in what manner will be governed by your particular situation.

* "Thoughts about Thoughts in High Places," The New York *Times Magazine*, October 11, 1959.

The aim of the following material, then, is to assist you in understanding your own situation and planning the measures of delegation appropriate to it.

What Delegation Is

Let's be clear about the nature of delegation. When you delegate, you don't give away responsibility. Even though you entrust performance to others, you remain the one who is accountable and who assumes the risks. Of course, you may hold others responsible to you for the way in which they carry out your work assignments, but should anything go wrong, you cannot point to them. In effect, the persons to whom you delegate become extensions of yourself.

In spite of the risk, delegation is an unavoidable fact of modern business life, even in the smallest of organizations. In the larger enterprises the ability to delegate is a prerequisite to the holding of responsible office.

Even further, the processes of delegation and subdelegation make possible the complete structuring of organizations from the highest offices down to the so-called working levels. Each is accountable in turn, up the line, to his immediate superior. On the other hand, from top to bottom, each point of authority distributes its responsibilities to others and looks to them to carry them out.

"This problem is as old as human history," wrote James D. Mooney in his classical work, *The Principles of Organization.** "It is the subject of one of the most practical and human passages in Scripture, the advice that Moses received from his father-in-law, Jethro, the priest of Midian, contained in the Eighteenth Chapter of the Book of Exodus. Moses, when he received this visit in the wilderness, was staggering under the same problem that has killed many a modern leader. He was attempting, in his own person, to perform the impossible duty of judging and governing all the people.

"Jethro observed his methods and saw what was wrong. 'The thing that thou doest,' he said, 'is not good. Thou wilt surely wear away, both thou, and this people that is with thee: for this

---

* New York: Harper and Brothers, 1947.

thing is too heavy for thee; thou are not able to perform it thyself alone.' Then he suggested the only possible remedy, the delegation of duties. So, in the words of Scripture, 'Moses hearkened to the voice of his father-in-law and did all that he had said. And Moses chose able men out of all Israel, and made them heads over the people, rulers of thousands, rulers of hundreds, rulers of fifties, and rulers of tens. And they judged the people at all seasons; *the hard causes they brought unto Moses, but every small matter they judged themselves.'*"

Delegation is not quite the same as referral or assignment. With the increasing degree of technological specialization that we have in modern society, we place more and more dependence upon experts and specialists. Even though the giving of assignments to such people may not relieve one of responsibility, there is a shade of difference. While you may yet suffer the consequences of the wrong judgment or of inadequate performance, the situation is more likely to be regarded by any who evaluate it in a somewhat different light. Thus, if you give an assignment to an ineffective staff medical officer or staff attorney, your business might suffer the consequences of a poor performance but your ability to delegate and to monitor the delegation may not be in question. If the incidents are repeated, however, the thing that might be questioned is the suitability of your staff.

How Well You Delegate

It is a strange thing but some of the worst delegators don't realize how poorly they are really doing. For that matter, very few of us are perfect delegators. The reasons may be simple or complex, readily apparent or buried deeply within our working personalities. Here are *some* of the reasons people may be unable or reluctant to delegate. See if any of them fit you.

1. You are so loaded with work, seeing clients, answering telephones, and answering correspondence, that you have no time to explain things.

2. You feel insecure about the people you have working for you: you are unable to take chances with them.

3. You may not know enough about the work yourself; the problems and courses of action may be so unclear to you that you don't even know what to pass on to others.

4. You are fearful of your ability to maintain control over the work once you let it get out of your hands.

5. The man above you may not permit delegation on specific matters.

6. You take the short-term view on each new assignment, saying that you can do it faster; you overlook the long-term gains through investing a little extra time in developing greater capabilities in your subordinates.

7. You simply do not know how to plan your work and supervise its execution through others.

Of course, these are only some of the simpler reasons for a failure or inability to delegate. Sometimes the reasons for non-delegation are so personal that we may not be aware of them or, if we are, we may not want to admit to them. "While it is not always fashionable to make reference to irrationality, it would be incorrect to overlook it," said Ernest Dale and Lyndall Urwick, the noted management consultants. "It is a vital and sometimes overwhelming factor working against effective delegation. Of these irrational factors, the strongest is probably the chief executive's desire for power and the fact that he likes the feeling of exercising it. These sentiments are linked with the instinct for personal survival. Executives tend to be reluctant to delegate because they fear the lessening of their personal power and the actual or potential strengthening of possible rivals. Hence one observes that presidents move to the board chairmanships but continue to act as chief executives. They fear—and their fears are often well-founded—that the younger men, their likely successors, wish to assume power as soon as they can. Therefore any reduction in their own power will push them that much faster toward a position of declining influence."

The matter of effective delegation is so important that I think it worthwhile to pursue even further our understanding of the barriers to effective delegation. A psychologist, Dr. Richard B. Cravens, and a psychiatrist, Dr. Addison Duval of the Missouri Division of Mental Diseases, have made up a catalogue of leader-types who have delegation blockages.

1. *The untrained leader,* they say, ". . . does not delegate because it does not occur to him to do so. . . . He simply cannot see the value in delegating duties he has taken care of for years. If the subordinates are eager for self-development,

they may threaten the uninformed leader, thereby creating an unhappy situation replete with suspicion, anger, and jealousy."

2. *The "I" leader* may try to satisfy ". . . needs that are unhealthy or destructive in nature. In order to meet relentless demands of a narcissistic makeup, deny feelings of weakness, prove adequacy, and enhance self-esteem, the leader may assume as much of the decision-making process as is possible. This person is unable to share the problems of a business. To do so may be viewed as evidences of personal defect, so ideas presented by others, regardless of excellence, will be discarded."

3. *The competitive leader* fears that he ". . . is in open competition with his associates. The motivation to compete may be based on such things as a desire for promotion, for power, wealth, control of people, self-enhancement, etc. In open form, he may plagiarize the ideas of others, but the variety of subtle competitive acts are too endless to mention except that all represent an attempt to present one's self in the best possible light at the expense of others."

4. *The fearful leader* is characterized by ". . . insecurity regarding competency and adequacy, with considerable emphasis placed on the latter. He has gone through life apprehensive and fearful of every step. It is not so much that he must be right and the other person wrong; he simply cannot tolerate mistakes. . . . He checks and double-checks his work. He strives for perfection."

5. *The incommunicative leader* is not the type, for our purpose, who deliberately refuses to communicate; rather, he does not know *how* to communicate. "This leader does not use written or recorded memos or the inter-office communication system. He stops a person in the hall and gives them what amounts to a garbled or incomplete picture of an assignment; he is often successful in alienating people through his informal discussion of issues with one person while not discussing the same topic with his entire staff; he has not developed the conference technique or the use of the agenda in order to facilitate conferencing. Interpersonal difficulties develop because people do not like to be in the dark, . . . to do a poor job, and do not relish redoing a job, all of which may result from defective communication."

Drs. Cravens and Duval remind us also of the overdelegating type of leader. "The reasons are varied, but influencing factors could be incompetency, feelings of inadequacy, or a life orientation based on a something-for-nothing attitude using manipulation as a main tool. They have learned the technique but have discarded the philosophy of delegation."*

Now, how well do *you* delegate? Is lack of delegation a serious problem for you? To assist you in finding out for yourself, I have devised the following questionnaire based on real-life experiences of a number of people:

1. If you're taken out, who knows your work sufficiently well to be able to move in and assume your work load?

2. Do you have to let one important task slip in order to take on another?

3. Are you unable to find time to plan ahead?

4. Are you unable to find a subordinate who is able to relieve you when you are under pressure?

5. Do you miss deadlines frequently or consistently?

6. Are you unable to find time for important public relations and professional engagements?

7. Do you have a waiting list of unanswered questions and requests for appointments from your subordinates?

8. Do you work long after regular office hours? Do you take a briefcase home?

9. Do you dictate most of the correspondence, memoranda, and reports prepared for your signature?

Positive answers to any of these—"yes" answers—are indicative of a need for delegation or divestment of responsibilities or both.

What to Delegate

Admittedly, there are things that you cannot properly delegate, but there are also many more things that you can. Here is a list of transferable duties:

1. Fact-finding and analysis prior to review and decision.

2. Formulation, but not final determination, of goals, policies,

* "Barriers Preventing Delegation," *Public Administration News,* Spring 1961.

programs, plans, and projects on which you must make personal decisions.

3. Execution of any of the foregoing after you have reached your decision.

4. Preparation of first drafts.

5. Performance of routines and carrying out of details and supporting activities.

6. Tasks others can do better, sooner, or cheaper.

7. Representation of you at meetings, conferences, and special functions where your point of view can be expressed in your behalf without your actually being there.

8. Tasks which will help develop your subordinates through exposure to new problems.

9. Parts of your work load, if you have overspecialized, to permit you to take on additional kinds of work.

10. Parts of your work, if you have underspecialized, in order for you to be able to devote more time to fewer tasks with greater effect.

The list of things you cannot delegate includes the converse of some of the foregoing items as well as a few additional ones. You must reserve to yourself duties such as the following:

1. Making of decisions at critical junctures of control, such as determination of goals, determination of policies, and approval of programs, plans, and projects which commit substantial resources or which are important to the success of the enterprise as a whole.

2. Execution of tasks where the goals are not clear, of policies where they are not clear or where they are so new as to require intimate contact during a trial period, and of new programs or projects where the commitments of resources and the risks are very great.

3. Personal representation where your own presence is highly important because of its implications for your organization's public relations or because of the effects on the morale of those who need and desire your presence.

4. The hiring, discipline, and firing of your immediate staff.

5. Items which must be handled under great pressure without time for feedback from someone else carrying out the work.

6. Emergency, short-term tasks when there is no time to explain or train.

7. Unique or highly personalized tasks which can never again come up.

8. Things which must be kept absolutely secret.

When to Delegate

The delegation of responsibilities is usually for categories of things rather than for specific acts. When a new matter arises for handling by a subordinate, it is assigned by you for handling within the previously understood pattern of delegation. In fact, you might not even see it; it might be referred by whoever opens the mail or it might be routed directly to the particular employee by someone else who knows that such matters are handled for you by him.

When there are drastic changes in the pattern of delegation, particularly when you want to take responsibilities away from someone or redistribute them, it is well to make such changes at times of readiness for change. If things are going along in a certain way and you make a change, eyebrows will be raised and the morale of affected employees may be unhinged. Following are some of the occasions which can be used as an excuse for reshuffling duties and responsibilities or for taking them back:

1. Personnel changes: key hirings, promotions, and departures which justify a redistribution of duties.

2. Reorganizations, because their effect is usually distributed over many people without putting the finger on anyone in particular.

3. Special events and crises which are of such importance or magnitude that they justify, in themselves, the emergency reassignment of responsibilities or their withdrawal to afford time for work on the more critical matters.

4. The creation of new activities or the assignment of brand-new duties which add to the already-full work load and hence call for redistribution.

To Whom to Delegate

In the well-ordered organization there are certain logical recipients of delegation. To depart from the pattern of acceptance could "rock the boat" if any employees feel that the delegation should be theirs for any special reason. It is hard to know what goes on in an employee's mind. You might think that you are getting a little better job done, but the employee may feel that the assignment comes within his purview and that your failure to give it to him may be some indication of a lack of confidence in him. Ordinarily, you should have an overriding cause for departing from the logical pattern of assignment.

The logical recipients of delegation usually are:

1. Employees in line of responsibility—who report directly to you.

2. Functional (task or technique) specialists.

3. Specially qualified or knowledgeable people—those with backgrounds of prior experience.

4. People designated as trouble shooters to handle emergency assignments which must be handled outside of the normal work load.

5. People with seniority who feel entitled to certain favorite assignments.

Notwithstanding any general rules which should be followed in the ordinary course, your main preoccupation is with getting the job done. In the final analysis, when you delegate responsibilities, you expect the job to be done. If you have any doubts as to this, you may need to find an excuse to do it yourself or to have someone else do it. In fact, if the situation as pertains to a particular employee is not remediable, you may need to replace him or to reassign him to other duties.

Following are some of the criteria which will aid you in evaluating an employee's ability to assume a delegation of responsibility:

1. Ability to absorb additional work loads.

2. Ability to lay out a work program with a minimum of direct supervision and to carry it out on his own responsibility.

3. Temperamental suitability for the assignment.

4. Acceptability to others with whom he must work or who have a major interest in the conduct of the work.

5. Availability of unused or untapped skills and initiative, especially where men are eager for responsibility or where they have potentials not fully realized in the interests of the organization.

How to Delegate

Now that we have gone through the preliminaries of recognizing our need for delegation and identifying what, when, and to whom to delegate, we are at that critical moment when we must do something about it. You will recall that one of the leadership types listed above was the uncommunicative leader—the one who simply was not able to put his ideas across. The recipient of delegation needs to know clearly what is expected of him. This subdivides into a number of topics, as follows:

1. Sufficient authority must be delegated, together with the responsibility, to enable the individual to carry out the task assigned to him. That is, he must understand fully what rights and powers he has—what decisions he can make on his own.

2. Clarify the resources to be made available and the limitations upon their use, in terms of dollars, personnel, physical facilities, time, and any others applicable.

3. Specify the conditions for checkback and feedback: when the individual should check back to obtain a go-ahead signal for the next phase and when he merely needs to send in reports of progress without interrupting his activity.

These are general specifications for the manner of delegating. As to the subject matter itself, you should provide as much background as possible. Consistent with the background of the individual, you should allow enough time for interactions with you, for questions and answers. If there are others who can give him additional background and guidance, you should refer him to them. Everything possible should be done to start the individual off adequately prepared and fully confident.

Of course, each case must be judged on its own. Some employees need be given only a brief identification of what is expected of them and they will take off on their own, requiring no additional guidance beyond that of a privileged nature which you feel you wish to communicate. Other employees may need to be taken in hand, cautiously, and guided along the path until they feel sure of their way—or until you feel sure of it.

How to Control Delegations

I remember a discussion with a businessman who was debating whether or not to take on a new employee. His main query to me was whether or not I thought the new employee would be willing to have someone looking over his shoulder all the time, checking up on his progress. Having been irked by this businessman myself in this regard, I looked him in the eye and said, in measured tones, "Nobody likes someone peering constantly over his shoulder."

Having delegated responsibility which you yet retain, as we discussed above, you cannot turn your attention away completely, no matter how much confidence you have in an employee. As with all things, however, there is a middle ground between too much and too little. In order not to weaken the employee's confidence in his own performance, the technique you need to develop for yourself is to look without seeming to look. Here are a few pertinent suggestions:

1. Establish the minimum number of checkback and feedback requirements at the commencement of the assignment. If you impose these controls later on, after the commencement of the assignment, the employee might interpret doing so as evidence of a lack of confidence.

2. Set up "lateral controls." These are requirements for the employee to tie his work in with someone else or to obtain guidance or review from another party without having to come back to you.

3. Give the employee a check list, if possible and convenient, setting forth the criteria of achievement or the sensitive points of performance which he should observe. If possible and convenient, suggest to him a model of performance—how someone else operates or an example of something else that has been done—so that he can have a tangible basis of comparison.

4. Use routine methods of checking, such as periodic staff meetings, periodic progress reports, and participation in other planning conferences at which it would be necessary to tie in a progress report on the particular area of assignment.

5. Be reasonably accessible for conferences with the employee to discuss key aspects only.

6. Use indirect reminders. For example, suggest the need for getting into a new area of activity and use this information as an excuse for inquiring about progress. Use a related memorandum or document, sent to the individual, as an excuse for attaching an inquiry about progress.

TEAMING UP WITH YOUR SECRETARY

A take-off from another famous saying goes like this: "If you have something to do, give it to a busy man and his secretary will do it."

Your secretary can be one of your most important multipliers of time. If she enjoys your confidence, if she understands your work problems and priorities, and if she can handle your relationships with others effectively, you can delegate to her a great many things which otherwise you would have to do yourself, which you could not delegate to anyone else. It is inherent in the role of the secretary that her mission is to make you as effective as possible. Osborn Elliott, in his book, *Men At the Top,* dramatized this somewhat with the following:

Boss: Where's my pencil?
Secretary: Behind your ear.
Boss: Dammit, woman, I'm a busy man. Which ear?

Things the Secretary Can Do

The duties you can assign to your secretary will depend to a great extent on whether she is your private secretary or whether you share her with one or more other people. The shared secretary can never begin to approach in effectiveness the private secretary but, of course, this is not always economically feasible. The private secretary is able to acquaint herself intimately with all aspects of your work and to help you in your efforts to achieve your goals. She gets to know your callers and correspondence more intimately and learns how to handle them in your behalf with a minimum of instruction. The shared secretary may do some of this but she tends to be restricted to stenographic, typing, and clerical duties, in addition to answering the telephone and receiving visitors.

Among the many different duties which can be performed by a private secretary, in addition to standard stenographic duties and telephone-answering duties, are the following:

1. Organizing and maintaining the informational resources which are most helpful to her superior.

2. Providing a work-reminder service for her superior, to assure that he gets things done when scheduled.

3. Following up with others in behalf of her superior.

4. Reviewing incoming memoranda and correspondence, prepared for his signature, to assure that they represent completed staff work and that there are no factual discrepancies.

5. Digesting or summarizing incoming materials; identifying key items of interest in reports.

6. Provision of a public-relations reminder service to her superior, to assure that he remembers birthdays and biographical facts about people with whom he maintains relationships.

7. Preparation of certain of his correspondence where she has adequate background.

8. Elaboration on her superior's correspondence, working from rough notes, or stylistic improvement on his more detailed correspondence.

9. Marking and clipping of trade literature and other reading matter.

10. Performance of research fact-finding on matters which should not be delegated to others (or for which others are not available).

11. Arrangement of travel and speaking engagements, including making of reservations and the preparation of expense reports.

12. The keeping of records of the ins-and-outs of important documents, visitors, and telephone calls.

Of course, these are highly generalized duties applicable to a great variety of situations. The secretary might also be book-keeper, petty-cash banker, order taker, procurement officer, chief of office clerical staff, and files chief. In a medical practice she would be expected to operate much of the equipment, to prepare patients for examination, to obtain specimens, etc.

These are examples of the many things a secretary can do to

multiply the effectiveness of her superior. Her ability to do these things, however, will depend in no small measure on the pains you take to explain how you operate and what you need.

Prerequisites for an Effective Relationship

George Washington was one of the most punctual of men. He looked upon time as a scarce resource and adhered rigidly to his schedule. It is said that upon one occasion his secretary arrived late, offering the excuse that his watch was slow. To this, Washington said, quietly: "Then you must get another watch or I another secretary."

Thereafter, one must presume, the secretary was as punctilious as his employer because otherwise he would not have survived in the job. How much better it would have been, however, if the incident could have been anticipated, if Washington could have told him in advance how important it was to him to maintain his schedules and how the lagging of a watch hand would not serve as an excuse.

The advance briefing of the secretary is fundamental. She must come to learn more about you and your operating interests, plans, hopes, and habits than even you might be aware of. If she is to be a mind reader, you must at least open the door of your mind.

In particular, she must understand how you want her to handle your personal working relationships. Your secretary should never be a substitute for you or a barrier. At most she can be your representative. Unfortunately, though, too many private secretaries get carried away by their identification with their superiors. Inevitably, this shows up in their own relationships with other employees who, in one way or another, will express their displeasure to you. This can provoke a great deal of time-wasting friction.

Since the management of your schedule is a very important part of your secretary's duties, you should have weekly and daily briefings in which you both review your respective and joint working schedules. You should convey a sense of the priorities and, sometimes, the specific things you want to avoid during the week.

THE HELPFUL USE OF ASSISTANTS

The very busy person, especially in a large organization, may need a great deal of assistance beyond that which can be provided by the most versatile secretary. The kind of help he will need will depend, of course, upon his own operating personality, the nature of the work, and the nature of the pressures on his time.

To illustrate, there are all-in-one aides, such as executive assistants, relationship aides who deal solely with people, action aides who follow up on situations or who act as trouble shooters, research aides, and counseling aides, among others.

The relationships between these special aides and your personal secretary must be carefully defined since your special aides may tend to operate, sometimes, as if they were independent of her area of cognizance. This is more likely to be a problem if you have an executive assistant or a general "assistant to."

The Functions of "Assistants To"

Sometimes the role of an "assistant to" is to protect the executive from himself, says Francis D. Tappan, assistant to the vice president of North American Aviation, Inc. "Some executives, like to be 'in' on almost everything, while others rely on their immediate staff to keep all matters from them except those relating to their own level of responsibility. This latter approach lends itself better to optimum utilization of time, but is most difficult to achieve for a vigorous executive with a large variety of interests and a strong urge to be in close touch with his subordinates."

The functions of the typical executive assistant or "assistant to" are probably as varied as there are such individual jobs. This is quite understandable, since the assistant must be an extension of the operating personality of his superior, even though he may be expected to complement him in some respects. In a sense he is a kind of super secretary. What distinguishes him from the personal secretary is his deeper involvement in the actual conduct of his superior's business and his mobility in attending to it. He may represent his superior away from the office. He may participate in conferences and follow through on execution of arrangements. He may possess certain special skills. His business maturity may make of him a confidante with whom his superior can converse in full confidence.

The privileged access which the "assistant to" will enjoy with you will not be without its complications. He may get to see more of you—or at least seem to in the belief of others— than those who have a direct operating relationship with you. This may be resented, along with the fear that the "assistant to" is monitoring their activities, even though it is done in your behalf. Much of this feeling may, in fact, be engendered by your assistant if he is not careful.

The "assistant to" must subordinate his own personality. He can function only as your personal representative, making it clear at all times that he speaks for you and not instead of you. Even more so than in the case of the personal secretary, you will avoid burdensome frictions if you clarify your relationships not only with your assistant but with your principal staff as well, so that they will understand clearly how you operate with an assistant. You must be careful at all times never to subordinate your principal staff, even seemingly, to your staff assistant.

In selecting an "assistant to" you might keep in mind the following qualifications:

1. Ability to grasp situations and their meanings quickly; ability to see the heart of the situation and to sense critical factors.

2. Ability to see the broad picture and to understand the interrelatedness of programs and activities, especially as they relate to the whole.

3. Ability to take particular situations, matters, and proposals and to relate their implications to past actions as well as to the unfolding series of actions to come.

4. Facility for absorbing, remembering, and interpreting facts; facility for knowing what additional facts are needed and where and how to get them.

5. Sensitivity to interpersonal implications.

6. Facility for oral and written communication; flair for brief expression.

7. Sensitivity to timing factors.

8. Ability either to complement his superior or to blend his personality and operating methods with those of his superior or to do both in varying degree.

9. Possessed of courage, ethics, and a passion for anonymity.

The Prudent Use of Assistants

As with personal secretaries, one of the chief complaints of the "assistant to" is that he does not have sufficient access to his superior. He may be pressed through a rush assignment only to find that he cannot check it out on some critical point. He may be working diligently on a certain matter, only to find after he has invested many hours of effort in it at the expense of other things he might do, that his superior has already disposed of the matter without telling him so. Worst of all, his entire confidence in his relationship with you may be shaken if you ever fail to support him in a pinch when he needs your support because he has actually done your bidding.

A difficulty may arise because the way in which he carries out an assignment may not be precisely the way in which you would do so. What Clarence Randall had to say about managers is also true of managerial assistants: "What comes particularly hard to the top man is to watch his next-in-line embark on a course of action of which he disapproves and still make up his mind to support him. Yet that must happen at times. So long as he stays within the area where reasonable men may differ, the junior manager must be given his head, or he will work in a constant state of frustration. Only when he completely oversteps the bounds of prudence, may he be overruled. If he has made a decision of marginal wisdom, he will find it out and be the better man for it."*

* "The Lonely Art of Decision-Making," *Dun's Review and Modern Industry,* June 1959.

SUMMARY

The ability to work through others is one of the hallmarks of success. Through others you multiply your effectiveness, for you are enabled to concentrate your time on those things which bring you the greatest return.

Many of us, however, are either unable or reluctant to delegate. The reasons may be found in a lack of training or they may be buried in the insecurities by which our behavior may be governed. Hence, if you are to be able to improve your own skills of delegation, you must first take stock of yourself, looking for the objective evidence of insufficient delegation, whatever the reason.

The essence of delegation is the retention of control. When you delegate, you never relinquish your personal responsibility for results. Accordingly, you can delegate, safely, almost anything which does not deprive you of that certain fraction of control. For this reason, you may delegate all but the key decisions, the making of the key policies, and the making of the key commitments. Additionally, you would not delegate certain matters of privilege and privacy.

In the actual making of a delegation you would be careful to select the recipients of delegation for their capability in accepting it. In addition to communicating adequately what is expected in actual performance, you must introduce elements of checkback and feedback to assure that at least as to the critical junctures of action, you would be informed.

For your most loyal multiplication of self, you will look to your personal secretary and to personal assistants on your immediate staff. In the truest sense they are the extensions of self to whom you will look for personal assistance and personal guidance. A successful relationship with your immediate staff depends upon the extent to which you take such people into camp, providing them with as much information as possible about your goals, your relationships, and your commitments of time. Finally, if you are to command their loyalty, you must give them yours, backing them up on errors of the head whenever the heart has been in your service.

VIII

More Multipliers

The employee to whom Arthur Gibbens had given an assignment came back later in the day with a worried look on his face.

"I don't think I can get this done by the end of the week, as you requested," he said.

"Why not? There shouldn't be more than about a half-day of work on this and you have four days left in the week."

"But," he replied, "it will take me more than a week just to compile all the data, let alone analyze it."

"Have you tried the library?"

"Uh-h-h-h, no."

"Well, if you ask the librarian, she probably has the information you will need in some reports of the Bureau of Labor Statistics. If she doesn't have the reports on hand, call Tom Street. He'll be able to help you."

This is a typical supervisory experience. The time wasted in recompiling information and in not taking advantage of other short cuts is incalculable. In the incident cited above, two time-saving techniques were mentioned, which we will cover in this chapter. They are (1) knowing people who can help you and (2) knowing the sources of information that have already been compiled. Other ways of multiplying yourself, which we shall cover here, are through (3) personal systems short cuts and (4) mechanical timesavers.

THE PEOPLE YOU KNOW

Through your co-operative relationships with your colleagues and with people you know in your profession, trade, or community, you can broaden your informational grasp tremendously. A single telephone call to the right person might make available to you the benefits of his own years of experience, his own informational files and resources, and his own access to other sources of information.

This is not a matter of one-way exploitation. In our daily business relationships we encounter many people with special technical knowledges and skills, acquaintanceships, access, geographical convenience, and physical facilities. *Potentially,* each is a source of assistance. Whether or not you can call upon any of these people will depend upon your relationships as well as the legitimacy and nature of your request.

How to Acquire Exposure

People can help you with more than information and favors. By exposure to the activities and ideas of others, you may be stimulated into avenues of useful development entirely upon your own. You can have none of these opportunities, however, if you keep entirely to yourself or if you refuse to share of yourself. You must make a deliberate effort to get out and rub shoulders —in moderation—with many different kinds of people with whom you might have a community of interest.

You should not expect a high rate of return numerically. If one in ten or one in a hundred of your exposures to people should develop into a mutually advantageous relationship, you would thereby add tremendously to your own resources. To your lifetime of experience, you annex the knowledges, capabilities, and insights developed during the lifetimes of others.

How do you find people with whom you can share mutual

interests? Of course, you must have actual exposure, but I think primarily it begins with a genuine interest in people.

Not long ago I ran across my neighbor, Arthur Turner, in the public library. I had known him only in the most casual way as the father of my son's friend and schoolmate. I had known also that he was a retail businessman and from that I drew surface conclusions as to his probable down-to-earth practicality.

In his hand, in the library, I noted a book on current world affairs. As we talked, a new image of him was built in my mind. I learned that he had written and published poetry, had a fluent command of many languages, and was addicted to many cultural as well as recreational pursuits. The ensuing discussion brought out, to his surprise, my own background in political science and public affairs as well as my own preoccupations which he had never suspected.

Of course, the moral of the story is that you cannot tell a book by its cover; you must dig into its pages. The point I wish to emphasize, however, is that mere probing alone is not sufficient. You must display genuine interest if you are to provoke a reciprocal interest.

This is illustrated in an experience which my wife had at a dinner party at the home of my old friend Harry Shaw. Ruth was talking to Paul Hendrickson, director of administration for the Emerson Research Laboratories. We had known of his prior background only as an FBI agent, but as Ruth conversed with him, much more came out. She learned about his early life, his boyhood family, his education, and that he at one time had been a high-school teacher.

Suddenly, he caught himself. With some mild embarrassment over his autobiographical excursion, he said, "But why am I telling you all this? I was trained to find out about people rather than to satisfy their curiosity."

"But I didn't ask you all the things you told me," said Ruth.

"But you seemed so interested," Paul retorted.

And that's the point of the story.

There is another point: You need not go too far afield to find the riches that are the personalities and backgrounds of people. They are found in your own neighborhood and in your place of business. These relationships you should cultivate and build in the normal course of things.

Additionally, you might budget your time for active participation in community and in professional and trade-association activities. The greatest benefits will be derived not merely from passive attendance but mainly from active participation, whether it be as a speaker, a member of a working committee, or the recipient of an individual assignment.

In our ordinary business intercourse we may have many opportunities for the making of real friendships, even among our competitors.

Edward Weeks, editor of *The Atlantic,* told how Alfred R. McIntyre, with the Boston publishing house of Little, Brown and Company, saved a competitor from great loss. Being a good businessman, McIntyre read his competitors' books as carefully as his own. One day he visited one of his greatest rivals who was about to release a novel of mammoth size. As Weeks told the story, McIntyre said: "Quite a book you've got there. Have you read it?" "Well, no, actually I haven't," said the publisher. "But everyone here who has is crazy about it." "Better read it," said Alfred. "Take a look at page 158!"

On that page there was a paragraph so offensive that it undoubtedly would have hurt the sale of the book. Somehow, it had escaped the notice of the five judges of a book club as well as the publisher's own editors. Grateful to their friendly competitor, the firm recalled the edition and revised the page.

What did this gain McIntyre besides the gratitude of his competitor? Some people would reason that to let a competitor hurt himself is to help oneself. Of course, this does not necessarily follow. Fortunately, there are some people in the business world like McIntyre, whose integrity must prevail. Inevitably they are discovered and placed in high esteem even among their most ardent competitors.

Friendliness, however, is a flower of slow growth. The bloom may require long nurturing. It will wither before its unfolding if it is not nurtured by sincerity.

The Art of Seeking Help

Friends can be very helpful but this does not mean that you should develop friendships in order to exploit them. While this may be the structure of relationships that many people try to build for themselves, in the long run it will prove faulty because it will have been made from base materials.

There is another approach. It is a recognition of life as a grand symbiosis in which people, in all their minute specializations, find mutually advantageous associations with others.

When you seek aid or favor, you are on safest ground when you do so on some basis of mutuality. Otherwise, you are quite likely to encounter reactions which range from simple reluctance to outright rejection. It is a paradox that the display of need should be responded to with avoidance. If you seek favor without it being based on some form of mutuality, you put yourself strictly on a market-place economics in which you will find people eager to be of assistance only when you least need it— when their own sense of opportunism tells them that you are on the rise and it might be the better part of expedience to do you a good turn.

The conclusion one might draw from this is that each should build his career and his business life on a base of self-sufficiency. His dependence upon others for voluntary assistance should be based on mutuality of interest, especially where the granting and receiving of favor is not each time placed upon a scale and weighed minutely.

Whatever the relationship, the seeking of favor or assistance should be done judiciously with due regard for the need of others to attend to their own concerns. Following are a few suggestions in this regard:

1. The person you ask should be in a position to grant your request or refer you to someone who can. To avoid embarrassment, as well as the waste of the other person's time, you should try to ascertain this in advance.

2. Before you decide to take up some of the time of another person, certify to yourself that your relationship permits this, or that the matter is of such obvious importance that the need speaks for itself.

3. Your request must be reasonable and proper. It must not be anything that would embarrass or jeopardize your friend's position; certainly, not anything unethical or dishonest.

4. Avoid imposing upon friends who occupy positions of influence. Remember that they are living targets for many favor-seekers. If your relationship permits it, the most you ordinarily

should do is to inform them as to your need without actually requesting assistance. If they can help—and want to—they may themselves offer their assistance (and, in fact, are more likely to when not requested). If they don't want to be of assistance, there is no embarrassment.

5. Find a way of putting your request which gives the other person a way out. It is only natural that you should seek an appeal which will engender some desire on the part of your business friend or acquaintance to want to help you. On the other hand, if this is not to be forthcoming for lack of desire or for simple inability to accommodate you, you will both appreciate it if you have provided a basis for easy disengagement.

6. The timing of your request should be appropriate. You would not want to ask a favor of someone who obviously is preoccupied with serious problems of his own or who is otherwise working under his own pressures.

7. Should the request be accommodated, it is quite appropriate for you to express your pleasure and gratification, but if you overdo your offer of reciprocal favor, this might be resented by anyone who does not want to feel that he is being bought. Should the favor be denied, it is equally important that you not show the slightest evidence of bad grace or rancor.

How to Evaluate Sources

In the preceding section we discussed the availability of assistance from others. We have yet to go into the question of *whose* assistance.

Sometimes the person to whom you turn can do little more than steer you to others. This is a worthwhile contribution. Sometimes the source you seek may be the only one. Then, you must consider whether it is better than none at all or worse than none. After all, you are better off with an informational vacuum than to take some action based on wrong information.

Whether it is information you seek or action, you must have some criteria for evaluating your sources both before and after you approach them, but mainly beforehand. One of the most important questions is: Is he a primary or a secondary source of assistance? If it is information you seek, does he have primary or secondary knowledge of the situation? If it is something you want done, is he the one to decide or to take action, or must he go to someone else? Now, the secondary source might not be the best, but if it is all that you can obtain, it might be wonderful in the circumstances. We are not here choosing; rather, we are ranking the preferences.

By way of caution, the well-known authority is not necessarily the best authority. The man's contributions might lie in another field. Success in one area does not necessarily carry over into another (even though we might ask a screen actress or champion pugilist to lend weight to great causes or to express their opinions on critical issues of the day).

The authoritative person represents all of his cumulative experience. It is to this body of experience that you must go rather than to his surface reputation if you want to evaluate its pertinence to your present problem. In other words, the authority by which he speaks is not his personal reputation but his actual experience and insights.

By way of example, to translate this into an everyday business-problem situation, let us assume that you want to market a product by mail. You seek advice. There are two kinds of information you need: One is the marketability of the item itself and the other is your promotional approach if you should go ahead with it. The right advice is important to you because it can save you from making some very expensive errors. You might be able to obtain information and advice from one source, but the greater likelihood is that you will need to go to two or three, each authoritative in his own way.

You will bear in mind, as you turn to others, that knowledge of product and market is not necessarily a qualification for advising on the mail-order aspects of your proposition. On the other hand, the expert on mail-order techniques might not be able to give you any useful guidance on your particular product. Finally, remember that ideas and information are where you find them. They are not the exclusive endowment of people who have arrived. Don't forget the unsung hero—the little fellow who has yet to make his way and his name, the little fellow whose ideas may one day make him king.

STORES OF INFORMATION

The people to whom you turn for assistance often will render you a service by directing you to public sources of information of which they have special knowledge, or they may send you copies of special studies, reports, speeches, memoranda, and other "fugitive" materials. Such items usually have limited availability. Rarely do they find their way into catalogued storehouses of information.

One very important source to which you should turn is your personal storehouse—both your recorded and unrecorded experiences, studies, and findings. This does not mean that you should save every scrap of information or every piece of writing you have ever done. Rather, you will need at least some rules-of-thumb to guide you in saving the kinds of things which might one day be useful.

What to Save for the Future

In general, you will want to save things that represent original effort, that cannot be re-created except at great expense, or that constitute convenient compilations of data not otherwise available.

You would not want to save any materials, even if they fall within the criteria just given, if they are abundantly available from other sources, or if they may be found in a central file. You would not save anything devoid of any original contribution. This would include information available from original sources or in more up-to-date form. It need scarcely be mentioned that without some special justification you would not want to clutter your files with routine correspondence and memoranda.

The accumulation of books is another matter. Books that relate to your main areas of interest can save you a great deal of time. The few dollars that you might save in not acquiring a certain book may easily be spent many times over if you need to develop the information yourself or if you need to run to some distant library to borrow a copy. Nevertheless, there is a limit to the collecting of books. One approach is to purchase books that you may want to read and *reread* from time to time. Try to build a collection of books which, together, represent a comprehensive coverage of subject matter in which you will have a future interest. Theoretically, you can find them in the library, but if you need information when the library is closed, your needs will then have to be deferred. Accordingly, in addition to the justification of frequent reference, add convenience on the spur-of-the-moment.

Effective Use of Reference Sources

One of the great problems of our day is the cataloguing of the tremendous stores of information being produced by government agencies, trade associations, scientific organizations, universities, and industrial organizations. The efforts to catalogue these materials are but preliminary to the main effort of retrieving from them the helpful information that may contribute to a current problem.

On a much lesser scale, within our own organization, even within our own file cabinets, we have more readily identifiable problems of retrieval. It is easy enough to store the information, but putting one's hands on it at the moment it is needed is an entirely different matter. The approach of vacation time for one's secretary has made many an executive shudder as he contemplates his inability to find the papers he will need.

Whether it be something you want from the library or something from a file cabinet, the finding of material of whose existence you may not even be sure many depend largely upon how you ask for it. You may think of the information in one context, while the librarian or file clerk may get either an entirely different idea of what you want or an erroneous assumption as to where to look for it.

One approach you can follow is to try to imagine the context in which the librarian or other informational custodian is likely to visualize the information you desire. A knowledge of the cataloguing or filing system would be helpful but not always practicable for you. More often, you will need to suggest a variety of possible reference headings.

Another technique is the finding of an informational springboard. If you can locate just one scrap of material in the pages of a book or the contents of a file, you can use this to stimulate the retrieving imagination of the person who is trying to help you. This also is a technique which you can use in your personal researches. Sometimes you will find actual documented references to other source materials which have been consulted by the writer. You may also find references to people who are authorities on the subject or who know about specific activities. You might find topical references that will lead you into additional areas of inquiry. Explain the purpose for which you seek information, if you are free to do so.

The business and technology divisions or the general reference divisions of most city libraries will have most or all of the following indexes to books and periodicals:

Applied Science and Technology Index. Monthly cumulative index to 199 periodicals in fields of engineering, applied science, and industry. For references prior to 1958 see *Industrial Arts Index.*

Books in Print and *Subject Guide to Books in Print.* The former is indexed by author and title. Both are annuals.

Business Periodicals Index. Monthly cumulative index to 120 periodicals in fields of business, finance, labor relations, insurance, advertising, office management, etc. For references prior to 1958 see *Industrial Arts Index.*

Cumulative Book Index. Monthly releases of new books, with bound annual, semiannual, and larger cumulations at other intervals.

Public Affairs Information Service. Five issues a year with an additional bound volume covering, by subject, materials relating to economic and social conditions, public administration and international relations, published in English throughout the world. Lists many types of directories, including industrial and manufacturing directories.

You can send for a *free* copy of *How to Use the Readers' Guide to Periodical Literature and Other Indexes.* Write: H. W. Wilson Co., 95–972 University Ave., New York 52, N.Y.

Two useful indexes to current news and comment are the *New York Times Index* and the *Wall Street Journal Index.* Bound or microfilm copies of both of these newspapers are available in most city libraries, at least in their main offices.

Consult the following general directories:

Economic Almanac. Annual handbook of useful facts about business, labor, and government; compiled by the National Industrial Conference Board and published by Thomas Y. Crowell Co., 432 Fourth Ave., New York 16, N.Y.

Encyclopedia of American Associations, 2d ed., Nov. 1958. Guide to trade, business, professional, labor, scientific, educational, fraternal and social organizations of the United States. Gale Research Co., 1116 Book Tower, Detroit 26, Michigan.

National Trade and Professional Associations of the United States, by Jay Judkins, United States Department of Commerce. (In production 1962, to be available from Superintendent of Documents, Washington 25, D.C.)

Poor's Register of Directors and Executives United States and Canada. Annual, indexed by corporation and individuals.

Sources of State Information and State Industrial Directories. 1958, 18pp. 35¢. Chamber of Commerce of the United States, State Chamber of Commerce Service Dept., 1615 H St., N.W., Washington 6, D.C.

Trade Directories of the World. 1958. $9.00. Croner Publications, Queens Village, New York.

Who's Who in America

Who's Who in Commerce and Industry

The United States Government, through its many departments and agencies, produces a tremendous amount of information that is publicly available, some of it from the originating sources and most of it from the Superintendent of Documents, Government Printing Office, Washington 25, D.C. A card or letter to the latter will bring a price list or catalog of printed matter on any given area of subject matter, if it is one covered by government materials—and the subjects that have not been covered seem few indeed! The following may be of general interest, all available from the Superintendent of Documents, unless otherwise indicated:

Business Cycle Developments. Monthly publication of the Bureau of Census. $4.00 a year.

Business Statistics. Biennial. A wide range of business indicators, from 1929 on. $2.00.

County and City Data Book. Summary census information, including metropolitan areas. $4.50.

Distribution Data Guide. Monthly, United States Department of Commerce. Annotated list of current publications of value to those marketing and distributing goods and services. Covers publications of federal, state, and local governments, associations and commercial organizations. $2.00 a year.

Facts for Industry. Seventy-two product series issued periodically containing information at factory level for different industries on inventory, production, shipments, and other indicators of business activity. List of titles and prices available from Bureau of the Census, Washington 25, D.C.

Federal Reserve Bulletin. Monthly. Comprehensive current and trade information on production, finance and banking, credit, commerce, construction, employment, carloadings, department stores, prices, international trade, insurance, etc. Special reports and analyses. $6.00 a year, Board of Governors of the Federal Reserve System, Washington 25, D.C.

Monthly Catalog of United States Government Publications. Most comprehensive catalog, including printed and processed publications, listed by agency. Includes congressional hearings, documents and reports. $3.00 a year.

Price list no. 36 Government Periodicals. Free.

Statistical Abstract of the United States. Annual. Standard source of national statistics. $3.50.

Survey of Current Business. Monthly report, statistics and articles, on significant economic developments. $4.00 a year, including four-page weekly statistical supplement.

United States Government Research Reports. Semimonthly listing of government research reports available to industry. $15.00 a year.

With the abundance of factual material available from all sources, not organized into specifically identifiable series, it is fortunate that there are a number of guides to informational sources, such as the following:

Business Information: How to Find and Use It. Marian C. Manley. 1955. New York: Harper & Brothers.

Government Statistics for Business Use. Philip M. Houser and William R. Leonard, editors. 2d. ed., 1956. New York: John Wiley & Sons, Inc.

How and Where to Look It Up: A Guide to Standard Sources

of Information. Robert W. Murphy. 1958. New York: McGraw-Hill Book Co., Inc.

Two useful bibliographical services, usually on file in libraries, but available through individual subscriptions, are:

Business Literature. The Public Library of Newark, New Jersey, The Business Library, 34 Commerce Street, Newark, New Jersey. $2.00 a year.

Business and Technical Sources. Bulletin of the Business and Technology Dept., Cleveland Public Library, Cleveland 14, Ohio. $1.00 a year.

Finally, it is advantageous to have access to a good research and reference service. As an example, membership in the American Management Association entitles one to use of its extensive research facilities through correspondence, telephone, or in person. All phases of industrial management, marketing, finance, international operations, production, and office management, among others, are covered.

In addition to the professional librarians and file clerks, you might turn to the specialists who are most likely to know what has been done in their own fields. They might be right within your own organization, in trade-association headquarters, on the staffs of trade papers, and on university faculties. If it's a matter of mere referral or identification of sources, these are usually free. Faculty members are usually so underpaid, in comparison with their industrial counterparts, that they are glad to have an opportunity to do some outside consulting work. The professional consulting field itself has become specialized to the point where you can purchase outside assistance covering intensive experience in given areas. When you buy this kind of assistance, you indirectly make available to yourself—and sometimes directly —the accumulated stores of knowledge of the consultant, covering a wide variety of related situations.

PERSONAL TIMESAVING SHORT CUTS

We come now to a variety of short cuts applicable to you personally as well as to your office procedures. Included in this section are reminder systems, communication short cuts, notemaking techniques, and the use of modern office equipment.

Reminder Systems

"This inexpensive device reminds you of many important things you forget in your busy daily routine," states a digest description of a recently granted United States patent. "Just write a note, drop into receptacle, and set at future date for month, day of month and hour of day. At that exact time the receptacle pops into view; also, bell rings which can be placed in any desired location of building. It is also a calendar clock, automatically changing name of day, month and year, compensating for months of less than 31 days. Manual resetting is required only at Leap Year. It may be used by secretaries, sales managers, follow-up in all businesses, lawyers, doctors, housewives, etc."

Can you visualize being summoned summarily from another part of the building by the insistent ringing of a bell which now commands that you read something you placed in the automatic tickler some eight and one-half months ago?

In the course of a year you might need to post ahead literally thousands of reminders. Each entry on your appointment calendar is a reminder. Systems technicians have developed any number of different kinds of "memory joggers" to help you keep track of the things you must do. They range from the very simple, such as "do" lists, to complex visible control systems and even to the use of electronic computers. Here I would like to comment on some of the simpler devices which you can use in your own work, especially if you do not have a secretary. They do not, however, replace that important functionary. Rather, they can be an important working tool of the secretary herself in her efforts to keep you on schedule.

The simple "do" list is most useful as a current inventory as well as a reminder of things requiring current action. You merely jot things down as they occur to you or, at intervals, you reflect on various things yet to be done and jot them down. Later, you might reorganize the list, assigning priorities or putting the activities into different groupings or on separate sheets according to their nature. Some people will prepare "do" lists the night before in order to get a head start on thinking about them or on planning their schedule for the next day. Others prefer to prepare the "do" list early in the morning, using a fresh mind with a fresh perspective.

Calendar systems are obvious and universal means of posting ahead on your reminders and commitments. For the busy man, one who has many visitors to receive or calls to make, the calendar is one of the most important tools of personal control. Particular note might be taken of the week-at-a-glance and month-at-a-glance calendars. These enable you to visualize all the things you must do over a span greater than that of a single day on a single sheet of a calendar. Their advantage is not merely in saving the turning of pages while you're working out an appointment with someone over the telephone. Rather, you can see the general configuration of your activities for a week or a month ahead.

For the man on the move, *pocket planners* may be convenient as reminders, time organizers, and note-makers. One commercially available system provides you with a leather pocket case, twelve monthly insert booklets, a telephone index for numbers called frequently, monthly summary cards, and a file chest in which to store the monthly inserts. The latter is thumb-indexed for each day of the month. When you turn to a particular date, you have a double-spread of two pages on which to enter things you must do that day as well as the things actually done of which you want a record. At the end of the month you post your expenses to a monthly summary card for expense reporting and tax reporting. Then you remove the completed calendar insert and insert one for the next month. The key to its effective use, of course, is to remember to consult it and to make entries in it. Unless you build it into your habit system, it becomes one additional pocket-stuffer.

Control-board systems are useful in much the same way as week-at-a-glance and month-at-a-glance calendars. The control board shows you the full array of activity which you must accomplish in the foreseeable future. The simplest control boards, such as blackboards and bulletin boards on the walls of your office, are mere visual inventories and reminders of things to do. More complex systems utilize visible file-card devices, with color coding on the marginal strips. As you get into more specific control of target schedules and progress toward them, you might turn to systems which utilize boards with time scales, colored pins or buttons, and colored tapes to chart your actual progress against previously scheduled completion times. If you want these for your personal use, you might observe these cautions: (1) Keep them simple, otherwise you will need a full-time person to administer them; (2) keep them current, or they will be worse than useless.

Colored signals are used to distinguish priorities or special tasks from the ordinary run of work. A colored sheet of paper covering an important document or work file will make it stand apart from all the other papers that come across your desk, thereby serving as a visual reminder. You cannot do too much of this, for then too many conspicuous colors will nullify the uniqueness of each. One way a variety of colors *might* be used is to have a different one for each day of the week. A distinctive color on a document would tell you that it must be done by the close of the day for which that color stands. This, however, like the complex control board, could become excessively troublesome. It might be more suited to massive clerical operations which require the precise scheduling ahead of completion times for each task.

Obviously, the mere availability of these various devices will not, in itself, provide you with the jogs and reminders you might like to have. You must make specific provision for feeding these into your reminder system. For example, you would take an inventory of all the cyclical events of which you must be reminded. These might include birthdays of customers and associates as well as of family, relatives, and friends. Then there are recurring special events or requirements, such as anniversaries, quarterly or annual reports, budget periods, conventions, rating periods, equipment-maintenance reminders, etc. You cannot keep all of these things in mind even if you try to, and if you did, you would be penalizing your ability to concentrate on the more important things.

If you work with a secretary, you might set up a system of "bring-up" in which you let her know currently about matters which you want referred back to you in the future. Rather than keep things on your desk or in your desk drawers, send them out to the secretary with a note slip saying, "Bring up in two weeks," or "Bring up after we get a reply from Smith." Some people make a habit of automatically entering a "bring-up" notation on the carbon copy of all action correspondence and memoranda which they sign.

Communication Short Cuts

Most of the suggestions now to be listed are intended to help you get extra mileage out of your regular activities. For example:

1. Floater files keep your associates or your subordinates informed of current matters on which you have been corresponding. Your secretary makes a floater-file copy of anything worthy of such treatment, binds the week's accumulation into a file folder, and routes it to a regular list.

2. Routed carbon copies of correspondence can be sent to specifically designated people who have specific interests in the subjects covered in the correspondence. In this way you save the time of telling them about the matters.

3. Tear sheets and clippings of useful information taken from trade journals, newspapers, and other literature, after you have read them, can be routed to others in the organization as well as to special customers or clients when you think they might also profit from the information.

4. The chain method of conducting staff meetings can move information up or down the line quickly and effectively. Important matters originating at top staff meetings, suitable for transmission, are discussed at the next lower levels of staff meetings by those who attended the preceding ones. Conversely, important matters arising at subordinate staff meetings are referred up the line for discussion and consideration.

For the busy executive, standard incoming formats will enable him to get very quickly to the heart of the matter. Here are a few examples:

1. Reports on the same subject coming from a variety of originating points, such as regional sales managers, should be in the same format so that key items can be identified uniformly and so that common information can be collated quickly.

2. Staff papers and studies, especially those recommending action, should follow generally the same format so that you can check them more readily for completed staff work and so that you can read them selectively, as you desire.

3. Correspondence briefs or digests superimposed on top of more lengthy correspondence files give you a bird's-eye view of the contents so that you can decide whether to go into them in greater depth. The brief itself might be sufficient.

Note-Making Techniques

As you proceed along with the conduct of your current activities, you will encounter many bits of information or you will think of things worthy of your further attention *but not at the moment.* If you let these go without recording them, you will have lost a great time advantage in the future when the information might be of current value.

Some people carry notebooks for this purpose; others use reminder pads on which they enter ideas, one item to a sheet. The three-by-five file card is used quite commonly because the notes then can be filed conveniently along with other notes made earlier. My friend Xenophon Palmer Smith, librarian of the U. S. Post Office Department, recommends the four-by-six file card. It's still small enough to carry in a pocket, big enough to record worthwhile amounts of material, and just the right size to fit into a desk card-file compartment. As a further refinement of these, you might carry some that are white and some that are colored, with the latter being used only for action matters as opposed to the deferred informational content of the others.

The notes you make before and after events of special importance can save you a great deal of time should you have to plan for the same kind of activities again. When Maurice H. Stans went on a safari to Africa, he jotted down an outline of his preparations. Two years later, when he planned a new safari, out came the old outline and, using his earlier experience, he adapted it to his new planning.

This technique is especially important when planning annual conventions, budget conferences, annual sales meetings, stockholder's meetings, trade shows, etc. It's a good idea to put all your working papers into a file for future reference. This should include any special notes on what not to do, based on actual events.

Your Office Equipment

The use of timesaving office equipment is important under some conditions. For example, an office photocopy machine will give you a copy in moments or minutes where it might take a secretary as much as an hour to make the copy on her typewriter. This may be worthwhile, but if your secretary has lots of time on her hands, typing a few extra copies once in a while would still be much cheaper than buying or leasing a machine. Quite apart from all considerations of cost-saving, if you operate under a system or a pace which dictates that you obtain your extra copies almost as soon as they can be put on the machine, then the cost becomes secondary.

DICTATING MACHINES

Dictating machines save time and money and they are a great boon for the man who travels. They are available when your secretary is not, either because she is out or because she is busy on other things.

The Available Hardware

The growing popularity of dictating machines has brought onto the market a great variety of different systems and models. You can take your choice of machines that use plastic discs, plastic belts, and magnetic tape or wire. Machines have been perfected, also, which will use sheets of paper coated with a magnetic material on one side. You have a choice between a permanent record made with a stylus and a magnetic recording which can be erased to permit re-use of the material.

For dictation purposes, you should have a machine with remote control, preferably in the microphone, although some machines have remote-control cables that can be operated by hand. The machine should also have a *very convenient* means of back-spacing so that you can hear what you last recorded—in case of interruption or in case you want to revise what you said. The remote control and the back-spacing are important features because if they are not conveniently available, you will lose time and you will be distracted through your mechanical manipulations of the equipment. While a foot control is advantageous for the typist who transcribes your material, it is not the best means of achieving remote-control convenience for the dictator. Co-ordination between mind and hand is much more sensitive than between mind and foot.

The Writer's Friend

I do not want to give the impression that dictating machines are universally used by writers. Many or most may use typewriters, recording their thoughts directly onto paper. Some prefer the slower method of very thoughtful expression through longhand writing. Others prefer the quick transfer of thought from mind to recording medium without the intermediate delay of the typewriter or the pen.

One free-lance British writer, Daniel F. Macrea, said: "Because I am not one of those gifted beings who can pour their thoughts straight into a typewriter, I have to take the more arduous path of thinking, marshalling my thoughts and clothing them in fitting language. Unfortunately, in the process I run into a snag; my pen cannot keep pace with my thinking. The inevitable result is that while I am mentally wrestling with the phrasing of one thought, others vanish and I must spend precious time in trying to recapture them."

Since he knew that an ever-present secretary to record his spontaneous expression of thought was out of the question, he turned to a tape recorder. Explaining how it solved his problem, in the British magazine *Tape Recording Fortnightly,* he said: "It took me precisely 15 minutes to speak an article to my silent 'friend.' A further 25 minutes in staccato playback enabled me to transfer the words to paper where the job of editing and polishing up was simplicity itself. From the time I first switched on the tape machine until the manuscript was ready for typing, a total of 55 minutes had elapsed, which made it the quickest-ever article I had ever turned out."

At least one dictating machine has remote control, back-spacing control, and play-back control at the mike. As an accessory for this machine—which makes it most interesting and useful for a writer—there is a sound pickup which activates the machine only when you talk. Thus, if you pause for a new thought, the machine will cut off after five seconds. It will resume only after you begin speaking again, so that there is no driving of the tape while you are silent. The dictator can pace around the room, unencumbered by any need for being close to the controls of the tape recorder. He can walk over to the bookcase, riffle through some books, and then, finding just the right quotation, record it while standing at the bookcase.

The Silent Secretary

The uses to which dictating machines can be put in business and industry almost defy the imagination.* Their versatility has been enhanced considerably by their new-found battery portability.

The first and obvious use for the dictating machine in the office is to have a secretarial recording service available without having to call the secretary in. Some people keep their machines "hot" all day so that they can record random instructions, brief memos, and other data without even the interruption of having to turn the machine on.

There are other important usages. For example, let us see how tape recorders are used by one of the busiest physicians in the country, Dr. Ethan Allan Brown, an internist-allergist in Boston, Massachusetts, who handles *up to 125 patients a day*. Not the least of his many streamlining practices is the use of tape recorders for the writing of correspondence and the detailed recording of medical histories. Instead of laboriously taking notes during a consultation, a voice-powered microphone starts a tape recorder going when the patient talks about his problems. Case histories call for a slightly different procedure. One or more questionnaires are mailed to the patient at the time his appointment is made. The returned questionnaires are reviewed by Dr. Brown, who makes notes about any additional information he will require. When the patient is shown in, Dr. Brown activates a recording machine which has an eight-hour belt. Everything the

* For a helpful booklet, full of hints, write for a free copy of *The Tape Recorder in Business and Industry* to the Minnesota Mining and Manufacturing Company, St. Paul 6, Minnesota.

patient says is then permanently recorded, but rarely is it transcribed in full. It is kept on file in the doctor's office in case he should need to refer to it at any time.

A good part of Dr. Brown's practice is referred to him by about six hundred other physicians. Immediately after treating one of their referrals, Dr. Brown writes a letter-report to the physician. Here again electronic wizardry takes over. The staff and equipment for this operation consist of Dr. Brown, two secretaries, two Auto-Typists, and a dictating machine. (An Auto-Typist reproduces, automatically, any material programed into it on rolls of punched paper.) One of the Auto-Typists is used to reproduce about fifty special paragraphs, keyed numerically to the push buttons on the Auto-Typist. The other is preset to reproduce any of thirty different form letters.

Dr. Brown takes his notes and then begins dictating. He records the standard information to be typed in automatically on the Auto-Typist as well as any special information unique to the patient.

As reported in *Medical Economics,* in which this story originally appeared, what Dr. Brown originally dictates would read like this if transcribed:

"History number 8087. Dr. Junius Parbold, address as shown. Dear Junie. One, Mr. Harold John Everett. Two, ragweed pollen. Three, skin tests. Four, ragweed pollen emulsified. Five, photocopy. Six, my regards to your charming wife. We so enjoyed meeting you both in Miami."

The letter which the patient might be able to take back with him the same day for delivery to his family doctor, when transcribed, would read somewhat as follows:

"Dear Junie: Your patient, Mr. Harold John Everett, came to this office today. As you know, he has a long history of discomfort caused by allergy to ragweed pollen.

"His skin tests were positive with an intracutaneous test of 1000 P.N.U./ml. He received a preseasonal injection of ragweed pollen extract emulsified in Arlacel A and Drakeol. The enclosed photocopy gives you the results of the physical examination, the pulmonary function tests, and the other laboratory studies deemed necessary. You are familiar with my discussion of this in Annals of Allergy, 17:358 (May–June), 1959. A reprint is enclosed.

"I have asked him to see you if he experiences any symptoms

of any degree or type, however mild or transient, and for whatever reason, during the pollen season. Should it be necessary for him to have any additional treatment, please telephone me at any time, but preferably not on a Tuesday, Wednesday, or Thursday excepting before 9 A.M. or between noon and 2 P.M. or after 4:30 P.M. These days, you will remember, are usually booked heavily, and during patient-hours I try to limit calls to those that are most important. But do remember that my secretary will always arrange for me to call you the moment I am free.

"My regards to your charming wife. We so enjoyed meeting you both in Miami."

Recorded Sound in Transit

A battery-powered portable recorder can be a tremendous timesaver when you want to record information away from the office. Here are a few illustrations:

1. Making notes while driving (but don't forget to tie the machine down securely or it may fall from the seat if the car stops suddenly).

2. Dictating correspondence, reports, and other materials while you are en route by airplane.

3. Making notes "on location" in the least time with a minimum of effort, such as when taking inventory, reading out the contents of files, and making notes in a library.

4. Making call reports and expense reports at the end of each day.

5. Sending detailed verbal reports to the home office when you are away on travel status.

6. Recording market-research data, especially interviews, on location.

Physicians seem to be important users of audio devices. Dr. Jack Schreiber hooked a tape recorder up in his car in order to listen to taped medical digests which he purchases from Audio Digest, a subsidiary of the California Medical Association. Every two weeks he receives a one-hour tape containing digests from leading medical journals as well as lectures by outstanding physicians. After he had become accustomed to the arrangement, he found that he had additional time so he used it to play back his taped notes on the lectures. When he makes a speech, he first

puts it on tape and listens to it over and over again in order to find
ways of improving it.

Another important professional use is the dictating of notes on
house calls immediately after each visit. Although this does not
exhaust the professional uses, Dr. Schreiber took along a library
of favorite classical recordings to be played in the car during
a long vacation trip of several thousand miles.

The Living Library

A record of a conference you have conducted, a speech you
have made, or some other important event might save you countless hours in preparing for some future event of like nature.

You may want to record special interviews and telephone calls.
These need not be played back or transcribed unless specific
need should develop for the information.

One college professor, when he is called away from the city
on other business, maintains the continuity of his lectures by
having a colleague or student play a prerecorded tape. Sometimes he has the students record their discussions of his lecture
upon the same tape so that he can listen to them upon his return.

A businessman makes a detailed record on tape after each
business meeting he attends. He records all agreements and dis-
agreements. Every commitment is recorded. Any other statements or reports that might have future significance are put on
tape. The tape is filed away and referred to only if there should
be a special need for recalling specifically what has transpired.

Paying Visits through Sound

Did you know that many people have a hobby of exchanging
correspondence recorded on tape? This hobby has its applications
in business life as well. Somehow, you are more freely expressive
when you say things orally than when you put them in writing.

Some executives multiply themselves by recording staff meetings and conferences and then sending taped copies to be played
back in subordinate departmental staff meetings. This keeps the
first staff meeting as small as possible, for good intercommunication, yet assures that important information is conveyed to those

not present without any distortion at all. Many other such uses will suggest themselves, such as reporting on company developments, greeting new employees, sending messages to field staffs about new-product programs or special sales events, etc.

SUMMARY

One's personal effectiveness can be enhanced many times over if he has the knack of inducing other people to render him aid. While some people may accomplish this through guile and insincerity, in the long run one is most likely to be favored by others when there is a relationship of mutual interest, mutual confidence, and mutual service. It is something at which we must work; it does not come of itself.

Among the various means through which we can multiply ourselves—that is, to use short cuts in the conduct of our business —are knowing where and how to obtain information which has already been developed instead of accumulating it through original effort; using procedural timesavers; and employing dictating machines and tape recorders to record the human voice swiftly and surely so that the thoughts it conveys may be retrieved economically and faithfully in the future at least expense.

IX

How to Manage a Desk

There was a story once current in Washington about two naval officers who were conversing. One had a reputation for keeping on top of things—for keeping a clean desk. This brought both favorable attention and promotion to him. The other was a forlorn, desk-weary lieutenant so burdened with his papers that he never could manage to clear his desk down to its wooden surface.

One day the lieutenant asked his colleague for the secret of his success. The lieutenant was no slacker nor was he inefficient. For some reason, he seemed to be getting more than his share of work and he could not dispose of it as fast as it came in.

"It's easy," said the clean-desk officer. "Whenever I begin falling behind or whenever I think I'm getting into more than I think I can handle, I merely write across the papers: 'Refer to Lieutenant Smith.' Then I throw them in the Out box and that's the last I hear of them."

"Very interesting," said the lieutenant, his eyes opening wide with a strange new look in them. "I don't think, however, that this technique will work for *me*."

"Why not?"

"I'm Lieutenant Smith."

The untidy desk has long been a subject for ridicule and moralizing. The clean desk, on the other hand, has become a symbol of efficiency. It suggests "moving today's work today." But not all people with cluttered desks are inefficient or unsuccessful. *Some* have reached the highest office in the land.

Nor can it be said that all those with clean desks are efficient whether or not they move their work; not even if they hold high positions. I would rather have a man with an untidy desk who does a bright job than one who sits behind a clear, shiny top, who does a lackluster job. As for a combination of both good qualities, who could want more?

The trouble with the clean-desk fetish is that we confuse the symbol with the real thing. That is, we confuse barren neatness with efficiency. What we should really seek is the well-organized desk—that is, the well-organized work center.

For an example of this kind of confusion, let's reach back to the year 1919, at a time when "efficiency experts" were really beginning to have their fling. That's far enough back to avoid arguments over current fads and practices. "The big man follows the program of the Clean Desk in his work and life; the small man does not," said Edward Earle Purinton, author of the Purinton Foundation Course in Personal Efficiency and head of a string of efficiency services. "The clean desk is first aid to clean work, clean profit, clean reputation. If you want to 'come clean' your work must travel on a clean desk. . . . A clear brain is back of a clean desk and an open heart is back of the clear brain. . . ."

In long perspective these words sound vacuous, which they are—or shall we say "corny?"

We get a little closer to modern perspective on desk management in the following, as stated in a training pamphlet of a national food chain:

"Did you ever stop to think that . . . the top of your desk . . . probably would tell a character analyst more about . . . *you* . . . than:

> your handwriting,
> or your photograph
> or the lines on your palm?

"Specifically—if your desk is cluttered, piled high, and disorganized, YOU undoubtedly would be classified as a haphazard, inefficient and untidy person.

"But—if your desk is neat, orderly and ready for work, YOU probably would be described as:
neat,
poised,
and efficient.

"Now—the watchword for a successful day of accomplishment at the office is . . .

Clear the Desk!

(And by that we *don't* mean sweep everything into the waste-basket!) What we do mean is
get today's work done today
so that desks are not allowed to become piled high with di-sheveled accumulations of unfinished business."

The key words are "neat, orderly and ready for work." They do not mean that your desk *must* be devoid of papers as some will suggest. While a clean desk may be the badge of an efficient worker, it may, in some cases, also be evidence of insufficient work or of file cabinets or desk drawers laden with work yet to be done.

The clean-desk fetish has been carried so far that some executives make a point of using *no* desk. They sit in up-holstered chairs where they work on a small lapboard. Using the work-center concept of the desk, the lapboard becomes a tiny desk on which one scarcely can do any work-sorting ef-ficiently—not unless he has a coffee table, which some do, on which he can also spread his work and writing tools. But then the coffee table becomes the desk!

HOW TO ORGANIZE THE DESK

Let's think of the delights of not organizing your desk. For example, if you have accumulated notes, reports, clippings, mag-azines, correspondence, and books on a wide variety of subject matter heaped in a bewildering disarray on your desk, think of the delights of rediscovery! While looking for last month's com-plaint analysis, you might run into the inventory record or you might chance upon an excerpt from an interesting speech someone sent you. Of course, you might also waste precious time looking for things and you might occasionally neglect to dispose of some important correspondence or other important matter. But, then, you can't have everything!

On the whole, most people cannot operate efficiently unless their work is also laid out efficiently. Very few of us can be like the character portrayed by the great W. C. Fields, in a notable movie comedy. He played the role of an executive whose desk was always heaped high in terrible confusion—a confusion that was apparent only to the onlooker. When asked to find a paper, Fields invariably would be able to reach into the middle of the mess and deftly withdraw the desired document. One day, though, he went away and, in his absence, an efficiency expert straightened things out. To Fields' consternation, he no longer could find any papers in the newly ordered arrangement. In desperation he stirred the papers around as though they were a tossed salad. After the dust had settled he studied the mess briefly, showed the light of recognition in his eyes and then, once more, deftly withdrew a desired document, surely and unerringly!

Although this is somewhat of a caricature, thereby depicting an unlikely extreme, it nevertheless points to the important principle that each must organize his ways to suit his own personality.

The Basic Principle

The same principle that governs housekeeping governs also the management of a desk. It is:

A place for everything and everything in its place.

Let us first define what is meant by *everything*. The desk is a workplace. Some things move across the desk quite rapidly while others tarry longer until all the papers or information are assembled for use in doing some kind of work with those papers. Still other papers and printed matter may be kept for reference use. Of course, the desk also holds miscellaneous items of stationery as well as a few personal supplies. All of these things need not necessarily be kept in or on the desk if you have another means of storing them.

If you do not have a secretary, the chances are that you will have more things on your desk than if you were able to route them to her with a note, "Please bring up two weeks from now."

If you perform a variety of tasks or if they are complex in nature, you are more likely to have an abundance of papers at your desk than if your tasks are simple or repetitive. Thus, it should be easier for some people to keep a clean desk than for others.

One way to have a place for everything is to store occasional reference materials on a table or in a bookshelf or file cabinet. Deferred projects should be put into the desk file drawer or into a file cabinet. If you do the latter, you will need to have some reminder system to assure you that you do not forget about important matters.

The first step in working toward a "place for everything," then, is to reduce the materials kept at the desk to those which you really need. The way to do this is to question every piece of paper you think you must keep on your desk and then, if you decide you do not need it for current use, you must find an alternate place for it to go.

What you do with the top of your desk may not be a matter entirely of your own choosing. For reasons of office security, you may need to have all papers off your desk top when you are away from your desk or when you lock up for the night. If you work in an open area, visible to the public, the office rules might provide that you leave a clean desk top when you leave at the end of the day.

This takes care of the nighttime aspect of your desk top. It does not, however, cope with the problem of how much you keep on your desk during the day. Some people prefer to see all of their current papers on the desk top where they can serve as reminders of things to be done. There need not be very many papers—only as many as might fit into a slim file folder—but their very presence serves as a reminder.

The top of the desk must be organized for the convenience of secretaries and messengers as well as for the convenience of the actual user of the desk. There should be a place for incoming materials and one for outgoing materials. If your work is pre-organized before it comes to you, you might need two or more In boxes into which different kinds of priorities of work are put. As for outgoing work, it sometimes saves writing brief instruction slips for certain materials. For example, you might have an Out box for file materials and another one for your superior or subordinates, as desired.

One manufacturer who has given attention to the "clutter-proof" organization of executive desks is Shaw-Walker with its Carlyle line of desks. The Carlyle desks are dedicated to the sanctity of the clean desk top. Drawer space is provided for just about everything, including letter trays, personal files, three-by-five and four-by-six card files, the telephone. There are reference pull-out shelves and side utility drawers in place of the center drawer in order to do away with the need for backing away from the desk when you want a fresh pencil or a paper clip. These desks even have in-drawer wastebaskets!

One thing you must yourself provide is a handy note pad or stack of note cards to use when you are talking over the telephone. Another thing you must provide is a habit pattern which will assure that you rotate work papers out of the desk drawers onto the top of your desk and from there to their ultimate destination. If you have a secretary, you must get into the habit of telling her what you have in your desk drawers or you must allow her free rein through them.

People who must have frequent access to the contents of their desk should consider where to store materials in accordance with their frequency of reference. Seconds saved while looking for a paper during a long-distance call could mean the difference between a minute more or less in the long-distance time charge.

The Globe-Wernicke Company, manufacturer of desks, reported on results of a time study which showed variations of as much as two seconds. Naturally, the time study had to assume that you could immediately put your fingers on just what you wanted. If you cannot, you must add the additional time. In that event, also, you still must figure the greater or lesser time depending upon the location of the materials. The time required to open the drawer, extract item, and close the drawer was least when it was located at the top right and greatest at the bottom left.

Commenting on the size of the desk itself, Globe-Wernicke says: "This much is true—that the mere size of a desk ordinarily has little to do with expediting paper work . . . and that unused top space is an open invitation to the accumulation of half-finished work."

"Modern office technique," advises the Art Metal Construction Co., "demands that the desk, the chair, the light, and the worker should be considered as a single operating unit, and each component should be carefully fitted to the others to produce the highest possible degree of working efficiency and working comfort." Too often overlooked is the chair. As to this, Art Metal states, "Fatigue is responsible for more errors and slow-ups in work production than any other cause. Correct posture seating reduces fatigue and helps to increase production and efficiency. . . . The weight should be on the bottom of the thighs and not on the base of the spine. The seat height is usually correct when the weight at the knees is supported by the feet and there is no pressure on the under part of the upper leg at the front edge of the seat."

Tables, Bookcases, and Files

Assuming that the desk is mainly a work center, an extra worktable, bookcase, and file cabinets should be regarded as extensions of the desk itself. The man with a private secretary may not concern himself with the file cabinet and its contents, but most people do their own traveling between file cabinet and desk. At one time some papers may be before you on your desk top. Then some or all of them may move into a file cabinet from which they are later to be retrieved. They might move directly onto your desk top for work or you might place them temporarily on a worktable in back of you.

From a practical standpoint the worktable offers a degree of privacy. It enables you to retreat from visitors and other distractions. Psychologically it offers a final separation from the task just completed at the desk. By a twist of the swivel chair you find yourself in another world.

The worktable offers another psychological advantage: even though the table is piled high with papers and other clutter, you may yet qualify as a clean-desk worker if the desk top itself is kept devoid of papers.

The L-shaped desk extension or attachment has become quite popular in recent years. The methods engineer would certainly approve of the arrangement if you need the additional working space, because all of the top area remains within easy arm reach as you swivel around in your chair. This arrangement does not offer the same degree of privacy and the same feeling of a psychological break which you have when you turn completely around to a worktable in back of your desk. Also, although you retain a little of the privilege of throwing work on the L-extension, this must be kept to a minimum or you will detract from the desired neatness of the desk surface.

Materials which are used infrequently should be stored in bookcases and file cabinets, as appropriate. The person who works without a secretary should have these immediately at hand in order to minimize distracting and time-consuming journeys away from his desk. Bookcases and file cabinets tend to conceal their contents so that after a while you may forget about them. With file cabinets the concealment is physical. With bookcases the concealment is psychological, because after a while you see *without actually perceiving or noticing.* Accordingly, you should take careful inventory of the contents of these repositories from time to time to assure that they do not contain files or reports which require attention and that they do not contain materials for which you no longer have a current need.

You will save a great deal of time in retrieving materials, from file cabinets particularly, as well as from bookcases, if your materials are stored in some logical pattern. The subject-matter groupings should relate to your areas of interest. As these change, you might want to reorganize your own working materials so that they are in parallel.

HOW TO MOVE PAPER

Purinton, quoted above, had an excellent description of the stagnant desk. "Before the development of the new science of efficiency engineering," he said, "the medieval business or professional man who never got anywhere much was likely to have a desk that looked about thus. Papers, letters and bits of half-finished jobs were scattered in all directions, without relation to each other or to the work of the day. People came in at all hours and dumped more papers on the desk without rhyme or reason. Elbow room was out of the question, so the man had to be a contortionist to do his work at all. When a certain paper was wanted, the only way to get it was to search through the desk, which was an old-fashioned roll-top with a dozen drawers and cubby-holes to catch the papers that dropped out of sight in confusion and disgrace. Hunting for lost articles took so much time that the man didn't have a chance to make a living. He never caught up with his work. . . . When a client or customer wanted immediate action or report, everybody in the office was seized in consternation.

"Among the total impossibilities of life was an exact knowledge of how the business was going. The only way to hide the man's inefficiency was to put a screen around the desk, which was done when a high official or a visitor threatened to approach and find out the shameful condition of the man's desk. . . . Often the atmosphere was rent with sharp words, because when the man lost something he blamed it, as men do, on somebody else."

The movement of papers off your desk is essentially a matter of system. It is surprising how a few simple techniques enable you to keep your desk load down to a minimum. One of the techniques is that of the preliminary screening. The other is to classify your work papers according to their importance and priority and to allocate time to them accordingly.

Screening and Classifying

The screening approach is in opposition to the FIFO approach, to use a term from accounting practice. Under the FIFO method each item is taken up in strict rotation, as received, and then work on it is carried as far as feasible. The theory is that once you pick a piece of paper up you have an investment of time in reading and identifying the problem and the attention required. Therefore if you put it down again without action, you will lose the duplicate pickup time. Accordingly, you should preserve your original investment and avoid rehandling time by carrying the matter through to completion.

Under the screening approach you dispose of some matters on first handling but you classify the others for attention after completion of the screening. As you pick up each paper, you make a quick judgment as to whether you can dispose of it in a few moments. This may be done by first reading the paper, and then throwing it away if it has no further value, marking it for file, or writing a brief note for action or referral. In such cases you are merely adding a little bit of additional effort to that already expended in picking up and identifying the contents of the papers.

The residual matters are those which are classified, as you read, for attention in various priority categories. Ordinarily, you would classify the papers by putting them in different piles. Thus, the technique of screening and classifying retains some of the advantage of the FIFO method while assuring that first things come first.

You may set up any system of classification that works best for you or you may use the following list:

1. Matters for prompt attention.
2. Low or deferred priorities.
3. Current informational matters for filing or for reading and disposal.
4. Pending: further study or information needed before action.
5. Defer: not for immediate action; extensive study or developmental effort required.

Matters for Prompt Action

In the prompt-handling category are those things which must be done today or as soon as possible. These include current correspondence, customers' orders, current-action matters of a wide variety, and long-lead preliminary actions in order to have certain things ready when needed in the future. In general these are all top-priority matters and they are characterized by being part of the daily flow and urgency of work.

Low or Deferred Priorities

Oddly enough, it takes more words to describe matters of low priority and the problems of handling them than to comment on matters of high priority. The low-priority matters are the things which we tend to set aside whether or not we have a plan for doing so. This can become very dangerous because even though such matters are not top priority or urgent, they are not unimportant. Sooner or later or on some timely basis they must be taken care of or there will be some discomforting or undesirable consequence. You cannot just keep deferring these matters because then they might never get done.

One solution is to budget your time so that you allow a given period for attention to low priorities. If you do this, you should mark the matters for attention on a certain day and then you should put them into your tickler or "bring-up" system. If your work schedule is such that you can handle them the same day they are received, you would probably set them aside for attention after the priorities are handled.

The matter may not be low priority. Rather, it might be quite important but something which needs to be deferred until a later date because something else must first happen or because the later date represents better timing.

From time to time deferred matters should be re-examined because priorities *do* change.

Current Informational Matters

Current informational matters include the wide variety of materials on which you may or may not need to take action. At least on face they do not require action even though you might decide to do something or write something as a result of reading them. Included in this category are carbon copies of correspondence and memoranda, reports, digests, pamphlets, periodicals, trade journals, etc.

As already suggested, some of these materials, if sufficiently short, you would read quickly upon immediate receipt and then you would dispose of them appropriately. You might throw them out, file them, or refer them.

Length is not necessarily a criterion for assignment of a work priority. Nor is the informational nature of the material a criterion for deferral. If the contents are of sufficient importance, you might even put an item of information into the prompt-attention category or you might keep it in the information folder in a "first-reading" subcategory. Remember that you might take important action based upon your reading of informational materials. The same pertains to trade journals and newspapers. These might have certain information in them which you should read immediately upon receipt. Then, if there are certain technical or other informative articles which do not have any priority, you can set the journals aside for later reading.

If you are not able to read important informational matters which are marked for routing to others, you might want to refer them to the next name on the routing list with a request that the document or publication be returned to you either next in line or at the end of the list.

As with low-priority matters, unless you set aside a time period for reading informational materials, whether at the office or at home or even while traveling, you are not likely to get this important part of your work done. If you do not cover your reading, you will be missing out on information that is vital to your profession or business.

Pending: Further Study or Information Needed

Pending matters are those which await additional information or action. In some cases the matter starts out as an "immediate-action" item because you need to write a letter or make a telephone call as a result of reading it, and then you put the item into a pending category for attention at a later date.

A variant of this is the project or problem folder. In it you would accumulate bits and pieces of correspondence and information papers until you had enough on the subject matter to permit you to write a final report or take other appropriate action.

Pending matters can change into a higher priority at almost any time, without warning, because of changes in the environment.

Defer: Major Effort

Those things which you would classify as "major effort" are really substantial projects or studies. They might involve only deep reading and analysis or they might require a full-fledged scheduling of manpower, time, and attention. In any event they are not the kinds of things that you would consider part of your daily paper-work load. Rather, they need to be worked into your weekly schedule. In some respects these deferred matters are handled in much the same way as things in the preceding category. It could be only a matter of degree. After all, very few things which fall into the paper-work category can be classified absolutely and purely.

HOW TO ELIMINATE PAPER

In the preceding discussion we covered techniques for moving the flow of paper—for preventing it from accumulating on your desk. In that discussion there was implicitly an assumption that the papers are ones that properly should be coming to your desk. This is not necessarily the case. All of us—especially those in a bureaucracy—tend to receive mail, reports, and other reading matter far in excess of our actual work requirements. One reason for this is that others send things to us because they think we might be interested or because they think we might possibly be offended if we do not receive them. Another reason for unnecessary paper work is that we change our work interests but the paper continues coming to us as though nothing had changed—except for the inflow of paper pertaining to our new interests.

To get at the unwanted paper, you need to get at the source, and to do this, you should from time to time reappraise your work interests as suggested in Chapters IV and V. Then, you can screen the kinds of things you are receiving and take steps to prevent the receipt of those no longer desired.

Apart from the unsolicited receipt of reading materials—and even action materials sometimes—very substantial savings in time can be made by streamlining some of your personal work methods. In the remainder of this chapter we will cover five suggestions for doing this:

1. Don't record it.
2. Don't ask for it.
3. Throw it away.
4. Discontinue it.
5. Use the telephone.

Don't Record It

Why make the record or notation? Will it help you in your work? What will it add? What would you lose if you do not keep the record? Ask yourself: Are you doing this (1) because you've always done so or (2) just in case. If it is something you have always been doing, without justification, a methods re-evaluation should ruthlessly prune it away. If it is something in the just-in-case category, you must think in terms of statistical likelihoods and the costs of the practice over a long term as compared to the remotely possible value of the record.

While conducting a survey of methods in a personnel office, an analyst came across a series of record books in the file room. He asked about one of them which contained a list of personnel folders, identified by the name of the employee, the name of the person looking into the folder, the date he did so, and the name of the file clerk who gave it to him. He was told that some years previously an employee had obtained unauthorized access to a personnel folder for reasons of his own not related to his responsibilities. The employees in the file room were reprimanded for their carelessness. Accordingly, they instituted the record book which they had been keeping for several years. When asked if they ever had had occasion to refer back to the record book under similar circumstances, they said that they had not. When asked why they kept the record, they said, "Just in case," which is a very common defense for paper work which has no real justification.

What they failed to perceive, however, was that since they now required some proof of need for a personnel folder together with some evidence of responsibility, this should make unnecessary the keeping of a record; unauthorized persons would not be able to have access to the files. Also, if someone did get to a file folder without authority, the keeping of the record would not correct the violation. Pointing this out was to no avail because people in such jobs often feel quite insecure and therefore rely upon such record-keeping to assure themselves that they are doing the right thing. Insecurity or a desire to fix responsibility or protect oneself in case blame is to be attributed at some time in the future are reasons behind a great deal of unnecessary record-keeping.

Another question to ask is whether the information is available elsewhere and if so will it be available to you if you really need it. Here, also, insecurity—as well as personal convenience—enters into unnecessary record-keeping. You will find people keeping records which duplicate those kept by others merely because they do not trust the record-keeping done by others. If they are to take action based upon recorded information, they tend to feel more secure if the records are their own.

Don't Ask for It

As you come across references to available information, it is so easy to ask for a copy of a report or pamphlet, a memorandum, or other data or reading matter. Unless you have a specific constructive purpose to which you will put any of this information, don't ask for it.

Sometimes people will ask for reports and other materials in order to create impressions of activity and importance. A survey in a very large organization which was becoming mired in an abundance of internal information material disclosed that a great many people did not need a great percentage of the reading materials they were receiving. When confronted with the fact, they objected to having their names taken off distribution lists. Some would agree to the deletion only if other names were also removed, which led to the suspicion—later verified—that they were interested in the materials not so much for their substantive content as for the maintenance of outward appearances.

These are questions you might ask about information or reading material for which you might send: (1) Does it fit into a current project, assignment, or correspondence problem? (2) Does it pertain to a possible area of future responsibility or interest—something you are very likely to do? (3) Is it something you should obtain for accumulation in a special file or information folder because you are monitoring this subject area? (4) Can you obtain it readily in the future from the original source, from the library, or from someone else's files?

Throw It Away

Many a file cabinet or desk drawer is like the attic loaded with relics of yesteryear which we keep for sentimental reasons or because they once had value and we simply cannot bring ourselves to part with them. You must be quite ruthless about this. If the informational content is absorbed and you have no further use for the actual material to support your action or to refer to again, *throw it away!* If the material is of intrinsic value—perhaps a book or an expensive report—and you have no further use for it, send it to the library or give it to someone else who might have need for it. Don't keep things which are commonly distributed, like press releases, monthly reports, house organs, etc., unless they have a high reference value for you. Otherwise, throw them away or send them to a central file if extra copies are needed there. You might be surprised to learn how much of this kind of junk is kept in office file cabinets even though it may never be referred to.

The same thing pertains to many other kinds of one-time information. If you receive a bulletin announcing a picnic for employees, why file it forevermore? Why file the reminder that you had not yet sent in a certain report? The thing to do is to send in the report; the reminder won't help you in the future. Carbon copies of memoranda and letters should be disposed of in the same way. If you received a carbon copy, it is obvious that someone else received the original. Unless you have an important reason for keeping the copy, you can always ask to borrow the file copy kept by the original drafter or the principal recipient. The time spent in saving things and in looking for things which are not retrievable because of a general clutter would far exceed the time spent in sending out occasionally for some piece of paper which you might have saved.

Discontinue It

We are creatures of habit. If once we begin receiving a report or commence the making of a record, we continue the practice. Whether it is something initiated by you or something which you receive from others, if you no longer need it, discontinue it.

If it is a report which you are regularly preparing which you disseminate to others, try to obtain some evaluation of its usefulness to them. If it serves no constructive purpose, you must either modify it or discontinue it. The time which you will save thereby is not alone that spent in physical preparation of the report. Rather, it also covers the amount of time and preoccupation which went into the accumulation and analysis of the material covered by the report.

Use the Telephone

It costs money to write a letter or memorandum but, unless you want a formal record of what you have to say, it is often cheaper to pick up the telephone than to use the written word. Moreover, in many cases you can get much better results and quicker understanding than if you had to rely upon a series of correspondence exchanges.

Of course, we all make great use of the telephone in just this way but then we tend, in many cases, to let some of the time savings leak through the practice of making telephone records. The telephone record is legitimate paper work where there are commitments or approvals or concurrences which you wish to keep on file. We will go into this subject, along with other aspects of the telephone and time, in the next chapter.

SUMMARY

The management of the desk begins with the physical organization of one's total work center. This includes the desk, the worktable if used, bookcases, and file cabinets, since paper may move from one to the other interchangeably. The central principle in arranging one's working materials is: a place for everything and everything in its place.

You can keep your paper work moving if you use the screening and classifying technique. Those things which you pick up for reading and content identification which can be disposed of in a few moments are handled in that way. The remainder of the materials is then given various attention priorities and handled in order, consistent with one's total work schedule.

Finally, you'll have more time for the more important things at hand if you avoid creating paper work for yourself. Ask yourself in each case: Do I need it? What loss will there be if I don't have it?

X

Mastery of the Telephone

Our schoolbooks and the institutional advertisements of the telephone companies tell us how much the telephone has contributed to industrial and economic progress.

Private polls of executives, professional men, and salesmen, among others—even the parents of teen-agers—bring forth expressions of utter chagrin at the amount of time lost on the telephone.

What a paradox!

A few years ago the American Management Association undertook a survey of how executives used their time. "On the question of wasted time," wrote Lydia Strong, "almost everyone named some pet gripe. Too much talk—on the telephone, at meetings, in unwanted interviews—led the list. 'Conversation with others which leads nowhere,' one man calls it. Many wrote just one word: telephone."

Nevertheless, like another famous saying, you can't live with it or without it. It will always be one of the most important media of business communication. Within organizations it is essential to internal direction, co-ordination, and general functioning of enterprise.

Wherein does it offend? It diverts time through unnecessarily prolonged conversations. It interrupts continuity of effort or thought. It interrupts important conferences and wastes the time of those who must sit around while the call is being completed. The telephone is an instrument of rudeness; with it people can interrupt you quite freely, using the cover of distance, whereas they wouldn't dare do so if they had to walk into your office and saw that you were engaged.

Recognizing both the virtues and the disabilities of the telephone, the challenge should be to learn how to master it. This has two aspects:

1. Using the telephone as an instrument for saving time and money.

2. Controlling access to you by telephone.

THE TELEPHONE AS A TIMESAVER

Whenever a cost-reduction campaign gets under way, the telephone is one of the obvious targets. Memoranda are distributed directing that personal calls be eliminated, that long-distance calls be kept to an absolute minimum and limited to three minutes.

A certain company required that written reports be submitted justifying any long-distance calls in excess of three minutes. This rule was enforced so arbitrarily that, in one case, an employee took a trip at much greater expense in preference to having to explain a long telephone call in a memorandum to a top corporate officer! In the same company employees would sometimes make their calls in three-minute sections—unbelievable as this may seem.

What was needed, apparently, in addition to the negative rules, was a list of criteria offering guidance as to *when* to make long-distance calls.

Occasions for the Long-Distance Call

Most of our formal and routine business is conducted by correspondence. Handled routinely, this is cheaper and it also provides records of the subjects communicated. The normal rule, then, should be to use the letter, but the following are among the occasions when it may be better to use the telephone:

1. Time is of the essence. If you delay as much as one day, the opportunity may be lost. Money also may be lost for every hour that passes before a deal is closed, instructions given, or information received.

2. The long-distance call will get you through where other means may not. It may not carry the imperative of a telegram but it still carries the connotation of importance and urgency. With it you can get through to people who just don't pay attention to their correspondence, who have efficient staffs that keep it from them, or who are more likely to respond to the human voice than to the dubious personality of a piece of stationery.

3. A ping-pong interaction is needed. With one long-distance call you may be able to obtain or give information and clarify situations that otherwise would require a number of exchanges of letters.

4. Convenience is best served. A letter might do just as well if you can be sure that inclement weather would not ground the air flights to a distant city. Or you might take a chance on the letter if you had someone to take and transcribe it. Then, again, you don't want to go on record or you are not clear as to the tack you should follow, so you prefer to "play it by ear." Sometimes you sense that a telephone call is the opportune thing, the courteous gesture which may create an atmosphere or set a tone which could not be achieved by letter.

Because long-distance telephone calls *are* costly, every effort should be made to complete them in the shortest time with as much accomplished as possible. The key to this is a little advance preparation. Be sure to have all papers, notes, and files on hand which you might need to consult. Make up a brief outline of topics you want to cover, unless you are going to work from a specific document which serves this purpose. Of course, you should have a pad and pencil handy.

If you are being called and need more time to prepare, it would be better if you were to report that you will call back at a certain time. The caller might not appreciate it at the moment but he would if he gets into a frustrating conversation because you're unprepared.

The Best Times for Making Calls

There are ideal times, from your standpoint, when you should be making your telephone calls, but there also may be ideal times of availability of the person being called. The two might not coincide. You know your schedule but you might have no idea whatsoever of the schedule or the availability of the other party. One rule of thumb is to place your call as early as possible in the day (with due regard to time-zone differences, especially when calling from west to east).

Some years ago the American Management Association's *Management Review* published the following item which it attributed to *The Mutual Link:*

"We don't know who drew up this schedule of the most appropriate times to call different types of prospects, but we suspect the telephone company may have helped. . . .

"1. Executives and business heads—after 10:30 A.M.

"2. Physicians and surgeons—between 9 A.M. and 11 A.M.; and between 1 P.M. and 3 P.M. Some between 7 P.M. and 9 P.M.

"3. Dentists—before 9:30 A.M.

"4. Lawyers—between 11 A.M. and 2 P.M.

"5. Stock brokers and bankers—before 10 A.M. or after 4 P.M.

"6. Contractors and builders—before 9 A.M. or after 5 P.M.

"7. Professors and school teachers—at home, between 6 P.M. and 7 P.M.

"8. Public Accountants—any time during the day, but avoid January 15 through March 15.

"9. Druggists and grocers—between 1 P.M. and 3 P.M.

"10. Publishers and printers—after 3 P.M.

"11. Merchants, store heads and department heads—after 10:30 A.M.

"12. Chemists and engineers—between 4 P.M. and 5 P.M.

"13. Clergymen—any time after Tuesday.

"14. Small-salaried salespeople and government employees— call at home.

"15. Housewives—between 10 A.M. and 1 P.M."*

* Earl Prevette had a similar narrative-style listing in his earlier work, *How to Sell by Telephone.* First published in 1941.

The foregoing list may or may not suit all cases, but at least it will give you food for thought. Specifically, you should keep records or make a mental note of availability patterns of people whom you may have to call with some frequency.

When making long-distance calls late in the day, take pause first to inquire of yourself whether the person being called could still take any kind of constructive action that day as a result of your call. A letter by airmail might do just as well. On the other hand, it might not be feasible late in the day to dictate and have a letter transcribed.

Making Internal Calls

In the very small organization you might find it just as convenient to walk over to someone as to call him on the telephone. In larger organizations, which generate many more bureaucratic formalities as an accompaniment of bigness, much of the business of the day is conducted through correspondence, as a means of getting things on record, if nothing else. Generally speaking, you would follow the same criteria as for the making of outside calls, with some exceptions. Within the house you would dispense with formalities which, if they were to involve outside people, might call for written communications.

Internal calls may be used as reserve business, something to be done between tasks and interviews. They may also be made during a period reserved for this particular purpose.

An office intercommunication system that bypasses the secretarial hookup may be used when there is a need for very quick and sensitive intercommunication among those tied into the "intercom." It could be very embarrassing if private information is conveyed within earshot of a visitor in another office. Hence, if an intercom is used, it ought to at least have built-in arrangements for privacy.

Some Conversational Efficiencies

You will save time for yourself and for the other party if you observe a few personal practices which should be quite obvious. Nevertheless, the telephone is handled so poorly by so many people that a few words would seem to be in order.

1. Answer the telephone promptly. Don't let it ring so long that the caller may actually give up.

2. Identify yourself and the person you wish to speak to when you are making a call. Get through the social preliminaries as quickly as possible and then identify your subject clearly so that thereafter you both will know what you are talking about.

3. When you are the recipient of a call which is answered by your secretary, she should identify your office and name. If you answer directly, you should do the same. If the caller has the wrong office, he will find this out promptly.

4. Speak distinctly. Keep things out of your mouth while you are speaking. Hold the telephone instrument close to your mouth. Avoid having to repeat or being misunderstood.

5. When the business of the telephone conversation is completed, bring the discussion to a prompt closing.

As you talk, you might be making notes, certainly of names, figures, and critical information. If this material is to be preserved, date it and add such additional information as you might need on file.

The Secretary as a Telephone Timesaver

The secretary can be a great timesaver in making calls but this is not without some risk. There are always some people who resent being called only to find that your secretary holds them in abeyance while you are put on the telephone. Such irritation is evidence of a sensitive ego or of ignorance. Either one causes an inability to recognize that the secretary can save you a great deal of time in putting calls through. For your part, however, you should be alert for your secretary's signal so that you will get on the telephone as soon as you hear it.

There is absolutely nothing wrong in having a secretary place calls. In the typical call she may look up the telephone number, dial it, get an outside switchboard, speak to the secretary of the other party and, finally, get you on the line when the other party is on. If the call is long distance, you must add to these steps the getting of your own operator, who dials for the long-distance operator, who gets the telephone routing and an open circuit and finally verifies the availability of both parties. Two additional hazards are that the line may be busy or the person called may be out or unavailable. For a busy man, then, it is certainly an economy to have one's secretary do all this waiting.

Very busy people can take a lesson from the practice of some physicians. Telephone calls which would interrupt office consultations are noted for call-back. Then, during a period reserved for making outgoing telephone calls, the doctor places them in rotation. His secretary will begin placing the next call before the preceding one is completed. If the doctor is not quite ready for the next call, his secretary will hold it, explaining that the doctor had picked up a line while she was placing the outgoing call.

HOW TO CONTROL INCOMING CALLS

Most of this section is written on the assumption that you have a secretary who answers your telephone. Those who answer their own, however, will find a few suggestions at the end of this section.

Preventing Interruptions

Refusing to talk to a caller is a sensitive public-relations problem. You never really know what the consequences of a call-refusal may be. It is much safer as well as more effective, then, if you can discourage unnecessary calls in the first instance or at least get them channeled into those hours when you are better able to take the calls. You might try the following:

1. Let people know when you're *not* available. You can do this with employees who are responsible to you and you can also do it in large measure with clients or patients if you have a medical practice. The constructive side of this rule is that you should also let all concerned know when they *can* get hold of you.

2. Don't invite people to "call back sometime." When you are closing a conversation, do so pleasantly but don't extend an automatic invitation for a repeat performance unless you really want it.

3. Get your business done on time so that you do not make others impatient as they wait to hear from you.

How to Refuse Calls

The typical persistent caller must feel that his business is important, else he wouldn't call. He may go to any extremes to make his contact. Mr. Frump calls saying that he was "referred by Mr. Smidge," the intent being to say that "you'd better put me through because otherwise Mr. Smidge, who is important to your boss, would be displeased and this, in turn, will bring repercussions for your boss."

Another trick is for the caller to simulate personal familiarity with the inaccessible person. Instead of asking for Mr. Lawson, he asks to speak to Harry Lawson or to just plain Harry. Sometimes he may trap himself this way because old Harry J. Lawson is known to all his friends as Jack.

The best approach for the secretary is to be quite frank about the situation. She can ask for the caller's business and, if it seems to be something that can be referred elsewhere, she can explain that her superior is very, very busy, she doesn't know when he will be able to return the call and wouldn't someone else be able to help in the meantime. If the caller still persists, the secretary might tell him that she will put him on the list but she cannot say when the call will be returned because of the crowded calendar.

The very top operators, whose positions speak for themselves, have an additional advantage in that their secretaries can politely but firmly decline to put calls through. An easy way to do this is simply to say, "One moment," and then to plug the call in to a special assistant who will offer his services to the caller.

In all of this effort to ward off calls, there is an element of calculated risk. Conceivably, you might miss a call that would bring you a fortune or solve some vexing problem. Thus, I know a president of a small company who patiently responded to telephone calls from dozens of stockholders and financial analysts. One of these brought his company a recognition which resulted in a twentyfold increase in the value of its stock in the market place. The incident would *seem* to prove a point: You never know what you miss unless you take every call! The fallacy, of course, is that these unusual episodes are rare exceptions.

For most people, the chances are that you will get more accomplished by conserving your time and eliminating interferences.

Calls from Special People

Not all of your callers can be treated alike. Some you wouldn't dare turn aside for obvious personal reasons and some you couldn't afford to refuse because what they have to say may be important for your continued economic welfare. The special people we'll take up here include: (1) wives and families, (2) office superiors, (3) clients and customers, and (4) salesmen.

Wives and families. The secretary who tries to control interruptions may feel awkward about cutting off the wife. One secretary solved this by transferring the burden to the wife herself. The secretary would say, "Yes, Mrs. Gerber. He has a roomful of people with him at the moment, but I will interrupt if you would like me to." This worked in practically every case. The secretary then followed through by having the husband return the call just as soon as possible, thereby letting the wife know that she was getting the attention she demanded.

Office superiors. Turning the boss aside is not very easy because he may think that he owns every minute of your time in the office—and sometimes out of the office. If your secretary doesn't think you should be interrupted while you are in a conference, she might try the same treatment that she used with the wife, with appropriate variations. For example, she might say, "Yes, Mr. Frobisher. He has Mr. Gluck in with him at the moment. Would you want to talk to him now or would you rather have him call you back?" It's even easier to do this—sometimes—when the call is put through by the boss's secretary. I say *sometimes* because each office has its own pattern of relationships. If the boss's secretary thinks that such a reply would be a challenge to her own effectiveness, icy tones will chill their way through the earpiece. Each situation, however, must be assessed by you or your secretary. If any rule applies, it is that when in doubt, take the call!

Clients and customers. Any reasonable client, patient, or customer would expect you to be busy and, hence, not readily accessible. He almost needs to find this to be the case as reassurance that he used good judgment in selecting you! The key word is *reasonable,* for there will always be some clients who are so wrapped up with a feeling of their own importance and the value of their patronage that they think they own a piece of you. Most cases can be handled by the secretary with a "He's with a customer (or patient)." He can also be on the telephone, with other calls waiting, and there is nothing wrong with saying so. The emergencies must be judged in their own right, case by case. As for the troublesome few, you will have to judge the value of their patronage as against the nuisance of having such customers. In some cases you simply will have to grin (or grit) and bear it.

Salesmen. The man with something to sell should not be pushed aside unceremoniously. He may be the source of some unusually good product, service, or idea. From him you can learn much about the market place and about technological trends. Admittedly, what you *might* learn must be balanced with other demands upon your time. When the salesman calls by telephone, he may want to make an appointment, to follow up on an order which you promised to place, to give you new information which you requested, or to sell you something by telephone. An original "sales pitch" by telephone is something, however, which can consume a great deal of your time. You should ascertain very early in the presentation whether it is of any interest to you. If it is not, you will do a favor to both of you if you politely cut the conversation short.

The Telephone Hour

Although the problems of the telephone hour are largely those of the physician, there might be implications for others. Typically, a telephone hour might be set for very early in the morning, with another one for patients who might call back to report their symptoms late in the day. The patients are advised by circular letter, a copy of which is given to each new patient, as to the hours when the doctor may be called for telephone consultation. The success of such a system depends upon a rigid disciplining of calls made by patients at other hours.

Dr. Stanley I. Wolf, a pediatrician in Silver Spring, Maryland, takes an opposing view which he explained in a prize-winning story in *Medical Economics* magazine.

"On the surface, the idea seems fine," said Dr. Wolf. "I thought it first-rate when I adopted it a few years ago. But here's what I soon discovered: Far too many patients, prompted by the knowledge that the doctor is sitting at his phone, actually *create* problems to discuss."

Dr. Wolf then gave the following example of an actual conversation:

"Doctor, my two-month-old finished her bottle an hour ago, and I don't know what to do."

"What are you worried about?"

"No burp!"

For the doctor just starting in practice, Dr. Wolf suggests, the telephone hour may be ideal because it will accommodate adequately all of his traffic. As his practice grows, the telephone hour becomes two: one for the morning and one for the afternoon. Eventually even this does not work for the physician or his patients, who find increasing frustration in their efforts to get through to him. "For some, it's a real achievement to get a call in during the period. One patient informed me that she used to take a tranquillizing tablet before starting to dial."

There were frustrations for Dr. Wolf, also. Although his morning telephone hour ended at 8:30, he might get a call at 8:29 which lasted for ten minutes, thus starting his day with a slipped schedule.

Dr. Wolf might have continued with the telephone hour if it had actually reduced telephone traffic. He found, instead, that those who could not get through during the telephone hour would call at other times.

After verifying with other physicians that they had substantially the same experience, Dr. Wolf announced to all his patients, through his nurse, that the telephone hour was not adequate time for the needs of all his patients and that thereafter they should feel free to call at any time, "which many of them were doing anyway," said Dr. Wolf. "And they've quickly learned to talk willingly with my nurse. She's able to take care of the majority of the calls, as she could have all along." The secret of it, he added, lies in the ability of his nurse to discuss the patients' problems understandingly.

"She's also careful never to let a worried mother get the impression that it's impossible to talk to the doctor directly. Even though the question may be trivial in the nurse's opinion, her voice implies otherwise. She gets across the idea that she's glad to help, and that if it turns out to be necessary, the doctor will be glad to help, too."

As a final note of interest, Dr. Wolf added: ". . . Your patients, knowing the wires are always open, may well become less demanding."*

For People without Secretaries

The man without a secretary cannot hide behind that defense but, if he must have periods without interruption, he can find substitutes.

When you answer the telephone, if you don't want to talk, say so politely to the caller. After a cheery "hello" and a friendly acknowledgment of the call, there is nothing wrong in telling the caller that you will have to call back—unless the matter is urgent—because you are in the midst of work that cannot be interrupted.

If you work at home, use your family as a secretarial service. Resist picking up the telephone when it rings. Let the family know whether you are available to take calls or, if not, whether you will take any special calls from certain people.

If you live in an apartment house which provides secretarial answering service, flip the switch so that you can safely ignore all calls during your period of concentration. Or you can use a telephone-answering service.

You can also obtain from the telephone company a private message recorder. Then, you can let the telephone ring or you can answer it, as you prefer. If you do not take your calls, you can play the message machine after you have finished your work.

SUMMARY

The telephone can be either timesaver or time-waster, depending on how well you use it. In many cases, in fact, it is more economical and more productive of results to use a long-distance call than to write a letter. The long-distance call may get you through to people where the letter will not. If the advantage is with the call, make it—but first prepare yourself with the notes or material you will need for an effective, brief discussion.

The local or internal call may not be regarded as seriously as the long-distance call because of the lesser cost, but this overlooks the time they consume. Generally speaking, you should handle them with the same economy of time-usage as though they were toll calls.

The control of incoming calls is a sensitive problem in public relations because callers do not like to be turned aside. A partial relief from the situation is for you to set aside periods when you are not available and to let your regular callers know about them. A constructive approach is to eliminate the necessity for follow-up calls to you by others by getting your work done promptly, meeting deadlines as scheduled.

Each of the people who call you may feel that his business is most important. Each must be treated in the light of his own special status but, in the final analysis, you can give only so much time to the telephone if you are to get your other work done.

XI

Life with Visitors

For those who work in organizations, internal visitors are usually predominant. This is largely true of top executives also, even though much of their work is outside-oriented. If the visitors are subordinates, they can have their schedules controlled more readily because of the obvious relationship (although I've seen organizations in which subordinates observed neither formality nor restraint whenever they felt it necessary to dash into the boss's office). Oddly enough, you may have more control with your superiors than with colleagues or people from other parts of the organization.

Those whose business it is to receive visitors or clients should, in many respects, have an easier time, mainly because they're set up for it and because it is expected by others that they must have some kind of visitor regulations. The main challenge for the man with a visitor clientele is to bring an interview to a close as promptly as possible while gratifying the purpose of the interview. Where the commodity sold is service or consultation, the guiding preoccupation very definitely is "time is money."

The man who works at home has his own special problems. Somehow, people don't take the home environment as seriously as they would an office. Hence, in the informal environment of hospitality which ordinarily prevails in the home, entirely different approaches are needed.

Osborn Elliott, in his book, *Men at the Top,* tells of presidents of companies who solve the interruption problem by starting their day at about 5 A.M. Charles B. Thornton, head of Litton Industries, gets to his office by that time for a few hours of uninterrupted work. President Robert Paxton of General Electric rises at 5:15 A.M. to catch a train about 7:10 A.M. for an early morning start. Apparently, some people like to do their uninterrupted thinking at night. Osborn Elliott reported that Robert Gross, chairman of Lockheed Aircraft, goes to bed for about two hours of sleep at about 8:30 or 9 P.M. and then wakes up, refreshed, to think through his business problems.

COPING WITH YOUR PUBLIC

Everyone who visits you or wants to do so has a reason or urge behind the visit. To him it is quite important, even if you may not think so. He may have been working the desired interview over in his mind for hours, days, or weeks before trying to arrange it. While most visits are probably routine, many are of sufficient importance to have a bearing on one's health, livelihood, or entire career.

While this suggests tolerances for the needs and urgings of your visitors, you must also accommodate your own need for working time or you, too, will suffer inconvenience and possible damage to your own livelihood. In other words, you, too, must maintain a balance. How you treat your visitor will depend upon your own time availability, the propriety of the visitor's claim upon your time, his relationship to you, and your experience with him in previous interview situations.

On this point, Dr. Hurst R. Anderson, president of The American University, said to me: "One of the problems which faces me every week of the year is whether or not to include Request A instead of Request B in a schedule in which it would be difficult to include either.

"My own feeling is that the evaluation must be made from two points of view—that of the person who is making the request and that of the recipient. The skill with which one effects the merger of these two will determine the skill with which one manages his time."

Mentally, you tend to put your visitors into certain categories, some of which will be covered below. Before going into them, we will review some of the general criteria which you should run through in your mind as you screen the necessity for the visit with a particular person.

Why Do People Visit?

People visit during office hours for one or more of the following reasons:

1. To seek information.
2. To seek aid or guidance.
3. To give information.
4. To respond to your invitation or request.
5. To socialize.

If functionally you are the one to provide certain information, then you should provide the time to anyone who has a real justification for asking for it. The two questions, then, are: Are you the proper source of information? Does the person seem to have a legitimate need for it?

The giving of aid or counsel involves a judgment on your part that goes beyond the mere commitment of time. In the first place, most people don't want advice; they want you to confirm or give aid and comfort to what they would like to do. In some business situations it even takes on an insidious character: Your visitor wants you to be apprised of something that he is doing so that, if it backfires later, he can say that you knew about it all along. Generally speaking, then, people experienced in the ways of business life will avoid such entanglements. They may see the visitor if the relationship is such that turning him aside would not be prudent. Due caution should be exercised with strangers and with those whose motives are not well established. Of course, with your superiors, your colleagues, or your subordinates, with whom you have defined continuing relationships, you will be called upon to render aid and assistance on a variety of occasions.

When people voluntarily offer information to you, they may do so in good faith with no other motive than to be helpful.

To screen this type of situation, you must first consider your need for the information, the authenticity of the source and the propriety of receiving the information in that way. It might be better, for example, for the information to come through some prescribed official channel or to be given to you in writing. Another situation you may encounter occasionally in some organizations or among salesmen or other marketing types is the dispensing of information as an excuse for prying other information out of you.

The visit in response to your request or invitation poses only two simple questions: Is this the best timing for you, and should someone else be present to participate in the discussion?

The pure social visit is often not as pure as it is made to appear. At its best the social visit may be a yielding to the gregarious impulse. A little of this goes a long way. You can indulge it for the occasional visitor from out of town but otherwise it should be reserved for the lunchroom. If you are in a position of power or have executive responsibilities, people may seek you out for purposes of impressing you or playing office politics. Naturally, as soon as you detect this, you will want to avoid involvement. In general, a nonresponsive, businesslike attitude will discourage this kind of socializing. When a subordinate wastes time with you, you might regard this not so much as an indication that he does not have enough things to do, but that it is an indication of some insecurity on his part—some probing for an expression by you.

"In public life time becomes particularly difficult," said Governor Michael V. DiSalle of Ohio as he told me of some of his pet aversions. "There is always someone dropping in who does not have an appointment, who just wants to say hello. He is a dear old friend, someone that you have known for a good many years and, even though you will find the time to say hello to 'good old Jack,' Jack often forgets that he just wants to say hello in his rush to tell you about a position he is interested in, or a brother who is in need, or a product that he wants to sell. So that you not only become disturbed that 'good old Jack' really didn't want to say hello, but by this time your appointments have piled up and those who took the time to schedule appointments are kept waiting because 'good old Jack' just happened to drop in and say hello. By this time Jack is no longer an old friend but a former friend and you have prepared to catch the time up at the latter part of the day.

"By the time this happens several times in the course of a day, the latter part of the day has assumed rather overwhelming proportions. I like to call this period 'the time that Jack built' and, although it is usually for constructive work, there is just a haze, as faint as it might be, of resentment in having permitted this to occur, knowing full well that in so doing you have broken the resolutions of months and years of experience.

"But don't think for a minute that there won't be more Jacks, because there will be; for in managing my own time, I have great confidence in my ability to stretch it over most of the hours of the day, when firmness in the first instance would have helped me maintain a planned, orderly, and efficient schedule."

Visits by Subordinates

As a supervisor of others, you must allow adequate time for regular as well as special interactions. The amount of time you give to one must be balanced with the amount of time you give to others, consistent with the respective nature of their duties. To seem to favor one excessively will create problems for him as well as for yourself in relationship with the others. Also, you cannot seem to be ignoring one or all of them. If this feeling should develop, you will have some serious personnel-relationship flareback, whether or not it is manifested openly.

To some extent, you are bound by the customs of the house. If an open door with unannounced visits is the prevailing practice, you are at a disadvantage if you alone attempt to introduce more orderly procedures for controlling your availability. The solution for this begins somewhere at the top of your part of the organization and must percolate down.

As a general rule, you should not be receiving visits from subordinates who do not report directly in line to you. When they seek interviews, your secretary should ascertain politely and discreetly whether the visit is with the cognizance of the intermediary supervisor.

All things being equal, some employees will require more time than others due to individual differences in their ability to express and to grasp ideas. Through experience you will become aware of these differences and you will know what adjustment in timing you need to make for each member of your staff.

To conserve time for the more important discussions, you should try to get extra mileage out of other communication situations for the transaction of routine or other less important business. For example:

1. Set up regular conference periods with each of your employees. You and they can accumulate items for these intermittent meetings. Special meetings will still be required for group conferences and for unusual items of business.

2. Hold regular staff meetings at which to take up matters of common administrative concern as well as to discuss work problems involving most of those present. Staff meetings are not a substitute for regularized individual meetings. The open staff meetings do not allow individuals to have the periods of privacy and intimate contact which they desire and deserve.

3. Hold occasional luncheon meetings or other non-working-time sessions to remove the pressures for social visits.

4. Encourage the use of other media, such as the telephone and office-mail systems, wherever direct personal contact is not needed.

Maurice H. Stans keeps a set of file folders in his desk— one for each person reporting to him. In each folder he accumulates items to take up the next time he has a general conference with one of those people. This helps eliminate the need for small visits.

Visits by Associates and Colleagues

Relationships with associates and colleagues require more sensitive care than in the case of your subordinates. Unlike your subordinates, they are not subject to the same direct control and discipline. Hence, because they have greater freedom to express themselves, you have more of a public-relations problem in responding to their requests for time.

This is not to suggest that your associates should be exempted from the imperative that they, too, must respect your working schedule. The difference is that you cannot be quite as direct.

(Nor does this imply that you can be brusque, abrupt, or inconsiderate of the feelings of your subordinates!) Here are a few suggestions:

1. Work for the long pull. Control your relationships with your colleagues by demonstrating a businesslike attitude.

2. On joint projects or work assignments, occasionally suggest handling certain aspects by telephone or memorandum—to convey the idea that meetings should not be called at the drop of a hat.

3. With troublesome colleagues who use too much of your time in unnecessary visiting, suggest your coming around to their offices when they call for permission to visit. After a while they'll get the hint.

Visits by the Boss

Your immediate superior—or even someone above him—may drop in abruptly to get a quick answer to an urgent problem with which he is coping. Of course, you will accommodate him. You might even have to excuse another visitor then present.

Being mortal, your superior may also want to socialize. He may want someone to hold his hand when he is troubled. He may like to hear your ideas. You should be flattered but you should also be concerned with your ability to gratify another requirement of his: that you get your work done. Therefore, if you feel under pressure, you might politely refer to your current preoccupation with a task in which he is specifically interested.

Another indirect technique might be to keep one's pen or pencil in hand, poised for action, with a reluctant air about engaging in conversation!

Clients

A troublesome client may not be worth it. He may come unannounced, come late to scheduled appointments, ask for emergency appointments, and stay too long. He may or may not be prompt about paying you, but he has no doubt that his problems are the most important things you should consider at the moment.

If he arrives without an appointment, his business should be extremely urgent to warrant any interruption in your schedule. At the risk of losing your client you must stand up to this kind of interruption, which is the most serious since it disregards all of your personal planning and may, also, jeopardize your relationships with other clients.

Calls for emergency appointments should be handled considerately because they may have merit. What you must determine over the telephone is whether an immediate visit is really essential. Your client must think so or he would not call, but you are expected to have the cool perspective to enable you to judge the situation more objectively. In any event, you must find some way of putting your client at ease whether or not you will see him as soon as he would like. Remember: it's what bothers the client that counts for him, whether the thing which distresses him is real or imagined.

Late arrivals show a lack of consideration, in most cases, even though they may not be deliberate. If the appointment is sufficiently late to throw your schedule off, your secretary or the receptionist should take command of the situation. The visitor should be told that his appointment is lost; that your next conference is under way. It is possible that the late visitor might be worked in sometime later, but the secretary doesn't really know just when. Should she make another appointment?

When clients stay too long, you may feel impelled to find some means of using one of the techniques in the section on "How to End an Interview" found below. Bear in mind, however, that some kind of insecurity may be impelling the client to stay longer. Your task is to try to put your finger on the insecurity and do whatever you can to relieve it.

Doctors and dentists, particularly, have a problem with the amount of time it takes to dispense much the same kind of information to their patients. One technique used by many professional men is to have a supply of preprinted statements on the most common informational topics, such as diet, symptoms during pregnancy, orthopedic exercises, massage of the gums, etc. My neighbor, Dr. Richard Gilbert, gives each new obstetrical patient a copy of his book on childbirth in which he provides answers to most of the common questions. Some physicians have periodic film showings for expectant mothers; husbands are invited to come, too. These media may not completely eliminate questions. They may, in fact, prompt more questions in some cases, but they will be the more important ones, often calling for replies unique to the patient's own condition.

The same "boiler-plate" technique may be used by salesmen. Question-and-answer bulletins may be compared on a particular product and services. Technical bulletins may be provided for customers who want to go more deeply into certain topics. In addition to saving time they assure uniformly correct communication of technical information.

Salesmen

The purchasing agent or buyer who deals with salespeople constantly will have his own procedures for arranging time with them. This section is more for the benefit of the man who meets only occasionally with salesmen who call upon him. While the time allotted to them must be controlled, you should not forget the valuable contributions they can make. The selling people who call upon you can serve as windows on the outside world. They can contribute a great deal of information to you about new products, services, applications, competition, market trends and practices, technological progress, and operating problems. Because they have a wide exposure to many situations, they may be able to help you with your own problems. While this is not true of all who may call upon you, occasionally you will find a salesman with rare insight who will identify himself with your own problems to your own great advantage. Thus, in your relationships with salesmen, you would want to give more time and consideration to the man who serves you well.

Usually you would not want to allocate prime time to salesmen; not that they are unimportant, but there may be other things more important. Of course, if the man is in town for only a limited amount of time, you would want to defer to his schedule to the extent that you can.

During the actual sales presentation, give the salesman your full and undivided attention. Actually, he will prefer this. If he is a good salesman, he will want to take as little time as necessary to make an effective presentation.

Ordinarily, salesmen who call on personal matters should be seen during your off-hours. They would like to get in some calls during the day, but they are accustomed to adjusting their schedules to meeting prospective clients during nonbusiness hours.

HOW TO SET UP BARRIERS

Under the best of circumstances and regardless of all else said here, the busy man in a busy office needs to have some privacy, some exclusion of the outside world. While it is easier to achieve privacy if you have an office to yourself, this is not always a deterrent to all visitors. Still, the man with a private office has an advantage over those who must share space with others.

This problem area has provoked many a bit of office whimsy. There is a story about the harassed man, desperately anxious to get on with his work, who groaned inwardly at the approach of a chronic time-waster. Maintaining an outer calm, he relaxed in his chair while casually pulling out the desk leaf on which appeared, in conspicuous print, the following: "What? You here again? Another hour wasted!"

The "Geography" of Relations

The location of your office or desk makes it easier or less convenient for people to have access to it. If you are one of the relatively few who have the authority to do so, you might even relocate others to deploy them away from you. The more likely solution is that you might move your desk away from direct view through the open door. You might also face away from the line of foot traffic.

The hallway presents a hazard in itself. It is a place in which to become spontaneously buttonholed into a conversation with which you may not want to be burdened. The "uncontrived" hallway conversation is used by some people as a convenient excuse for violating protocols and channels.

Hallway conferences may be avoided by:

1. Walking briskly with a businesslike demeanor which says that you are in a hurry to get where you are going.

2. Anticipating a buttonholer by greeting him graciously and continuing on before he has an opportunity to reply.

The Closed Office

If you have a private office, the tactful use of a truthful secretary ordinarily should be the means of preserving your privacy, but this does not always work. Secretaries complain bitterly of men who walk right past them, as though they did not exist. Others make it difficult for them by saying, "Will you tell him that I'm here?" rather than asking about his availability. With subordinates you can usually control this, but with your other associates, more indirect suggestion over a period of time might be necessary.

Some executives use a "closed period" during which they do their private desk work. They announce this to their own staffs and also spread the word to others through informal means. To minimize violation of the closed period, they may ask their subordinates to use the same time period in the same way.

The psychology of an open door is that people can walk in. When you do not wish to be disturbed, close the door. This *should* tell most people that you do not wish to be disturbed.

One way of limiting an interview which you cannot entirely avoid is to come out of your office into the reception room. This accedes to the visitor in part, lets him know that you are very busy, and usually succeeds in keeping the interview short. You can almost terminate it at will.

The Open Office

In a busy office which you share with others, your chief defense against unwanted visitors is a busy demeanor. You can't claim to be "in conference." What is called for is skill in deferring conversation and in terminating it. You must be able to maintain your poise in the face of interruptions because this gives you some advantage in mastering the situation. Actually, you may suggest to your visitor that you are in the midst of a rush job and, if convenient to him, or unless it is an emergency, you would prefer visiting with him later.

A partial physical solution to the problem is to install low partitions, about 5 feet 6 inches high. They serve almost as well as the completely enclosed offices.

HOW TO MANAGE AN INTERVIEW

Like a letter, an interview or personal conference has a beginning, a middle (or body), and an ending. The substance or meat of the interview should come out of the middle, with as little time as possible spent in getting under way and winding up. In practice anything can happen. In more cases than one might imagine, there is no substance to any part of the interview! Some visitors are so poorly prepared to present their thoughts that they don't get around to the heart of them until the last moments of the interview, if then.

You cannot do very much about the preparation of your visitor, unless he is someone who works under your supervision. You can, however, follow certain procedures, for your part, which help you get the most out of the conversation and also help you limit the amount of time spent with visitors.

The topics to be discussed here are:
1. Preparing for a visitor.
2. The art of listening.
3. The art of guiding an interview.
4. How to end an interview.
5. How to be a good visitor.

Preparing for a Visitor

It is common practice in business and in government to obtain a "rundown" on a visitor before he comes in for his appointment. Important people are referenced with their biographies in a variety of standard sources. Many of the professions publish biographical registers. For a fee, personal reports can be obtained from various of the credit-reporting organizations, a number of whom do a big business in conducting personnel investigations. In very few cases will you need to go to this extent to find out about your visitor, but the principle holds, nevertheless, that you should know *something* about him if he is a stranger to you. If he is from within your own organization, you will have your own internal sources for this purpose. You can also find out a great deal about your visitor, quite often merely by asking him to tell you something about himself.

The things you will need to know about a person will vary widely depending upon the purpose of the interview. A physician may review his patient's entire medical history, briefly at least, before undertaking a current examination of him. If he is a new patient, the physician will usually have his nurse or secretary enter as much information as possible on a history card before the examination takes place.

Similarly, in many business situations you will want to know information such as the following about your visitor: his status, background, probable goals and motivations, and his operating personality. These pertain to the individual as such before you get into such questions as what he wants and expects.

Why do you want to know as much as possible about your visitor and his interests? The most important reason is that you need to catch up with him. Before coming to see you he may have put a great deal of thought and effort into his own preparation. He might even have engaged an entire staff of people in preparing exhibits. He will—if he prepared well for an important presentation—have rehearsed even your own probable reactions. Then, if you have not had an opportunity to prepare for his presentation, he will have you at a disadvantage. You may not be able to see the flaws in his arguments. This is one of the advantages enjoyed by salesmen: They get to know their products and the selling problems they encounter much better than their prospects get to know the objections—unless their prospects are equally prepared in depth.

I recall a very interesting situation that arose during hearings in 1953 conducted by the U. S. House of Representatives Post Office and Civil Service Committee. The postal-employee organization had pulled together a rather impressive comparison between cost-of-living and wage-increase trends in the economy as a whole and wage increases in the U.S. postal service. The presentation was replete with impressive charts and graphs which, however, contained many classical statistical fallacies. Still, the members of the Committee, not prepared in advance for what was to be presented, might well have been swayed by the arguments. Unfortunately for the postal-employee organizations, the hearings were recessed over the weekend. Meanwhile, a copy of the presentation was obtained by the Post Office Department from the press table in the Committee offices. Postmaster General Summerfield and his staff analyzed the presentation in detail, developed counterarguments, and briefed friendly members of the Committee before the opening of the hearings the next Monday. You can imagine how surprised the employee organizations were when their testimony was challenged rather successfully on almost every point.

This story has applicability in your everyday relationships with any visitors who have important matters to discuss. You will get more out of the interview and, in the long run, save time, effort, and expense if you prepare for the discussion in advance of it. Find out the background of the problem: past discussions, decisions, and actions as well as probable developments currently and in the future. Anticipate the possible or probable courses of action you might want to take. Anticipate the kinds of questions you might want to raise.

Now, there is a very interesting aspect of being adequately prepared. You will have more time available for listening during the interview. This brings us to one of the neglected arts of conversation.

The Art of Listening

Imagine two people seated in a luncheon booth, talking and eating intermittently. Imagine, also, everything they say is being recorded on tape. When the tape is played back and edited with a pair of scissors, you will, in a surprisingly great number of cases, be able to reassemble the pieces into the two separate monologues that made up the conversation. Each was so intent upon telling his story that he made no effort to listen. He may have heard words being sounded but he took no meaning from them.

Listening is an active process. It requires positive effort. A conversation between two people, if it is a true conversation, calls for an exchange of thought—a sharing of ideas and meaning.

You cannot really take meaning from a conversation unless you concentrate on what the other person has to say, and you cannot do this if you are preoccupied solely with your own thoughts. If you do not listen carefully and take meaning from what you hear and observe, you really have wasted your time grievously. Your conversation may turn into a dual monologue like the one conducted in the luncheon booth.

My friend Harold P. Zelko, professor of speech at Pennsylvania State University, suggests that one of the ways to start improving your listening habits is to first catalogue your listening faults. He lists nine that are typical and suggests that you might be able to add some of your own.

"1. Are you *preoccupied?* Do you have so many other things on your mind and so little interest in what your visitor has to say that you withdraw into your own thoughts?

"2. Do you *daydream?* Do you let things arrest your attention so that you wander off into ideas and reflections different from those to which the speaker is addressing himself?

"3. Are you *prejudiced* for or against the speaker? Do you let your feelings toward the speaker govern what you think about what he has to say? Do you let your feelings toward the speaker cause you to accept or reject his statements?

"4. Are your *attitudes* locked in to such an extent that you do not let yourself accept any new approaches or contrary arguments?

"5. Are you *self-centered* to such an extent that you can only see things from your standpoint to the exclusion of any other point of view?

"6. Are you *argumentative?* Do you see in everything the other party says an opportunity to negate him? Do you have a compulsion to be right which makes you shut out the meaning behind the words of another?

"7. Do you *tune in and out* of the speaker's wave length? Since you can hear about four times as fast as the speaker can talk, do you hear a little, think of something else and then hear a little more—at the risk of losing the speaker's train of thought?

"8. Are you guilty of *busy-ness?* Do you fail to give your full time and attention to the speaker? Do you look at other things, sign letters or allow other things to engage you while the visitor is speaking?

"9. Do you *jump to conclusions?* Do you reach conclusions before the speaker has had a chance to give you all the facts or arguments or even state what he proposes?"

"Our lives would be longer and richer," said Wendell Johnson, noted authority on communication, "if we were to spend a greater share of them in the tranquil hush of thoughtful listening. We are a noisy lot; and of what gets said among us, far more goes unheard and unheeded than seems possible. We have yet to learn on a grand scale how to use the wonders of speaking and listening in our own best interests and for the good of all our fellows. It is the finest art still to be mastered by men."

If you listen well, this will be apparent to your visitor. You cannot just seem to be listening for he will sense this and resent your treatment of him. Your visitor would prefer active perception on your part rather than a passive reception. While your visitor will not really object to a businesslike and economical handling of your time with him, he will resent being rushed. He will object to the implication that your time is worth so much more than his.

Thus, the senator or congressman who refers a constituent to a public official—even goes along with him—is often more concerned about the way his constituent is treated personally than with the content of the decision on the constituent's problem. True, he would prefer a favorable decision, but whatever it is, he wants his constituent to feel that he obtained for him a prompt hearing and a considerate one.

Hence, if you are not likely to please your visitor with what you have to say, you should at least please him with the way you receive him as a guest in your establishment.

Now, the substantive part of listening is to be able to take meaning out of what your visitor has to say. Here are some suggestions for doing this:

1. Distinguish between facts and everything else. Nonfacts include beliefs, opinions, attitudes, reports of rumors, hopes, desires, and feelings. It is well that you recognize these for what they are but you must also understand what they are not.

2. Trace out the logical framework or structure of the speaker's presentation. A logical framework of facts and ideas may not coincide with the actual sequence in which they are presented to you.

3. Identify the apparent feelings and attitudes of the speaker, even though he does not put them into words. While these are not the same as facts, they communicate a frame of mind which probably influenced the selection by the speaker of the things presented by him to you. The speaker may try to control his

expression of feeling but you will find evidence in his tone, inflection, pace, facial expression, and hands.

4. Make a conscious effort to avoid hearing what you want to hear. Identify your own attitudes and predispositions and try to put them in abeyance. Reserve judgment until the speaker has concluded his presentation to you.

5. Compare the statements made to you with your own knowledge and past experiences. Look for similarities and differences.

6. Look for the speaker's real purpose, whether or not he expresses it or is even aware of it. To do so you may need to perceive out of the context of all that he says and does.

You may ask how you can have time to conduct this mental inquiry while yet actively listening to all that the speaker has to say. True, you must work at it, but it is easier than you might think. Since you can listen at about four or five times the rate of speaking, you can outpace the speaker with your thoughts. In a sense you can think between his lines! While you are listening, in addition to probing for meaning, as outlined above, you will draw tentative conclusions, think of questions to put to him, make interim summaries, and regroup or reorganize into your own logical patterns the information obtained during listening.*

The Art of Guiding an Interview

Let us not forget that conversation cannot consist entirely of listening. What if both of you were to try this simultaneously? At times the conversational ball will pass from the visitor to you and then back to him. An important aspect of this may be called "guiding." This is a gentle coercing of the conversation to assure that the speaker stays on the main path.

When the discussion becomes nonproductive, you may throw in a question intended to bring him into a more useful line of talk.

If the speaker seems to have overlooked pertinent topics, you might suggest them.

If the point being made seems to be labored excessively, you may want to summarize it for the speaker so that he can move on to the next one.

* For a thorough treatment of the techniques of listening, read *Are You Listening,* by Ralph G. Nichols and Leonard A. Stevens (New York: McGraw-Hill Book Co., 1957).

If the conversation turns into an area of sensitivity—something which should not be discussed—you can indicate avoidance in whatever tactful way the situation allows.

If the speaker is not logical or adequately expressive in his presentation, you can guide him along the desired logical path while avoiding the implanting of ideas.

How to End an Interview

Good or bad, all interviews must come to an end. If your visitor does not seem to have a terminal facility, like the famous "Man Who Came to Dinner," you might need to help him along. In the list of "windup" methods given below, some employ more gentility than others, but then the desperation of your situation will vary with each case and you alone must judge how far is far enough.

1. Make a summarizing or concluding remark.

2. Bring the business part of the discussion to an end by changing to small talk.

3. Look at your wrist watch or at the wall clock.

4. Show boredom or ennui.

5. Stand up.

6. Walk your visitor to the door.

7. Begin reading correspondence while the visitor continues talking.

8. Buzz your secretary so that she can interrupt you with a message that you have another date.

9. Become a little more brisk and somewhat hurried in your discussions.

10. Tell your visitor in advance as well as toward the end that you have another date coming up and that your time is limited.

Practiced politicians have their own ways of terminating interviews. Here's one familiar procedure: The politician stands up. So does the visitor—usually. With a booming, laughing voice and a great show of palship, the politician walks to the visitor. He puts his arm under the visitor's while grasping the wrist from underneath. Chatting gaily all the while, he propels the visitor to the door.

My neighbor, Dr. Richard Gilbert, tells of one physician who uses a bell-ringing timer to terminate interviews. He informs the visitor beforehand that he has fifteen minutes and that the bell will tell them when they're gone. When the bell rings he rises. It may seem hard, but Dick claims it works for that busy doctor.

On your own account, you should not contribute to unnecessary conversation directly or indirectly. One physician had to get rid of an aquarium full of attractive and conversation-inducing tropical fish because his patients paid too much attention to them. A Detroit physician, quoted in *Medical Economics,* said, "Keep your consultation room clear of avant-garde paintings, photographs of your children, and other items that invite nonmedical questions and comments."

The same applies to anyone else. Figure it out: five minutes wasted each visit, six visits a day, adds up to two and a half hours a week.

How to Be a Good Visitor

If you have read this chapter well, you will by now have catalogued the various things that a visitor should and should not do. Since a good part or your life is also spent in calling upon other people, apply the lessons learned to yourself.

By way of emphasis:

1. Don't call upon a busy person unless you have something of reasonable importance to take up with him.

2. Prepare yourself in advance, knowing well what you want to cover, how you will cover it, and what you want to take away from the interview.

3. Be careful not to be so carried away with your own presentation that you fail to give the other person an adequate opportunity to communicate with you. After all, you can listen to yourself at any time.

4. Be alert to any expressions of attitude on the part of your host. Above all, respect any sign from him that the interview should be concluded.

SUMMARY

Much of the management of your relationships with visitors will fall under the heading of *avoidance*. This may begin with the avoidance of the interview itself. From an editor who had had long years of experience with eager writers, I once received the following letter:

"I have before me your letter of August 16, which I have read with interest. While I do not feel that I could contribute anything along the lines of a social-psychological study of the various influences on T—— W——'s life, I shall be glad to see you for a brief discussion, provided you can let me know well in advance when you plan to come to town, so that we can arrange an hour mutually convenient. I am rather busier than usual this autumn, and that is why I emphasize the word 'brief.' But you, doubtless, are equally busy, and will not want to take up much time.

"Finally, I might add, though you do not raise the question, that ——'s would not be interested in another book on T—— W—— at this time."

This editor had successfully practiced avoidance. I read his message clearly and concluded that avoidance of an interview would save time for both of us.

The conduct of an actual interview should be an active engagement for both participants. Both should be prepared for the occasion. While one talks, the other should listen. Listening consists of the active process of looking for meaning.

Both the host and his visitor should have clear understanding of the amount of time to be devoted to the interview. This should be respected by the visitor and, if he does not monitor his own pace, bringing himself to a timely conclusion, his host may need to help him along.

XII

Conquering the Conference

"I hate most conferences," said Don Herold.* "I have sat in many a business conference and squirmed in pain at the spectacle of so many high-powered, high-salaried men fiddling their time away so childishly.

"A conference can often get nowhere faster than any other form of human cooperative effort."

In spite of this despairing note, whose sentiments are shared by most people who have anything to do with conferences, including some of the worst offenders, Mr. Herold concedes: "But conferences are necessary, and they will always have to be held, and some of them move fast and get things accomplished."

Conferences offer one of the greatest opportunities for time-saving in most business organizations. The savings will come out of those unnecessary conferences and meetings which you eliminate as well as through more productive accomplishment from the remainder. "Four out of every five business meetings could be eliminated without being missed," said Charles A. Cerami, the Kiplinger organization's noted business writer. "Just how many hours that might return to you depends on your own situation."

* *How to Harness a Conference,* by Don Herold (Hammermill Paper Company, 1956).

If the biggest loss is in holding unnecessary conferences, the second and third complaints against them are that they consume too much of the time of too many people. A fourth black mark is that they are often too inconclusive.

No one should get the idea, however, that conferences should or could be eliminated. We can indulge usefully in brickbatting them only if this leads to learning how to get more out of them.

We can even tolerate some of what appears to be loss of time in chitchat if it leads to something. What appear to be the time-consuming preliminaries of many meetings are really the necessary social amenities through which people break down the barriers of communication between each other.

"I think it is a necessary characteristic of committees that they do not get to the point as quickly as you can in a man-to-man conversation," said Wesley H. Sowers, president of the Frontier Chemical Company. "But I think that this is also part of the benefits—perhaps a large part of the benefits—of committee meetings. This exchange of comments frequently leads to interesting new viewpoints on the problems at hand. So while a committee's deliberations are somewhat time-consuming, I think they are necessary. I don't know of any way to bring the viewpoint of all the salient divisions and departments to bear on a problem as effectively as through committee action."

TO HOLD OR NOT TO HOLD

When someone says that you can eliminate four out of five meetings without missing them, this does not necessarily mean that those which could be dropped should be dropped. The statement really only holds true if you judge by results rather than by how much better the meetings could be if they were to be managed more effectively.

For the purpose of this section, we'll have to assume that you will have good conference management and participation as a prerequisite to holding a meeting. If we cannot assume this, there is no point in proceeding further. The next question, then, is whether anything is to be gained from the meeting.

You can easily talk yourself into a meeting. To test your need for it, suggests Don Herold, "write it down."

"There should be a lot more writing and a lot less talking in connection with every conference.

" 'Let's get the boys together and talk things over' is a poor start for any conference. Specifically *what boys?* Specifically *what things?* Specifically from *what angles?* And who will say *what* on *what subject?"*

When the man who addresses himself to these questions puts the answers down on paper, he begins to find himself more reflective and selective. "In this act," said Herold, "he may discover that the conference has no purpose and that he doesn't have to call it. And *that* will be just so much velvet for everybody concerned—or unconcerned."

When to Hold

In the following list you may find one or more important reasons for calling a conference. While you only need one to justify this, several may be applicable to your situation.

1. The matter concerns some important change from existing practice. It should have an important bearing on the operations of the participants or require their *collective* judgments in reaching a position.

2. A variety of *interacting* knowledges, opinions, and judgments must be exercised simultaneously. Minds must be mutually stimulated.

3. Time is not available for the handling of the matter step-by-step, referral-by-referral, through ordinary administrative channels. The meeting is expected to produce the instantaneous feedback between the chairman and the participants or among the latter themselves which will permit a timely decision to be made.

4. A new approach is needed—even an excuse—to take a matter out of ordinary administrative channels where it has languished or become stalemated.

5. The decisions reached are more likely to be acceptable—and hence more enforceable—if they have the participation of those who will be affected by them.

6. The matter requires a continuity judgment. That is, the group called together has had prior experience in collectively reaching judgments on matters such as this. Usually, intangibilities

may be present, thereby placing a greater premium upon consensus. Collective judgments are frequently needed on matters affecting personnel or the making of awards.

7. The decisions reached in the meeting will be followed by action carried out by the various participants. Each should be informed as to his own role and as to the roles of the others to assure properly co-ordinated action.

8. The discussions have a training value for some of the participants, at least, because of the typical nature of the subject matter or because of unique opportunities for them to observe how people interact and reach judgments.

Or Not to Hold

Either of two general rules may dictate that you not call a meeting. One is when the matter is of such a nature that you can and should handle it through normal channels of responsibility. The other is when the matter properly comes within the framework of established policies, procedures, operating plans, and budgets.

Many meetings are called when responsibility is not clear. Undoubtedly, when responsibility is not clearly defined or when it is shared collectively, there may be no alternative to decision by conference. This is more likely to be the exception, however, for in most cases responsibilities *are* clearly defined. The reason many meetings are called is to *evade* responsibility, rather than to *assemble* it. This, then, is the question to be decided before the meeting is called.

On the second count, matters which already come within some framework of prior judgment, there should be a clearer case for action through ordinary administrative channels. For example, if policies have already been established governing award of contracts, each new contract need not be the subject of policy discussion. It either comes within the specifications of the policy or it does not. The same applies to budgetary decisions.

This is a rather simple and clear-cut rule and should, on surface, give no trouble unless people are trying to evade responsibility. There is also the question of magnitude or special consideration. The amount of the expenditure may be so large that, while it fits within the budget, it deserves special consideration. While another action may clearly come within policy, events may have changed sufficiently to justify reconsideration in the light of the new circumstances.

It should be obvious, but meetings should not be held to read proposals or memoranda when this can be done within the privacy of the participants' offices. At the very least it is unfair to those who may have read the materials beforehand. This topic, however, we should consider as part of the discussion in the next section of this chapter.

SAVING TIME THROUGH GOOD PREPARATION

"My husband had a great love for detail," said Eleanor Roosevelt. "In preparing for conferences, he would carefully go over the locale in which the conference was to be held, the objectives he hoped to achieve, the people he expected to meet. This, I think, was one of the most important things in his preparation for a conference. He had a great interest in people and a great confidence in his own ability to make contact with every type of person, but he wanted to know all he could about a person before they actually met. I think he studied the make-up of the people who were going to attend a conference even when he was not actually going to be engaged in the conference himself."*

Observers have told how President Roosevelt, a grand master of conference strategy, would spend countless hours doing his homework, reading through memoranda, reports, and files. He had a special facility for anticipating questions that would arise and the answers that they would require. Nothing should be left to develop of itself nor should any wishful assumptions be made about the other parties. "The American people see Khrushchev as a crude, drunk, poorly educated person," said Vice-President Richard Nixon, "but of all the world figures I have met, not one was more smooth, or quicker on the trigger, or did more homework on me before I arrived."

The great work of the conference is not really done around the table; it is done beforehand in the quiet of one's office. This is of the essence in good conference preparation.

* "A President's Planning," *The Saturday Review*. July 8, 1961.

The Agenda for the Meeting

The purpose of an agenda is to advise all participants in a conference, beforehand, as to the matters which will be taken up, so that they can prepare adequately. Not all conferences require a formal agenda, but at least the participants should know for what they should prepare. For some things, though, the identification of the topic alone would not be sufficient. For example, if a conference is to be convened to decide on the disposition of some complex case, a file of information—either the original file or a duplicate for each participant—would have to be circulated beforehand.

The same would apply to papers in support of proposed new policies, programs, and procedures. A great deal of time can be wasted if a draft of a procedure is to be read, word by word, laboriously, in a meeting with all present. The meeting, then, is held back by the least common denominator—that one who comprehends at the slowest rate.

The agenda as well as any supporting papers should be distributed sufficiently ahead of time. How far ahead cannot be stated as a fixed rule. Probably in most business situations no more than a week should be sufficient. If the participants are expected to come to the meeting armed with elaborate analyses of their own, supported by position papers and counterproposals, much more time may be needed, perhaps as much as a month.

The agenda will be ignored or respected in direct proportion to the way in which it is used. If meetings are conducted as scheduled, if the agenda is followed, and if unscheduled items are not taken up, the agenda is more likely to be given the advance attention it deserves.

Participation

Each person you invite to a meeting adds to its cost. If he is not really needed, he could be doing something else much more constructive with his time. Therefore, when you ask yourself *who* should attend a meeting, you should also ask *why*.

These criteria may be considered:

1. Will be affected by decisions to be taken.
2. Possesses specialized knowledge of the subject matter.
3. Will carry out the decision.
4. Has had prior experience with such situations or knows the conditions or personalities that are involved.
5. Has administrative or legal responsibility for reviewing or deciding.
6. Will provide a detached view, serve as elder statesman, or balance out a known contrary view.

These criteria should not be used as excuses for letting participation get out of hand. Rather, they should be used more as a basis for restricting participation. In general, depending upon the personalities, the ideal number of participants is about five, with seven as a workable upper limit. Beyond that number the conference becomes too unwieldy.

Although four will not give you the same flexibility as five, you can frequently do quite well. Three gives you some rigidity as well as risk. A division of two against one does not necessarily mean that the two are correct. Although the majority can be wrong in a larger group, the added numbers help cut down on this risk.

"In selecting participants," said James O. Rice and Edward O. Malott, Jr., New York management consultants, "it is important to recognize that most members of organizations operate in three hierarchical roles simultaneously—as superiors, equals, and subordinates. Mixing levels in a meeting may be absolutely necessary if it is the only appropriate combination of resources. But people do tend to behave differently in these different roles and there is a strong tendency to 'filter' contributions to avoid censure. Thus the energies of the group may be devoted to coming up with what is safe or palatable to the exclusion of what is really needed."*

Related to this problem is the matter of bringing assistants along with you loaded with files as well as mental stores of information. For some meetings, this may be appropriate, but in many situations their presence may have a limiting impact on conversation, especially where sensitive matters of policy or personality must come out into the open.

* "Using Meetings Effectively," *Public Administration News,* Spring 1960.

The Physical Aspects

Things you must not overlook are scratch pads, pencils, ash trays, reference materials, easels, blackboards, chalk, erasers, and any other materials for which you may have call during the actual course of the meeting. It should not be necessary to send out for any of these things, for to do so may interrupt a train of thought.

For more elaborate meetings, slide or motion-picture projectors, opaque projectors, or overhead projectors may be needed.

Of all the comfort aspects, good air circulation and ventilation are most important, especially if smoking is permitted, which usually it is. A long meeting should be broken up by coffee and a stretch. While this may seem to consume time, the refreshing effect will usually make the remainder of the meeting more productive. A good meeting chairman will use the coffee break as an intermediate goal toward which to work.

MAKING MEETINGS PRODUCTIVE

A story is told of John Locke, the distinguished English philosopher whose wit and wisdom were in great demand by the great noblemen of his time. It seems that one evening he had been invited to attend a very select party. When he arrived, he thought he would be introduced, go through some of the social amenities, and then spend the rest of the evening in stimulating discussion. The important topic they were to discuss never came up. The distinguished noblemen were playing cards when Locke arrived and they continued to do so for another two or three hours while he sat, wondering whether they were really conscious of his presence.

Eventually he took a little black book from his pocket and began to write in it. After some time the noblemen took note of his writing and asked what he was doing. He replied:

"My lords, I am improving myself the best I can in your company; for, having impatiently waited this honor of being present at such a meeting of the wise men and great wits of the age, I thought I could not do better than write down your conversation, and here I have in substance all that has passed for this hour or two."

As the story goes, the noble lords were so taken aback by the record of frivolous talk which Locke recited to them that they immediately put aside their cards and proceeded to the serious discussion which they had scheduled for that evening.

Locke had put his finger on one of the troubles with many meetings: They lose much time getting under way. Had he been the chairman, undoubtedly he would have proceeded to the main business with much less diversion of time into frivolous talk.

Although the greater burden of success rests upon the chairman of a meeting, one must not forget the participants, for they, too, have a contribution to make. Even as Locke did, a businesslike participant can do much to keep a lagging meeting "on the ball."

The Art of Chairmanship

The chairman of a meeting has the obvious task of covering the subject matter assigned to that meeting. He needs to bring the meeting to a successful state of coverage, apart from the nature of the decisions reached, if any. His background in the subject matter itself is not really as important as his skill in managing the flow of expression from the participants and the interplay among them.

The task of the chairman should begin in advance of the meeting when he familiarizes himself with the subject matter, the issues, the personalities, and the sensitivities. In the conference room itself he is called upon to demonstrate personal skill in getting the participants to make contributions and in blending the outputs of a wide variety of personalities. The participants may vary from each other in their backgrounds, personal stature, intelligence, temperament, expressiveness, motivations, and personal security.

The operating goal of the chairman is to bring forth discussion that bears on the subject. It must be a balanced discussion, neither excessive for the subject as a whole or for any of the participants. This is more easily said than done. Some people won't talk. Others will talk more than they should. Occasionally, discussions will become heated and even antagonistic. People ramble and interrupt. Some will use the meeting as though it were a public forum for the expression of pet ideas.

The skilled chairman needs to cope with a variety of these situations as well as many others. He needs to know how to handle the individual personality types—the troublesome ones.*

The chairman will recognize certain critical points at which he should come into play to exercise his leadership. These are:

1. *Diversion.* Restate the topic or goal of discussion. Ask whether continued discussion will be in order.

2. *Floundering or wandering.* Throw out challenging questions; call for comments by those who have not yet spoken; restate over-all objectives, agreements reached thus far, and residual goals.

3. *Dissension.* Shift the discussion to someone else; bring up a related matter; appeal to sense of humor, if appropriate; use a "let's-see-where-we-stand" approach, analyzing the issues and then getting someone else into the discussion.

4. *Deadlock.* Find means of getting the parties to see things in a new light; back away from the deadlocked issue, taking up some other aspect of the related discussion, in hopes that new facts or new perspectives might come up; identify agreements reached thus far and attempt to get participants to *agree* on basis of disagreement; call for a coffee break, tell a story in light vein, or use any other appropriate means of relieving any emotions that are overflowing.

5. *Hasty conclusion.* Slow down a conclusion reached too quickly; make sure all discussants have had an adequate opportunity to express themselves; raise questions or implications that might not have been considered; challenge the adequacy of facts used to support the conclusion; state the implications of the conclusion and make sure that all present accept them fully.

6. *Wrong decision.* Find some excuse to delay—some hypothetical question, some new facts, or someone else who needs to be consulted; decide contrary to the judgment of the group if

* For a discussion of some of these, see Chapter VII of *The Art of Decision-Making*, "Decision-Making in Meetings," by the same author (Garden City, N.Y.: Doubleday and Company, 1961).

you have the authority—if that is the only way to head off a decision which you believe to be wrong.

7. *Conclusion.* Recapitulate what has been accomplished so that all who leave the meeting will come as close as possible to a common understanding of decisions and understandings; identify what remains to be done in the future, especially action that is to be taken and by whom.

The Art of Participating

Good participation calls for a positive effort. It begins with the reading of the agenda and of any documents to be discussed in the meeting. It calls for reflection in advance and for preparation of any thoughts or contributions expected from the participant as well as from anyone he will represent in the meeting.

Rice and Malott say that the effective member of a meeting group:

"1. Shares responsibility for seeing that the task and maintenance functions of the group are performed appropriately —shares but does not monopolize these functions.

"2. Has the courage to express his true feelings and to encourage others to express theirs.

"3. Recognizes the importance of timing and controls his own contribution.

"4. Does not use the group for personal ends (to show off, air grievances, justify himself, etc.).

"5. Learns from each situation—he is not merely a passive presence."

When they refer to the "task and maintenance functions of the group," they mean, respectively, getting the job of the group done and facilitating the relationships within the group itself to enable them to get on with the task.

The good participant carries his work on after the meeting is closed. He carries out assigned tasks, as agreed, and prepares for any successive meetings at which the discussions may be continued.

Before going further into this aspect of getting results from meetings, I would like to quote selectively from a rather humorous guide to obstructing conference progress. It has applicability both for chairmen and participants. Of course, I do not suggest a literal application of the points listed below. Rather, they suggest *things not to do*. The authorship of this material is, obviously, anonymous.

HOW TO RUN AWAY
FROM A CONFERENCE PROBLEM

"Most discussions become, sooner or later, a desperate attempt to escape from the problem. This is often done clumsily, causing unnecessary embarrassment and leaving the group without the comfortable feeling of having disposed of the problem. A "cultural lag" is evident in this situation. Both military and educational leaders have long since worked out an adequate battery of techniques for dodging the issue.

"The following list, of course, is only tentative, partial, incomplete, a mere beginning, etc., but it should at least give group leaders a command of alternative modes of retreat, enabling them to withdraw their forces gracefully and to leave the problem baffled and helpless. . . .

"1. Say that we must not move too rapidly. This avoids the necessity of getting started.

"2. For every proposal set up an opposite and conclude that the 'middle ground' (no motion whatever) represents the wisest course of action.

"3. Look slightly embarrassed when the problem is brought up. Hint that it is in bad taste or too elementary for mature consideration.

"4. Say that the problem 'cannot be separated' from other problems; therefore, no problem can be solved until all other problems have been solved.

"5. Ask what is meant by the question. Then ask for the definition of a word in the answer, and so on until when all is finally clarified there will be no time left for the problem.

"6. Discover that there are all sorts of 'dangers' in any specific formulation of conclusions.

"7. Retreat from the problem into endless discussion of various techniques for approaching it.

"8. Put off recommendation until every related problem has been definitely settled by scientific research.

"9. Retreat into generalities on which everyone can agree but which suggest no content and no changes in the present state of affairs (as, 'Evaluation should be in terms of performance on the job').

"10. Retreat into analogies and discuss them until everyone has forgotten the original problem.

"11. As soon as any proposal is made, say that you have been doing it for several years, even though what you have been doing bears only the faintest resemblance to the proposal.

"12. Point out that some of the greatest minds have struggled with this problem, implying that it does us credit to have even thought of it."

The Meeting Follow-through

Unless the meeting is conducted purely for informational purposes, some specific form of follow-through is needed in order to assure that the decisions reached are translated into action. Minutes of the meeting should be kept in appropriate detail and distributed to all concerned. If extended description of what took place in the meeting is not considered necessary, the chairman or the secretary (if designated) of the meeting should at least hand out memoranda confirming the action to be taken and the dates of action.

The significance of recording the conference or meeting transactions cannot be overemphasized. An interesting illustration of this point was reported in an experiment conducted by two British psychologists, J. Blackburn and E. J. Lindgren. Privately, they had recorded a discussion at the end of a meeting of the Cambridge Psychological Society. After a lapse of two weeks, they asked the attendees to write down whatever they could recall about this discussion. The written reports of what was remembered were then compared with the actually recorded discussion with these results:

1. The average number of points remembered by each person was only 8.4 per cent of those actually recorded.

2. Forty-two per cent of the items remembered as having been discussed were incorrectly remembered—substantially so.

3. Many of the things remembered were not said at all or were said upon some other occasion.

4. Some of the things remembered in some detail were scarcely more than hinted in the actual discussion.

The moral of the story, of course, is that you can avoid many subsequent time-consuming debates if you reduce the understandings to writing *immediately* after they are reached.

Since action is the purpose of most meetings, the mere recording of decisions reached is not usually sufficient. Unless some positive effort is made by a person in authority to follow up on the action requirements of the meeting, there is a good chance that nothing will be done about them. One way to follow up is to call for a report of action taken, at the next meeting. Another method is to put the minutes or a report of agreed-upon action into the regular follow-up system of the responsible executive or supervisor.

SUMMARY

Meetings and conferences are one of the greatest sources of time leakage in most organizations. You have but to consider the arithmetic of attendance to realize the potential for loss.

The first economy is to eliminate meetings which are not really necessary. Next, one should restrict participation in meetings and conferences to those who have a legitimate contribution to make. Finally, the techniques of conducting conferences should be so improved that they become much more productive of results.

The good meeting actually begins in the advance preparations. Participants should be informed as to what they are to discuss so that they can become acquainted with the topic and prepare their contributions to the discussion. If several topics are to be discussed, an agenda should be distributed sufficiently in advance, usually about a week beforehand. Lengthy proposals, memoranda, reports, or other documents which are to be considered at the meeting should be distributed beforehand with sufficient time allowed for them to be read and digested thoroughly.

Apart from technical discussions in which a technically qualified chairman may be expected to participate, the main contribution of the chairman is in using his skill to bring people of varying backgrounds, interests, and points of view into some form of concerted action. This burden is not his alone. The participants must have the same objectives. That is, they should contribute their views constructively, keeping in mind the larger interests and goals of the group as a whole.

XIII

The Spirit and the Flesh

"Each man at some point during each day should set aside a shred of time in which to do absolutely nothing. That's right— nothing. I have come to agree with Cicero who said: 'He does not seem to me to be a free man who does not sometimes do nothing.' Bravo!"

So wrote Eric Johnston, president of the Motion Picture Association of America, adviser to Presidents, and holder of many distinguished honors for his public-service contributions, in response to my question "Time for What?"

What do people such as he do when they do nothing? They reflect and muse over what has happened. They may let their minds go free to mull things over. They may conjecture their way into the future. They don't really "do nothing."

The value of a time for nothing is one of a number of topics to be covered in this chapter, each concerned with a psychological or physical aspect of the efficient production of work. Much has been done by industrial engineers and industrial psychologists in studying the performance of production workers and clerical workers under a variety of operating and environmental conditions. Little is really known, however, about personal productivity when the work is more creative—when ideas are the product of effort. The topics covered in this chapter have, in part, been suggested by the observations and findings of others published in scattered researches and by reflection that grows out of one's own experiences.

The reader might use these as a basis for personal experiment with his own work cycles and his own approaches to creativity. He might also find it helpful to compare his own experiences with those described below, for in so doing he will identify more clearly those things which have helped him be more mentally productive in the past, if previously he had not reasoned why.

THE SPAN OF WORK

Here we will discuss three different characteristics of work which I shall call (1) the saturation effect, (2) the short-stroke effect, and (3) the game-board effect.

The Saturation Effect

What happens when you work too long at a task? How does this affect one's ability to absorb information and ideas? How does it affect the ability to generate ideas and solutions to problems? We may find answers to these questions in the limited knowledge we have acquired of what happens in problem-solving, studying, and learning.

It seems that when you approach new material there is a warm-up period during which you sample the information and look for the basis of relating it to what you already know. This is followed by a period of progressive intake. In any continuous or concentrated period, however, a point of saturation is reached after which absorption and understanding of new material begin to decline.

During the absorption period you attempt to synthesize what you have taken in and consciously derive from it new understandings and conclusions. As with most tasks, greatest headway may be made in the least time. Beyond a certain point the going becomes much more difficult. The return for added effort becomes disproportionately less and less.

You can feel yourself drawing upon your energies just to maintain your efforts at concentration. This should be a signal that it is time for withdrawal—to take a relief break. This interlude should be used to relax and reflect *passively* or, as a busy person is more likely to do, to engage in other work which does not require directed mental attention. The relief break operates as an incubation period in which ideas are turned over, sifted, and organized without conscious effort.

In planning your work schedule, then, you would avoid assigning too long a period of uninterrupted time for any activity that requires that you absorb and think. How long is long enough will depend partly on your experience and feelings. A stretch of two hours would seem to be a rule-of-thumb limit if you want the greatest return for your effort. We should recognize also that this will not always be realistic. You may not have time for efficiency; the task must be done as well as possible but it must be done now!

Even in the face of pressure it might be best to compromise by taking a little time out for an intervening task. If related, it is better that it be of a passive nature, not requiring very much directed attention of a creative or analytical nature.

The Short-Stroke Effect

In the performance of a task over a continuous period of time, whether short or long, there are at least three distinguishable phases: (1) the build-up (warm-up), (2) the fully productive period, and (3) the wrap-up or put-away.

When you get under way with a new task, you build up toward full productivity. Obviously, there will be less return for effort during the build-up period than at the peak. Similarly, there will be a decline in productivity during the period of wrap-up. In a short task the time spent in build-up and wrap-up will represent a bigger percentage of the whole than in the case of a longer task.

A concrete illustration of this is noted in the following explanation by the Eastman Kodak Company to photographic dealers on costs for the repair of Brownie and simple box-type cameras:

"Each piece of equipment that is received by us must necessarily be subjected to certain minimum handling operations. This is true whether it is a Brownie or other simple type camera or a more complicated mechanism. For example, the package containing the item must be received, opened, contents recorded, item examined, instructions read, and a work ticket prepared. After repairs, it must be packaged and shipped. The handling operations are the same whether a camera is to be completely overhauled or some minor repair made, and in the case of simpler cameras make up a rather large portion of the charge."

The point of the discussion, then, is that the middle part of your work must last long enough to make up for the diminished productivity during starting and stopping. On the other hand, it must not be too long or you will encounter a decline in efficiency due to the saturation effect.

As a practical matter, if you have small tasks to perform *immediately,* requiring little time, you do them. If possible, however, you try to batch together a number of similar or related tasks. Sometimes these might require the use of the same reference material, the same tools, or the same personnel. A familiar illustration of this, in almost every office, is the accumulation of enough work to make it worthwhile for your secretary to come in rather than the calling in of the secretary for a single memorandum.

Where the task is to be sufficiently prolonged, so that it must be done in more than one sitting, you should avoid subdividing it into too many small bursts of activity.

Once more, let's be practical about this. If you should suddenly have fifteen minutes or a half-hour available because an appointment was canceled, you would not let that time go entirely, merely because you might not be able to use it with utmost efficiency. You would use it for fill-in activity or to get a head start on something important.

The Game-Board Effect

The term *game board* suggests a field of activity divided into many blocks or paths upon which you move the playing pieces, which can be buttons, beans, checkers, or chessmen. The game board suggests variety, complexity, and the unexpected.

To play a game is one thing, but to have one's work organized as though it were a simulated battle is another. Dr. Melvin T. Copeland wrote of this problem in his book *The Executive at*

Work. He commented on the shifts in the executive's attention from production to sales, to finance, to merchandising, to personnel, to public relations, and so on and over and over again.

He said: "When we ultimately discover the basic test of executive ability, I expect that the capacity to make quick mental switches will rank high on the list. From my own limited observations, I judge such activity to be rare. A great many people —a large majority, I judge—do not have either the interest or the capacity to acquire the knack of making quick mental switches in the consideration of substantial problems. The mental wear and tear of continually making such switches is heavy. . . ."

The avoidance of this wear and tear is essentially a matter of work-planning and scheduling. The constant effort should be to put related kinds of work into categories in order to minimize the strain of building up to each different task. An executive cannot always do this because he is subject to pressures from many different people on a variety of different problems. It becomes a game just to match their schedules with his. One solution for him is to assign continuous periods of time for visitors, for desk work, for outside activities, etc.

Many physicians have learned to save time as well as personal wear and tear by making appointments during certain periods reserved for special types of patients. To some extent, lawyers can make use of the same technique, but not as readily because they do not see clients with the same frequency. Salesmen, however, can make use of the "batching" principle in planning their sales calls and in planning their sales presentations.

PERFORMANCE UNDER PRESSURE

The preceding discussion of the span of work covered the duration of tasks. It did not take into account the pressure under which work may be performed within varying periods of time. This is our next type—another one about which little is known.

There is a theory among psychiatrists that people who are always late for appointments, who cannot comply with deadlines, and who do not like schedules of any kind are subconsciously trying to *kill* time. The theory is that they are expressing their hostility, as adults, to the pressures which their parents put upon them when they were children, first learning the meaning of time—learning to finish eating under a deadline, learning to go to bed by a certain time, learning that they had only so much time in which to play, etc.

We all know people who rebel against complying with time schedules or deadlines of any kind. At the very least they inflict upon their associates a great deal of inconvenience and burden.

Not counting the comparatively few dynamic self-starters, most of us fall into the big middle group in which we conform to most schedules but for the unusual effort we need an unusual pressure. This is the basis of incentive programs and of imposing systems of reward and penalty which are used in every phase of life.

The Conflict between Pleasure and Pain

The effort to achieve something desirable, some gain, whether it be pleasurable or remunerative or gratifying, we may call *the seeking of pleasure*. It is a positive incentive.

The effort to avoid discomfort, loss, or unhappiness, we may call *the avoidance of pain*. It is a negative incentive.

In practically everything we do, we seek to maximize pleasure and minimize pain. It is the realism which imposes itself on the making of choice when we must give a little and take a little—the process of compromise. In business judgments it is the process of seeking to maximize gain and minimize loss.

In the performance of work, with which we are here concerned, it is the response of the work horse to the lure of the carrot and the fear of the whip, an almost classical example of the conflict between pleasure and pain. If the carrot does not draw, the whip will certainly drive.

The philosophy of pleasure and pain and the conflict between the two has preoccupied men of thought from the earliest times. "Pain compels all things," said the Greek philosopher Seneca. Aristotle's counsel was that the wise man does not seek pleasure; he seeks freedom from care and pain. Spinoza set happiness up as the goal of conduct. He defined happiness as the presence of pleasure and the absence of pain.

In our daily work lives we are spurred to performance by both incentives, positive (pleasure) and negative (pain). Some of us are impelled more by the one than the other. We have before us a variety of positive incentives: the making of quotas, the reaching of goals, the breaking of previous records, the production of quality, and the satisfaction that comes with the completion of a task in good time. Negative incentives include: financial loss, lack of advancement, dismissal, reprimand, and other forms of disavowal.

Although rewards and penalties for the prompt performance of work are customarily imposed upon us by others, we can also impose them upon ourselves. When productivity wanes or when we find ourselves faltering in other ways in our efforts to achieve work goals, we can ask ourselves: If I complete this on time, or ahead of time, or in good manner, how will this benefit me? If I fail in any way—if I don't get as much accomplished as I should—how will I suffer loss? If, for example, I am a salesman, how will my earnings be affected—what bills will I not be able to pay if I do not make a sufficient number of profitable sales calls?

Some people will defer pleasurable acts until they have completed things which are not quite as gratifying in their accomplishment. Then, there is pleasure in the relief from the added pressure they have imposed upon themselves.

Deadline Pressures

The deadline is the most commonly imposed medium of getting things done on time. There are deadlines for filing reports, for filing tax returns, for completing projects, for exercising options. As you approach the deadline, you feel added pressure to get the task done and you organize your work accordingly.

"I work better under pressure," is one of the most commonly heard expressions. There are advantages to performance under pressure. You get into a driving spirit that countenances fewer marginal actions, fewer interruptions, fewer dalliances, and fewer hesitations. Your pace quickens, you become more decisive. You infect others with your own businesslike effort. You discourage them from interrupting you or otherwise tampering with your own rate of progress.

There is an art to working under pressure. Some people come by it quite naturally. I noted with interest how my son set himself to the completion of a science-fair project at age fourteen. "I divided the project into little pieces," he told me. "Each night I had to finish another piece or I would not go to bed." Of course, with this method he finished in good time and won his Honorable Mention. In his own way he had come upon one of the most important techniques of deadlining, which is to subdivide the work schedule into segments with intermediate deadlines.

The intermediate deadline keeps you going at a more measured pace without forcing you into a crescendo of frenzied activity toward the final target date.

The deadline is not without its dangers. Some people go to pieces when they work under pressure. They impose upon themselves a rather curious kind of pressure: they organize their activities and schedules to be sure that they have enough time for everything and they assiduously pursue whatever they are doing in order not to be caught up in last-minute pressures. Actually, it is the *frenzied* pressure which they are avoiding, because they have imposed upon themselves a *distributed* pressure under which they operate from the very beginning.

The frenzied pressure must be avoided as much as possible. It is not a time for the rushing of creativity. Under the pressures of the moment the inadequate or the absurd may be rationalized into being the panacea. For creative work, there must be deferred judgment and reflection.

The rush job is a risk on many other counts, too obvious to mention. Suffice it to say that one risks calamitous error or, if not that, loss of quality, equipment, and materials, and damage to the nervous systems of all concerned.

More about Stress

There is a great deal yet to be learned about stress mechanisms in people. It is not important for the present purpose that we be informed as to the specific biological forces and mechanisms behind behavior under stress. It is important, rather, that we know something about working with stress situations—which brings up a warning and a suggestion.

The warning is that you not impose upon someone else or upon yourself a pressure that cannot be borne comfortably. Of course, you must rely on your past experiences and observations. If, after a pressured activity in the past, you have vented your feelings upon others or upon yourself or if you have had to undergo some personal repair, whether it be in the form of a pill or an absence from work, you should be careful not to strain your own limits of pressure. The same applies to your observations of the pressure performance of others and your assignments to them.

The positive suggestion is that you recognize and take advantage of your emotions and drives. If you should feel a great inspiration or if you should feel angered to the point that you want to do something, you can take advantage of this gland-stimulated energy.

Our example can be quite typical. In a time of low spirit everything you do seems to be a drag upon your energies. You are listless and unmotivated. You find yourself in a downward spiral. At what seems low ebb you are electrified by some good news. Suddenly, all is light and bright. It would seem that energy must now exude from every pore. From a sliding momentum of despair you now soar upward in a momentum of success.

The suggestion, then, is in two parts. First, when you have difficulty in being productive during an emotional or physical low, stop what you are doing if at all possible. Try, then, to do something—anything—out of which you will take a satisfaction. Try to arrest your negative momentum. Success breeds success, we know, but we may not give sufficient credit to even the tiniest of successes which can start us on the way to the greatest.

The second part of the suggestion is that when you feel carried by a burst of enthusiasm, ride on its crest. It may be an anger or a tremendous inspiration; whatever it is, if it unlocks your stores of energy, be ready to exploit the opportunity.

TIME FOR PRODUCTIVE THINKING

Thus far we have taken up two aspects of work: how long to stay with a task and how hard to work at it. Now, we take up the best times and conditions under which to work—especially when thinking is involved.

Unlike other kinds of work, you can invest a great deal of time in mental work without appreciable results. Productivity in thinking depends upon many things, not the least of which is how much you know about your subject. Assuming that you are covered in this respect, there are at least three other aspects that will influence your productivity: the psychological, physical, and procedural. The psychological has to do with your inner feelings and your personal readiness. The procedural has to do with the techniques of defining problems, securing and analyzing facts, and exercising judgments. It is with the physical that we are concerned here as we examine the mind-and-body relationships that seem to influence creative work.

When to Do Creative Work

The time to do your most creative work ordinarily is when you are most alert. At least this seems to be the case for people who must think to some definite purpose in business and professional work. It may not necessarily be the case for certain artistic types who wish to produce ideas without conscious restraint. We are not, however, concerned with the latter.

Considering the normal workday, most of us are at our best from about 10 to 11 A.M. and from about 2:30 to 3:30 P.M. Before each of these peak periods, we go through a warm-up, and after each peak period we go into a slight productive decline. This is true also of production workers, but people who work mainly with their minds take less time to warm up and experience less of a decline from their productive peaks.

Generally, your most critical thinking should be done during those periods which tend to correspond with your own peaks of alertness. I used the word *generally* because you must individualize this. Some people get under way sooner, while others take longer to build into a peak of alertness. We hear of early-day types and late-day types. What counts is how you feel at different times of the day and what your experience is about your productivity in mental work during those times.

Your personal experience may be that you find very little difference in your thinking capabilities and in the results you achieve, regardless of when you do any creative work during any part of a normal workday.

It is when you try to do creative work at the end of a period of sustained effort or late at night that you may begin to sense very significant differences. You may become conscious of a physical effort to keep going and to keep your attention concentrated. Sometimes your thoughts may take longer to come. At other times you may have no problem in generating ideas but upon cooler reflection the next day you may wonder about your judgment the night before. Ideas seen by daylight often fail to look anywhere near as brilliant as those generated by candlelight.

This brings us to a very important rule: If you must do important creative work late at night, you should avoid mailing it that night or turning it over to someone else the very first thing in the morning. Allow time for a fresh look at your work in the morning.

Incidentally, when working late, do the most creative work first, leaving the tasks requiring less analysis and judgment to the end.

The Muscular Side of Thinking

"We think with our muscles," said the great psychologist William James.

It appears that our muscles contract and tense in keeping with the nature of our action thoughts. Psychologists have demonstrated that some invisible muscular activity goes on during all thinking. One manifestation of this can be observed in the faces and bodies of television and movie viewers. If a viewer's attention is concentrated on a physical struggle, as an example, you might, in some cases, observe that he is leaning into the action, tensing his own body.

Experiments have been conducted which show that even while

a person may seem to be physically inactive while thinking quietly, muscular flexing and tension are going on. The conclusions are that thought is not possible without some kind of visible muscular activity. In other words, if you are thinking you are not relaxed; if you are relaxed you cannot be thinking.

What are the practical applications of this? Primarily, it comes back to the concept of "a sound mind in a sound body." It argues for enough sleep and recreation, especially physical activity. There are also more direct applications in individual situations.

This concept explains a number of things which we do mainly as a matter of commonly accepted practice. For example, when we have been concentrating upon a task without interruption, we may take a relief break for coffee or a cigarette or just a walk around the corner. This relieves muscular and nervous tensions somewhat, giving us an opportunity to relax and start afresh.

It explains also the value of the physical warm-up after a period of inactivity to enable you to think better. Sometimes, if you should begin some thinking activity very early in the morning, the thoughts may not come. The house may be very quiet and there may be no distractions; you have had a good night of sleep and feel quite rested. Still, the ideas won't flow. Then, you fix a pot of coffee, take a shower and shave, after which the coffee will be quite ready. At this juncture you have been moving around rather briskly and as you sip the coffee, the ideas begin popping, demanding instant recognition.

This explains, too, why many creative people have talked about their early-morning and late-day walks, or at other times after a concentrated bout with their work or when the ideas have ceased to flow.

Finally, what little we know about "thinking with our muscles" may explain why a deep, comfortable, stuffed chair may be good for rambling reveries, while for hard, directed thinking you need a more solid seat which keeps you in alert attendance upon your immediate task.

A Time for Nothing

Alex F. Osborn, author of books on applied imagination, presently chairman of the Creative Education Foundation, has devoted most of his lifetime to the study and application of the techniques of creating ideas. He has reflected, lectured, and written on many different aspects of creativity. "One of the most important steps—the one to which least attention is often given—is that of 'deferred judgment.' I wish you would emphasize this," he told me, "and be sure to use the words *deferred judgment* in order to draw attention to the importance of postponement."

Dr. Osborn referred, in more appropriate terminology, to the stage in problem-solving called the period of *incubation;* sometimes also called *mulling over.*

In everyday life your work schedule would dictate that you set the problem aside and move on to other things while the mulling over goes on subconsciously. When you are ready to return to the problem, the solution may come to you in a moment of what is called *illumination.* This may occur when you deliberately return to the problem or it may be one of those flashes of insight which made Archimedes famous and the ideas-while-shaving story rather trite though true.

There will be other times, however, when you will not be able to set the work aside. There are pressures on you to complete the work, to solve the problem, to find the answer. It is upon occasions such as this that you might be able to make the most headway by taking some time out for nothing. Nothing but enforced idleness.

In the organization of your day's activities, the thought with which we opened this chapter, you might provide for this period of doing nothing as a means for bringing forward the day's events and projecting beyond them to what yet remains. In the solution of a problem where you cannot defer judgment to another day or even to later in the same day, you must take your moment of apparent idleness then and there. It is not easily done. "The attainment of this masterful idleness is in fact the hardest part of the creative discipline," said Dr. Eliot D. Hutchinson, in his book, *How to Think Creatively.*

Taking time out for idleness may not seem consistent with the hastened pace at which we are expected to operate. If, however, it produces a better judgment sooner than otherwise, its practicality will be well established for you, at least, if not in the eyes of the beholder.

The technique is to bring your analytical work to the point of what is called *frustration*. You have studied all of your materials, observing, evaluating, and discerning interrelationships. You have looked toward possible conclusions. At this point you do not pursue the matter further. Rather, you defer judgment until after some lapse of time beyond the moment of frustration at which you cease trying to be creative. Now, you have consigned the problem to the subconscious. No longer bound by your specific directions, the mind runs its own course, often producing solutions that might never occur to you through conscious deliberation.

SUMMARY

In applying ourselves to specific tasks we are wise not to go beyond a point of diminishing return where little benefit is yielded for the added effort—where, in fact, the quality of judgments may be strained. As a rule of thumb, about two hours would seem to be a worthwhile limit, while somewhat less might be more desirable, depending upon individual experience.

The work span should not be too short, however, for then a disproportionate amount of time is spent in warming up and wrapping up. If you have many brief tasks to perform, do them in sequence, to make common use of information, mind-set, people, equipment, or facilities.

When the attention must shift from one kind of work or problem to an entirely different kind, a great strain is imposed. One solution is to limit the range of activity. Another is to perform related kinds of work together to the extent feasible.

Working under deadlines provides reasonable assurance that a task will be completed when needed. A deadline is a pace-quickener. It makes the effort slightly faster than comfortable. It should be evenly distributed over the entire effort, maintained through intermediate targets. When, however, the pace begins as an easy one and builds to a frenzied crescendo, the results can be disastrous.

Under stress individual productivity can suffer or soar. Try to arrest a negative momentum with a positive counterattack, apart from removing the specific causes of depression. Ride the crest of a winning mood.

During certain times of the day we can be more productive than at others. Generally, the peaks of productivity are found about midmorning and midafternoon, although individuals vary. Work done late at night may seem quite satisfactory under the strained judgments of the hour but to the well-slept eye of the morning, it may look ridiculously different.

Muscular activity seems to be an accompaniment of thinking, even though it may not be visible. One's best thinking to a purpose should be done, therefore, in a state of physical alertness.

Finally, there is a time in which to do nothing. It may be at some juncture in the day when one must pause to take stock of how far he has come and where he has yet to go. It may also be an interlude during problem-solving when the mind is given a chance to mull over what it has taken in thus far.

XIV

The Art of Concentrating

The ability to concentrate—to persevere on a course of mind without distraction or diversion—is a power which has enabled men of moderate capabilities to reach heights of attainment which have eluded genius. They have no secret formula other than to persevere. Such men must have learned early their limitations and they must have learned, also, that concentrated effort over a protracted period can be more productive than a brilliant, but inconsistently followed, endeavor.

Let us not concern ourselves here, however, with the Horatio Alger implications of perseverance. Rather, it is sufficient if we look into the several techniques for learning to concentrate better on the single task before us. The achievement of personal success then will take care of itself, for if one can learn to concentrate on a single task, he will apply the same skill to other tasks.

The problem of concentration is that it takes positive effort. Hence, if there is some diversion, and the level of positive effort is low, you lose the ability to concentrate. Our effort in this chapter, then, will be to minimize the diversion and maximize the positive effort. More specifically, the formula offered here consists of: (1) a proper setting for work, (2) a conducive mental and physical condition, (3) adequate facts and materials on which to work, (4) motivations for sustained effort, and (5) a knack of knowing when to quit.

HOW TO GET STARTED

"The time lost is in the beginning," said William Hazlitt, "or in stopping after we have begun. If only we go forward with spirit and confidence, we shall soon arrive at the end of our journey." In short, the way to start is to start—that is, to lay into the task with a will.

This is true regardless of your field of work. "The best art director I ever worked with," said James R. Adams, the advertising executive, "picks up his drawing board when it's time to work and commences to visualize. He doesn't telephone or talk with someone or go for a cup of coffee. He knows, from long experience, that he will never get anywhere until he puts some marks on paper. . . .

"I would not wish to imply that creative people are lazier than other men and women," he continued. "It is only that they have chosen work which is tremendously hard to do, and they fritter away a lot of energy shadow-boxing with the job. . . ."

The Work Environment

Some of this shadow-boxing has to do with getting set physically. When we talk about work environment, however, I do not wish to imply the ideal situation depicted in trade journals showing modern office interiors, such as you may also see in motion pictures which attempt to portray the modern executive in his habitat. Very few of us have or can afford such plush privacy, replete with conveniences and comforts and devoid of distractions. This is not what we have in mind nor is it necessary. A good work environment, apart from considerations of heat, ventilation, and illumination, is one in which you feel comfortable. It should have a minimum number of distractions and opportunities for intrusion upon your privacy. If you have to work with others in the same room, you cannot have all this, but then, if you are highly motivated to get on with your work, it is amazing how much of the outside world you can shut out of your mind.

More important is the organization of your work center. The physical paraphernalia ought to be conveniently located or quickly accessible. Calculators, tape recorders, files, dictionaries, special references, catalogues, and any other facilities or work tools for which you may have some reasonable need should be available to you without inconvenience or distraction. Naturally, if they are items for which you will have only the most occasional need, you might have to obtain them from someone else or from a central reference or supply service.

Next, to the extent feasible, you should eliminate environmental distractions. For example, there is the case of one doctor who could see the feet of passers-by in the corridor through the space below the bottom of a swinging door. Somehow he started a personal game of guessing the personalities of the owners of these feet. One day he realized what a distraction he had created for himself by this bit of diversion. By then it was simpler to replace the door than to try to correct his own foible. The moral of the story is to remove any temptations, especially those of the eye-catching kind.

A more difficult suggestion to be followed is that you control the demands on your attention. It is not a new problem even though we are so impressed with it in the modern age in which we work. More than a half-century ago, in 1911, Walter D. Scott said, in his book *Increasing Human Efficiency in Business,* *"The modern businessman is exhausted no more by his actual achievements than by the things which he is compelled to resist doing.*

"Appeals for his attention are ceaseless," wrote Scott. "The roar of the street, the ring of telephone bells, the din of typewriting machines, the sight of a row of men waiting for an interview, the muffled voices from neighboring offices or workers, the plan for the day's work which is being delayed, the anxiety for the results of certain endeavors, suspicion as to the loyalty of employees—these and a score of other distractions are constantly bombarding him.

"Every appeal for attention demands expenditure of energy—to ignore it and hold the mind down to the business in hand. The simple life with its single appeal is not for the businessman. For him life is complex and strenuous. To overcome distractions and focus his mind on one thing is a large part of his task. If this single thing alone appealed to his attention, the effort would be pleasing and effecting. It is not the work that is hard; the strain comes in keeping other things at bay while completing the pressing duty."

The important thing, therefore, is not so much what goes on in your environment as whether it distracts—whether it makes demands on your attention. If, for example, news reporters in a busy city room or customers' men in a busy stock brokerage were to be distracted by the hurly-burly of their respective environments, they would get nothing done. Each, however, is able to preoccupy himself to such a degree with his own tasks that he is able to shut out most of his environment of distraction.

Physical Condition

Since a positive effort is required to concentrate, you should aim to do your important work when you are in the best part of your day's energy. Work with your own energy curves, as discussed in Chapter XIII. If you are working late at home, take a nap to refresh yourself. This is said to have been one of the techniques used by such men as Thomas Alva Edison and Albert Einstein to enable themselves to work their long, long hours with such a high order of creative output.

On the mental or emotional side, those things especially which relate to your feelings of personal security will intrude themselves upon your consciousness as you try to concentrate. While this is more easily said than done, you should try to eliminate or reconcile problems and anxieties before you buckle down to your stint of concentrated activity. In other words, if your neighbor upstairs hasn't yet dropped the other shoe, call him up—if you know him well enough—and ask him to get done with it!

The ordinary guidances, such as "a sound mind in a sound body," are certainly applicable here. This covers adequate sleep.

If you don't get enough of it in spite of knowing better, try to tackle your more difficult mental problems during those hours when you feel most alert. While the injunction not to overeat fits in here, try not to violate it on a sleepy day.

Informational Preparation

When you have felt mentally blocked—when you have not been able to see solutions to problems or even approaches to them—later events may have shown you what was happening. Apparently you had not provided your mind with sufficient information or had not given it sufficient opportunity to take inputs, absorb them, and integrate them. After some brief lapse of time during which you may have acquired new information or new insights, a further attempt to solve the problem may have met with success.

It is best, therefore, not to try to cram too much into one session. If you do, it all may end up as one big jumble out of which you cannot draw anything intelligible, as with the student who crammed too hard before an exam. If you are working with a lot of complex, new, or difficult materials, you might assemble and organize them in one work session and then complete the work of analysis in another.

Personal Goals and Motivations

It doesn't take much effort to concentrate on things in which we are deeply interested. The other side of the coin is that when we are not too interested in doing something, having more time available for it won't in itself be fruitful. This is why long deadlines for the completion of reports or work tasks don't bring fulfillment. If the deadline is enforced, the major effort probably won't get under way until the very last minute and then the deadline is apt to be missed anyway.

A philosophical explanation for this is that we tend to do those things which give the greatest pleasure (yield greatest return or gratification) or which minimize or avoid pain (hurt, loss, dissatisfaction, discomfort). Hence, to goad yourself to action you must ask: What will this do for me if accomplished? What disadvantage will I suffer if this is not done? In other words, if you do not spur yourself to action with anticipation of pleasure, you might do so through imagining the painful consequences of inaction.

Sometimes a man may goad himself into concentrated action through imposing specific and general goals upon himself. John Adams, in 1759, at the age of twenty-three, wrote in his diary a self-admonition over his propensity for frittering away his time. "I am too lazy to rise early and make a fire," he wrote, "and when my fire is made, at 10:00, my passion for knowledge, fame, fortune or any good, is too languid to make me apply with spirit to my books. . . . My mind is liable to be called off from Law by a girl, a pipe, a poem, a love letter. . . . What am I doing? Shall I sleep away my whole 70 years? No by everything I swear. . . . I will push myself into business. I will watch my opportunity, to speak in court, and will strike with surprise—surprise bench, bar, jury, auditors and all. . . . I'll not lean, with my elbows on the table, forever. . . . I'll have some boon, in return, exchange, fame, fortune, or something."*

Such broad aims or goals may not in themselves provide the compelling motivations sufficient to override lethargy as well as subconscious claims upon one's attention. You need more specific plans. You need to provide yourself with specific deadlines —openly announced and committed—so that you will be subject to some censure if you violate your deadlines, even those which you have imposed upon yourself voluntarily. You should give yourself rewards for completion and penalties for noncompletion. That is, allow yourself some liberty or indulgence after you have finished a task. If you fail to stay with and complete your task, deprive yourself of some desired indulgence.

Getting on the Way

We've had more than enough of the preliminaries. At some point you must get under way. You must get to the heart of the task. You must start somewhere. Here are some suggestions for doing so:

1. Retrace your work from where you last left it. This should give you a starting momentum. With this in mind, when you put away an uncompleted task, leave it in such condition as will

* From *The Adams Papers* (Cambridge, Mass.: Belknap Press, 1961).

enable you to retrace your last steps easily. Also, go a little bit beyond: When you put away the task, tell yourself how and when you will start again.

2. When you are working with fresh material, look for some familiar element. If present, you might use it for a starting point, if for no other reason than to get a momentum under way, sufficient to carry you into the unknown.

3. If you do not find any directly familiar elements, draw comparisons to your previous experiences or to other situations of which you have knowledge. Then, by analogy, you might find an approach to your problem.

4. Identify a pivotal point and attack it. Once conquered, other pieces will fall into place. Try making a game of this.

5. Identify the key elements in the situation and note them on paper. Then try to interrelate them in some meaningful way. You may come up with several patterns of relationship. If necessary, put them away for a second look after a brief lapse of time.

6. Finally, if you can find no other logical approach, start at any point where you think you can get under way.

HOW TO STAY AT A TASK

A good start is the first step in undertaking any big effort. Along the way, however, you may encounter many hazards, all tempting you into diversion. They may be caused by your own mind-wandering or by outside distractions. They may result from a simple wearing down of your mental and physical energies or from a loss of interest.

How to Build Interest

Interest and motivation work hand in hand. They bolster your effort to overcome the ever-present forces of distraction. Absorption in one's task, in fact, can be so powerful as to make one oblivious of all else. Thus, you are driving on a turnpike. You are alert for signs of your turnoff, concentrating on that alone while mindful of traffic. Then, your wife suggests another trip to Europe. This becomes the central thought as images are

conjured up of all the things you've been saving up to do during
your next journey abroad. As compared to casual chitchat, the
topic is so absorbing that before you know it, you are miles
beyond your turnoff.

Unfortunately, not all of our tasks are uniformly so interesting that they automatically command undivided attention. In
particular, in any prolonged effort, however interesting, the attention is likely to wander.

Here are some interest-building techniques:

1. Look at the task from different viewpoints. If one facet
fails to hold you, find another bearing on the same task.

2. Create an image in your mind of a larger undertaking of
which the present effort is only one part.

3. Think of the final product of your effort and visualize
the satisfactions of achievement, as an incentive to completion.

4. Take some measure of success out of your work. Create
a challenge for yourself, whether of quality, speed, preciseness of
detail, etc. Seek to build a reputation which you then must
retain.

Thus, Kenneth Roberts told of how his writing career had
languished and then how a bit of financial success changed all.
". . . With this lush new field unfolding before my eager eyes,
I abandoned lethargic habits. Instead of reading at night, I
worked. Each day I held out a verse or an idea in which I
saw possibilities. On Sundays I crouched over my desk from
sunrise to midnight, elaborating those ideas, polishing them,
twisting them, rewriting them, typing them. At the last possible
moment I packed them up, caught a street car for the big post
office in Boston, and put them on the last train for New York,
getting back home around 2 A.M., exhausted but pleasantly
speculative."

How to Acquire Habits of Concentration

The ultimate in concentration is to make it a way of life.
Instead of inducing yourself to persevere—this requiring a positive effort—you acquire habits of exclusion as well as habits of
continuity.

Start with the habits of exclusion. If you can resist interruption or distraction, you more easily acquire habits of continuity. Admittedly, to acquire a habit of exclusion is difficult at first. If you can resist diversion of effort once, then again, and then a third time, the effort will become less and less apparent. Eventually, it becomes a way of life for you.

Many people do not have much confidence in the various exercises in memory and concentration that one sees in certain books. Perhaps it is because of their esoteric nature—some of them approaching the "oddball"—or perhaps it is because of the unlikelihood of their being practiced by most readers.

Here is an exercise, however, that appears to be an exception. It is from a volume of essays on personal psychology by A. R. Orage (1873–1934), ". . . best known in America as a lecturer on psychology although Americans had been impressed before his arrival in New York in 1923 by his fame as the editorial genius who directed the London weekly, *The New Age*."

His exercise has the appeal of "portability." No paper, pencils, or other props are needed. Only a watch with a second hand—carried by most people.

"Take out your watch and observe the revolution of the second hand. It performs its circle in sixty seconds, or one minute. Watch the hand as it begins a fresh circle and let not your eye wander from it to the little dial; but keep your eye focussed on the moving hand. When you are honestly certain that you can keep the focus of your attention on the moving hand for one revolution, you will have made an important step in the deliberate development of your thought-power.

"Now take another step. Keeping the focus as before, count mentally the numbers one to ten and backwards, slowly, during the course of one revolution of the hand. This requires a double attention, as it were. You are observing the movement and counting deliberately at the same time. At first it may be easy, but do it again and again until it becomes difficult; and *then do it!* This is a very important piece of advice.

"The next step is to add to these two simultaneous activities a third. While continuing to observe the moving hand with the eyes, and counting with the mind, repeat to yourself some familiar piece of verse.

"The exercise can be made progressively difficult by adding

fresh subjects for the attention. Two or three minutes at a time is enough.

"Practice this often, whenever you have a spare minute, and the effect on thought-power or concentration will speedily be marked."

How to Bolster Your Efforts

While self-discipline is the essence of concentration, it won't hurt to bolster your efforts with external aids or supports.

1. At the office, if you have a secretary, she can help shield you from interruptions, remind you of deadlines, keep diversions in abeyance.

2. At home the entire family must come to your rescue when you want to get important work done. The big problem is the unanticipated caller or visitor.

3. Goad yourself to action with a deadline—a meeting coming up, a client coming in or someone who can't get started with his work until he gets yours.

4. Involve yourself in a joint effort but not with an inconstant type of person. Each should set a pace for the other. Try, also, to express ideas to another. In doing so you will be converging all your efforts on the expression of your thoughts.

How to Take Breaks without Leakage

Advertising man James R. Adams said: "My own time limit at hard writing is two hours, almost to the minute. After that I become dizzy—dizzier, that is, than even an advertising man is supposed to be—and I have to get up and walk around. Sometimes I actually stagger around the room a couple of times before I can gain my equilibrium."

There is some similarity, it seems, between the mind at work—for many of us—and the performance of an electric battery. Used in relatively short bursts, the battery will give more output than if used without pause until exhausted. The mind at work seems to weary of uninterrupted input or output. It is as though it needs to withdraw to regroup its resources. Each of us must find his own pace and duration of effort. Hervey Allen, author of *Anthony Adverse,* put it this way: "The mind makes its own time, keeps to its own schedule."

At some point in a continuous effort you will feel the need for a retreat from the pressures of either absorbing or producing ideas or information. The trick is to break away from your main effort without really diverting your mind into unrelated areas. Try these:

1. Change to a different facet of the same work, preferably something that does not require active thought, such as transcribing notes or rearranging your materials or papers.

2. Have a cup of coffee, a soft drink, or a smoke, while you reflect aimlessly. If you're with others, keep the conversation on noncompeting chitchat or on aspects of the work topic not requiring active mind process.

3. Take a nap—if you're working at home—or go for a walk.

How to Stop Usefully

When finally you must quit to resume work at some other time, do so in a way that will maximize the effort just made. Wind up your work so that you can make a new start most effectively.

1. Quit on a point of satisfaction, if possible, thereby associating the effort with gratification.

2. End, if possible, at some natural point of intermediate accomplishment, some subgoal.

3. Clarify or identify your frustration, if you end without the success you desire. Put it down in writing. Give the frustration a good kickoff into the subconscious for nondirected attention there until you resume.

4. Put your work into such physical shape as will enable you to take off promptly and easily the next time. Take stock of your accomplishment. Summarize. Draw conclusions. Put your working materials away in orderly condition. Avoid having to unravel knots when starting.

INTENSIFIED CONCENTRATION

The art of concentration calls for more than an ability to stay with a task. There are times when you need to immerse yourself in a task in some depth, as in memorizing and recalling. We will cover these, briefly, as well as techniques of narrowing your area of concentrated attention.

Memorizing

The suggestions which follow do not call for complex practice exercises, such as you may find in certain memory courses. Rather, they are easily followed and can be woven into your ordinary work. First, let's list a few general techniques.

1. Take your inputs in digestible chunks. You must find your own balance: not too much for not too long, nor too little too briefly.

2. Repeat the material several times. If you're more concerned with content than mere word sequences, study and memorize the items or ideas from more than one approach.

3. Space your learning. Start with a review of what you last memorized, to make up for the rapid decline in recall shortly after input.

4. Associate the material with familiar ideas, events, people, symbols.

5. Arrange the ideas into a single formula or system. Even a code word made up of initial letters will help, such as AIDA for "arouse *A*ttention, create *I*nterest, stimulate *D*esire, and move to *A*ction."

6. Group many items into subcategories. Thus, it is easier to remember three groups of five each than one of fifteen.

For a deeper effect, try these techniques, each of which involves you in some intense interaction:

1. Trade ideas with others. Examine their points of view. Advance and defend your ideas. Involve yourself in controversy. Ask others to help clarify uncertainties. In these ways, give living dimension to thought.

2. Write down things to be remembered, putting them into the form of lists, summaries, analyses, and conclusions. While relieving your mind of burdens, the act of writing while thinking implants material more firmly in the memory. It is like the speaker who writes his speech, then puts it aside to make his remarks extempore.

3. Diagram your ideas. Use doodles, schematics, block diagrams, organization charts, abstract symbols, etc. This kind of symbolization is an abbreviation which, when remembered, unlocks stores of supporting ideas and information.

Recalling

In the main, the methods of recall—when you must dig deeply for forgotten facts—are the methods of memorizing used in reverse. For example:

1. Associate ideas with occasions when you discussed them. Then, think of the people who participated in the discussions— their ideas and arguments and what you said to them. Think of those who agreed and disagreed and what their positions were.

2. Think of people and their connections with events, situations, and ideas. People and what they stand for are more tangible and more subject to recall than impersonal ideas.

3. Re-create events and situations themselves, recalling any details. Trace the sequence of events. Look for any scrap of helpful information. One familiar item will recall another, like reliving the past with an old crony. If you're stumped, a joint effort with someone who was there may help.

4. Reformulate the logical system of which something is a part. What are all the parts that go together to make up the entire category? Into what larger category would you put an item?

Limiting Ideas for Treatment in Depth

It may seem contradictory but I have found, often, that to concentrate on one tiny aspect of a problem I must first see the whole of it. Then, by subdividing the task into its separate parts, I can see them more clearly in themselves and in relation to each other.

The finer the subdivision of thought, in this way, the more easily you can concentrate on details appropriate to the depth of analysis.

SUMMARY

The problem of concentrating well was expressed in an old Latin proverb: "Our perception, when intent on too many things, is less able to grasp matters singly." In other words, during the moments of concentration you must exclude all things from your mind which are not of your immediate purpose.

In the first place you must start well. Your work center must be laid out for convenience, comfort, and freedom from distractions. Face up to any unresolved problems and anxieties before you begin work. Procure, beforehand, all the information and working materials you may require.

Finally, you must make a start and it must be a good one. You can look for some carry-over from your last efforts. A familiar or easy facet of the work may be more to your liking in getting a running start. You might prefer to attack the more difficult points first, feeling that when you have succeeded, the rest will come easy, like running down the other side of the mountain. If you can't find anything familiar, simulate it by analogy to previous experiences and situations.

It is possible to improve one's general powers of concentration through the practice of certain psychological exercises. The most potent force for continuity, however, is interest. For most of us, though, even when highly motivated, there will be times when the spirit will falter momentarily. Then, it is useful to have external prods upon our consciences, whether a secretary, the wife, or some deadline-reminder system.

In a single work session you may need to take one or more brief breaks. During these interludes you will be careful not to divert your mind into new challenges. When you have worked long enough, turn yourself off in a way that enables you to get off to a good start the next time, if possible at some point of intermediate accomplishment.

The techniques of deeper concentration provide the ability to memorize key items of information. Even greater concentration may be required to recall information stored away at some time in the past.

For concentration on the most limited aspects of a problem, you must first be able to see it in its larger context so that you will the better know how to define the limits of your inquiry.

XV

How to Read More in Less Time

"The main difficulty for me is to find enough time to read all the newspapers, periodicals, reports and books that I should peruse as Editor of *Newsweek*," said Osborn Elliott. "I keep telling myself, I will take a speed-reading course but, alas, I haven't time to do so. The result seems to be that I get up earlier and earlier and go to bed later and later; mathematically, my sleeping hours should dwindle to absolute zero within another few years."

Mr. Elliott is, of course, an editor, so you would expect him to be floating in a flood of reading material, but actually this is a typical complaint. It might have been voiced by almost anyone in business or professional life—scientists and engineers, economists, salesmen, doctors, lawyers, teachers, psychologists, and many, many others, who try to cope with the problems of keeping abreast of developments in their technical fields, their own organizations, and the outside world. There are so many things to read for so many different action, information, or discussion purposes: correspondence and office memoranda, operations reports, trade publications, technical bulletins and articles, internal instructions, technical digests, business digests, news magazines, business publications, and books.

How do we cope with it? Time is usually found for reading those things on which current action must be taken, like letters, memoranda, and other action documents, but if there is no current imperative, then the pending reading pile tends to accumulate, getting bigger and bigger until some measures of desperation are taken.

Several years ago *Business Week* surveyed the reading problems of top executives and drew some less than optimistic conclusions.

"In all truth, there's little likelihood that the modern manager will ever catch up with his back reading. He may be able to control the flow a bit more efficiently, but he'll never be able wholly to dam it up.

"By the very nature of his job, the top executive has to assimilate as much information as he can. If his intake slows down, or reaches him in a form whereby he can absorb more in less time, he promptly expands his field again. Some facts he can get by word of mouth, but most of them have to come from reading. So the executive, whirling the treadmill of reading, wonders wistfully how to escape—and how the other fellow is doing."

The other fellow could just as well be a member of any of the occupational categories I listed above because, while the top executive may be loaded exceptionally, the others have voiced the same complaint relative to the scope of their own work.

One possible solution to the reading problem which has come into vogue in recent years is the taking of a course in rapid reading. The claims made in behalf of these courses, by their sponsors, range from modest to amazingly incredible. *Business Week* said: "At one time it looked as though lessons in speed reading would be the answer. . . . Reading courses successfully doubled the executives' reading speed without diminishing his comprehension but instead of cutting the time he spends reading, this frequently merely enables him to jam more reading into his waking hours. Only if the executive is selective in his reading, can these courses give him free time."

The key to reading more in less time, then, is selectivity—deciding whether to read it in the first place and, if so, how much of it to read. It is to this that most of this chapter will be directed, although we will also give some coverage to the rapid-reading techniques as such.

THE TECHNIQUES OF SELECTIVE READING

The suggestions which follow are applicable regardless of your basic reading speed, whether you read a word at a time or a line at a time. There are some capabilities which we will not cover here, although proficiency in them should make a faster reader out of you. These include a good vocabulary, a broad general knowledge cutting across many fields of interest, and a deeper knowledge of the specific field of information covered by the reading matter. You will do even better if you have a facility for analytical thinking.

The steps in selective reading, to be covered below, are:

1. Screen for a purpose.
2. Read for a purpose.
3. Read for the gist of it.
4. Trace ideas instead of words.
5. Look for thought signposts.

Screen for a Purpose

Your first rough cut is to eliminate materials at source which you do not want to receive. Apart from adding to the clutter and the time they take merely in handling, they get in the way of things which deserve your prompt attention.

The next screening can be done by a secretary or an assistant, if you have one. In this case you must communicate your long-term and current interests to assure that you are given things that you should really see and that other things of actual interest are not kept from you, in some cases things which you may be awaiting eagerly. As your interests change, you must communicate the new interests as well as those which you are ready to flake off.

Whether it is done for you or whether you do your own screening, the following criteria ought to be considered:

1. Is it *required* reading—something sent or referred to you by someone in authority over you or something you must do for a client?

2. Is it *pertinent* to your area of responsibility? If it is merely

interesting but not pertinent, eliminate it or put it aside for your off-hours recreational reading.

3. Is the material of *current* interest or something that can be deferred for the future? If the latter, you can (a) file it, (b) put it in a deferred reading pile, (c) give it to your secretary with a "bring-up" note, or (d) return it to its source, making a note to obtain it later.

Read for a Purpose

It is said that Daniel Webster, when preparing to read a book, would first make a list of the questions he would want answered through his reading. Doing this presumes an over-all familiarity with the work through prior exposure to it or through knowledge of the author and subject matter. In the absence of these it can be done by quickly turning through the pages of the book or other document in order to obtain a preliminary grasp of its contents.

The depth and thoroughness of the reading in the material will then be governed by the use to which its informational content is to be put. For example:

1. *To answer a letter,* after having covered the entire letter in a quick first reading, identify for closer attention those points requiring action or reply.

2. *To follow instructions,* identify the successive actions, relating each to a progressive unfolding of the entire sequence of action.

3. *To prepare for a conference,* read carefully those materials on which you might have to talk and merely identify other materials to which you might have to refer in the discussion without necessarily covering them in depth.

4. *To form an opinion,* trace the writer's line of reasoning and look for supporting facts and authorities.

5. *To read for information,* cover the *new* facts or opinions which add to your store of knowledge.

6. *To solve a problem,* look for pertinent points but also identify them in context so as to make sure of their pertinence.

Read for the Gist of It

In the preceding material, mention was made of the technique of prereading which is intended to give you an over-all picture of the material before you read any parts of it more selectively. With some materials all that you might want is a single light reading just to get the gist or drift of the material. This is a kind of reading for highlights. Some magazines, recognizing the reading burdens of many of their subscribers, make it easier for them by abstracting the main articles. *Fortune* and the *Harvard Business Review* give you the abstracts in the table of contents. *U.S. News and World Report* puts the highlights on the same page with the article. Technical journals, increasingly, publish abstracts at the heads of articles.

In a book the table of contents and the index will give you a quick structuring of the subject matter. Years ago it was more common to include exceptionally detailed tables of contents, sometimes running to many pages. Where this is still done, it is advantageous for the reader because it gives him a clearer idea than the chapter headings alone, which sometimes can be journalistically deceptive.

Forewords, prefaces, and introductions should be read, by all means, because they usually prepare you for what is to come. If you desire, you can skip across the personal histories, apologies, and indebtednesses or acknowledgments which may abound in such prefatory materials.

In lengthy materials, scan the pages, looking for paragraphs that introduce or summarize informational content. Scan paragraphs for lead or concluding sentences.

While looking for main ideas, there are some things you can deliberately omit. These are the built-in appendixes such as lengthy supporting statistics, extended descriptions, asides, supporting proofs, and miscellaneous digressions or hobbyhorse riding of the author. You can skip right over these unless for some particular reason they are essential to your analysis or evaluation of the author's line of argument.

Trace Ideas Instead of Words

As we scan for the thought content of the material, we should put words in themselves in a secondary role. Ideally, the paper whose thoughts are well organized would be replete with revealing headings, subheadings, signal-thought paragraphs and sentences, summaries, and all the other devices that make thought content readily identifiable. Rarely, however, is this the case. Even if it were, the idea structure of the writer might not necessarily be the one which you want to pick out of the material for your own purposes.

Tracing the writer's pattern of thought can be fairly easily accomplished if you keep in mind certain typical lines of thought development, such as the following:

1. Presentation of a simple chronological report with or without conclusions and recommendations.

2. Tracing of a condition or effect to its cause, in order to explain it; proceeding from a known cause to an anticipated condition or effect.

3. Explanation of a point by analogy to similar or related situations.

4. Statement or proposal supported by arguments or elaborating details.

5. Presentation of a fund of facts, analysis, and conclusion, followed by recommendation.

6. Mixed lines of presentation.

With practice most people should be able to trace mentally the organization and flow of ideas in material of average difficulty—average for them. A knowledge of the author's previous materials and ideas as well as a knowledge of the subject matter will help greatly. If you have difficulty in finding idea structures in your mind, make a running list, without any attempt to organize it, of all the ideas that you encounter as you read through the material. Don't pause, while doing so, to think the material through. When you have finished your first rough list, go over it quickly to discern from it how the ideas themselves are organized and what total message and what subsidiary messages they convey.

Look for Thought Signposts

Another way of reading for main ideas is to be on the lookout for thought signposts which are included by the writer. Some of these are readily apparent, including headings, underscorings, indented statements, and tabular listings. Others, which require a little more alertness on your part to discover them, are verbal signals which are built into the written presentation itself. These include (1) introducing signals, (2) amplifying or elaborating signals, and (3) idea countersignals.

Introducing signals include such expressions as: accordingly, because, for example, if, provided, specifically, therefore, thus, etc. Each in a somewhat different way introduces a governing, subsidiary, or illustrative point. When you catch such an expression or word, you should pause to pick up the idea immediately preceding it as well as the idea which follows it.

Elaborating signals serve a similar function except that they concentrate on amplifying an idea already presented just before the signal is reached. Examples of these include: additionally, also, as well as, besides, furthermore, moreover, too, etc.

Idea countersignals tell you that a change in the line or trend of thought is about to take place. Look for such words or expressions as: although, but, contrary to, either . . . or, however, nevertheless, notwithstanding, on the other hand, rather, regardless, still, etc.

READING FOR DEEPER UNDERSTANDING

One of the obvious reasons for reading selectively is to save time which, in turn, can then be used for more careful reading and study of the things that are more important. Reading in depth has two functions: (1) to enable you to relate the new material to your previous knowledge, experience, attitudes, beliefs, and desires and (2) to enable you to retain what you read for future recall and application. The following four points are involved in reading for greater comprehension and retention:

1. Sharpen your reading purpose.

2. Reflect imaginatively.
3. Intensify the learning experience.
4. Stretch out your learning.

Sharpen Your Reading Purpose

You must have felt, when you selected the material for deeper reading, that it would be of benefit to you. Now, you should redefine your specific goals in reading for deeper coverage and understanding. As you examine the material and as you read it further, relate it to your current and future informational needs. Think of the specific problems to which the information may be applied. Your reading will be more practically oriented, you will retain more and you will perceive aspects of information which otherwise might escape you.

Remember that in the scanning stage of your reading, you looked to see if you had any purpose in giving further attention to the material. Now, you must read only for purposes of making specific use of the material.

Reflect Imaginatively

Add what you read to what you already know and reflect as to the change. What new problems do you now have? What new lines of inquiry are stimulated? Who else needs to know about this?

Perhaps the new information or ideas must go through an additional preliminary stage of reflection before they can be assimilated. You may need to prepare or verify information with your past ideas, understandings, and experiences to see if you agree or disagree or to ascertain specifically how the information may fit into your mental frame of reference.

Apply the information to specific problem situations. Consider the implications of what you might do with the information —the conclusions you might reach and the actions that you might recommend or take.

Intensify the Learning Experience

Bore in deeply on specific points. If you can do so on the written material, underscore the key points. Make marginal notes. Make notes on a memorandum pad. Organize them. Amplify them with additional thoughts and notes on paper. Keep organizing and reorganizing the material in your mind as you read along. Study the interrelationship of individual ideas and concepts to each other and to the whole framework of the situation as well as to your total knowledge of such matters.

Explain your understanding of the material to others as well as to yourself. Try to write a summary memorandum, if only for your own convenience in gaining understanding.

Read the new material in conjunction with your examinations of other things you have on file. Make comparisons. Consider how your framework of ideas or plans may be modified by the new material.

Stretch Out Your Learning

It is a fundamental principle of the learning process that you must not cram too much into any continuous session. If you do so—as anyone who has crammed too hard for an examination will recall—all your thoughts will become jumbled. After a certain point you stop absorbing and very quickly after the cramming period is over you will forget most of what you learned.

In reading, the amount of material you can cover is governed not so much by its length as by the amount of information, your familiarity with the subject matter, and the novelty and complexity of the ideas. In other words, it is informational saturation that you want to avoid rather than mere length or bulk.

The amount which you can absorb is something which you must sense for your own case. Individual differences play a big part here. The most important rule is that when you feel that your absorption is beginning to wane or that you are not able to comprehend as well as you did when you first started, you should stop right then and there. You may pause for a little quiet reflection or you may move into some other activity. If you want to derive the maximum benefit from your reading, however, any other activity you undertake should be passive, so that your mind will continue to mull over and digest what it absorbed a bit earlier.

If you have read to the point where you feel a blocked reception of any more information, you have really gone too far. At that point you are not getting the same batting average as when you started out. It would have been much better, then, if you had slipped in some intermittent refresher pauses—mental rest periods. They don't necessarily have to be inactive. In fact, a constructive use of the brief pause would have you summarizing what you have already learned and posing questions whose answers are to be found in your further reading.

When you stop for any substantial period of time, or as little as a day, do a little backtracking before you go forward with the new reading material. In as brief an interval as one day, you forget much more than you might realize. The review of what you covered previously both restores and reinforces your prior learning. Thus, you get a combination of repetition and spaced learning, both of which are essential for good retention of information and ideas.

This kind of reading for comprehension and retention may seem to involve a little extra effort. It may seem to be a bit more costly in time. Actually, it will take more effort and more time but this is much more economical than reading and forgetting, for this can be a total waste.

READING SPECIAL MATERIALS

Now that we have covered the general principles for reading selectively and intensively, we can apply some of these rules to some of the most frequently encountered types of business and professional reading matter, such as correspondence, instructions, reports, trade books, and journals. The suggestions which follow are designed to help you get to the heart of the material. In each case, for greater retention, you would apply some of the principles covered in the preceding section.

Correspondence: Letters and Memoranda

The first thing you've got to decide is whether you want to see new communications as soon as they come in or whether you want to have the previous correspondence on the matter withdrawn from the file and attached to the new communication when it is sent in to you. One way is to leave this to the discretion of your secretary, letting her judge from the contents of the new communication whether you do need the background materials. Where the attachment of previous correspondence is the exception rather than the rule, the new correspondence might be sent in without delay while the background files can be procured on an exception basis, as needed. The practice to be followed must depend upon the nature of the correspondence received.

With the correspondence in hand you scan first to identify the source, subject matter, and true purpose, looking for a clue as to what is expected of you. This information is obtainable from the subject line, if any, the identity of the writer, and a quick scanning of the contents.

Usually you can skip right past the courtesy opening paragraphs. You can also, usually, skim the surface of the succeeding paragraphs, looking for clues to the meat. This may be found somewhere in the middle or toward the end. A friend of ours who does a screening job for a United States senator says that almost invariably he finds the writer's request for something—a favor or a demand that the senator vote a certain way—almost at the very end of the letter.

Unless you have a particular reason for not wanting to write on the surface of the incoming correspondence, it is helpful to underscore key points, particularly dates when action is to be taken. Otherwise, write this information on a note sheet to be attached to the correspondence file.

As you read paragraphs, you should not assume that they are written in accordance with the classical rule of one subject only to a paragraph and one thought only to a sentence. You may find many thoughts in a paragraph which might consist only of a single sentence. Hence, sometimes you may need to pause for a more careful analysis of such passages.

Such communications may also be full of obscure or strategic language. The writer may have labored at writing what he considers a strategic communication. He may have put hours into a single page. For your part, if you read that page in a minute or two, you may not get all the meanings. While you can slip past the various jargonistic phrases that some people erroneously think must go into correspondence, be on the alert for any trick phrases that point to special writing strategies on the part of the sender.

Finally, read the communication in the light of your knowledge of the sender and his interests and problems. This may tell you much more than the communication itself or, at the very least, it should help to round it out.

Instructions (Directives)

The term *instructions* covers a wide variety of communications. For example, there are instructions on how to fill out a form, how to prepare a report, how to use a piece of equipment, how to decide certain matters in the future in accordance with specified criteria, how to participate in a meeting, how to go somewhere, etc. Some tell you about changes in the way you have been doing things, while others tell you about entirely new things to do. For our purposes here, we are not concerned with the directive or instruction that merely tells you to take an action without telling you how. Rather, we are concerned with the techniques for following a prescribed action, step by step.

The ability to follow instructions is not necessarily related to intelligence. Sometimes it helps and sometimes it hurts. What is more important is that you approach instruction-reading with patience and deliberation. This is no time for rapid reading. Intelligence will come in handy when you have some obscurity in the instruction or some adaptation to your own situation which seems not to be covered by the instruction. Unfortunately, too many instructions are poorly written and difficult to understand—incomplete, poorly organized, too technical for the reader, or even inapplicable to the reader's situation. These deficiencies in themselves impose upon the reader the burden of careful study and analysis. The following suggestions may be helpful:

1. When you pick up an instruction, make no assumptions as to why, when, and how you do things until you have read

the instruction fully. Without doing so in detail, you should at least get an over-all view of the purpose, total logic, and system.

2. Break the total operation down into its separate or successive steps or sequences. Make sure you understand how each is related to the others, individually, as well as to the total activity. More particularly, be sure as to the relationship of one step to the next preceding and succeeding steps or to something which must be done in parallel with it. Underscore key words or otherwise identify the critical points of action.

3. Identify and mark any special conditions, exceptions, provisos, warnings, etc. These are important because instructions may tell you what must be done in general, with modifications for particular circumstances. They may also tell you what you may do and what you may not do.

4. If the instruction relates to anything you are already doing, it may call for a change or a discontinuance in existing activities. Hence, you should look for the new, the different, and the things to stop.

5. What is unclear? What has not been covered by the writer? Remember that the best of writers might not anticipate every conceivable problem or question which might arise.

6. When must something be done? How long should it take? Are there any specific dates indicated?

7. Must you obtain any verification, review, approval? Is anyone else to be involved in this with you?

8. Do you have everything you will need: information, materials or supplies, tools or equipment?

9. How will you know whether or not you have followed the instructions satisfactorily? Have any standards or criteria been included in the instructions or must you develop these yourself?

10. Go through the entire instructions *before* you do anything. Then, repeat your reading of the instructions as you follow them, step by step.

Narrative Reports

Narrative reports vary widely in their scope, content, and purpose, and hence may vary just as widely in their actual treatment. A fact-finding report may attempt to be thorough in coverage, analytical, and conclusive. It may try to tell so much that it tells too much. At the other extreme a so-called progress report may attempt to use many words to cover the fact that very little has been accomplished. The task of reading each will differ: for the one, you must look for the organization and logic of the material and for the essence of its factual content; for the other, you must be able to distinguish factual from impressionistic writing. We'll discuss each separately.

The fact-finding or study report may be organized, in some cases, in accordance with a standard or prescribed format. This may help you somewhat, especially in identifying introductions, summaries, conclusions, and recommendations, if any. In any event the following suggestions may be helpful:

1. Read the introduction or statement of the problem, any summaries, and the conclusion and recommendation. If these are not specifically identified, scan the report to find them. This preliminary coverage may be all that you'll need. If, however, you feel that you should read in greater depth, continue your reading as indicated in the succeeding paragraphs.

2. Scan the report for key facts, observations, and findings. Skip past any built-in elaborations and appendixes which might just as well have been attached as supplements to the report. Read these only if you want to go more deeply into particular matters or if you want to check the writer's methodology and factual adequacy.

3. Distinguish carefully between fact and personal opinion, whether that of the writer or of someone whom he is quoting. Look for evidences of bias or subjective interest.

4. Consider the total credibility of the report in the light of what may be known about the author and his sources.

Progress reports are usually of two distinct types: (1) those which make an accounting for work done over a period of time, such as a week, a month, a quarter, or a year, and (2) those which tell how a specific assignment was carried out or how a specific deadline for full or partial completion was met. In either case the tendency is for a lack of deed to be covered by a profusion of words. Try these:

1. Compare the volume of work, when that is important, against what had been accomplished in the preceding period.

2. Determine the actual progress since the end of the preceding period.

3. Compare actual progress against goals which were to have been reached by target dates.

It is not at all unusual for a progress report to be replete with references to difficulties; delays upon the part of others; meetings which were attended or should be attended; additional studies which should be made; additional facts or replies to correspondence which are being awaited; and vague references to inappropriate timing for certain actions, among other self-relieving obfuscations.

I am reminded of a top-management report which had been designed for a certain organization. Every project of interest to top management was included in the monthly report and identified by a number so that continuity would be assured from report to report. When the individual reports of progress were received, for inclusion in the over-all report to top management, it was usually easy to tell which had little to say. These were more likely to be the longest reports because it somehow takes a writer with an insecurity or a guilty conscience many more words to report on the lack of activity than on actual progress. These lengthy reports were scanned and if they did not show tangible progress, their contents were summarized for top management in two words: "No change." Oddly enough, all concerned came to accept the "no-change" interpretation as one of the fair rules of the game, even though its application might sting.

Statistical Reports

In the business world it is quite fashionable to criticize the profusion of statistical and financial reports with their masses of data which no one has time to read. It has always seemed to me that business people have found a very quick way out: they don't read them. In spite of their complaints and their disuse of the reports they receive, they are nevertheless unwilling to discontinue them for fear that they might miss something or they might be regarded as showing disinterest or for other reasons. While much can be done to improve the format and presentation of reports, the fact remains that in the best of organizations such a desired state is rarely attained. The reader's best defense is to use a check list of critical indicators or comparisons which will enable him to pull out the exceptional information that he desires. For example:

1. Check *first* for pertinence of the material to your actual interests. Do you have a need to know (direct interest) or is it nice to know (curiosity interest)?

2. Check now for timeliness, because this will often determine usefulness. How current is the report? How much time has elapsed since the end of the reporting period and its receipt by you?

3. What change has there been since the preceding reporting period? How does it compare with performance for the same period a year ago? How does it compare with performance against some predetermined base period?

4. What trend do you see and how does it project into the future? What are the trend *percentages?*

5. What is the performance against a standard? Toward specific goals?

6. What relationships or comparisons are found between key related factors? These may sometimes be expressed as key ratios or indexes of performance.

As with narrative reports, the technique of reading is to look for the key ideas and information. Appendixes and subsidiary facts need be consulted, usually, only to amplify some of the main facts.

Trade and Technical Publications

In almost every walk of business and professional life the alert individual tries to keep abreast of the latest developments. He leafs through one or more trade or technical publications in order to read of new products, technological progress, business practices, case histories, important personalities, and business opportunities. The alert reader may find important ideas which might not even be seen by a more casual reader.

1. The first rule is to know the editorial and advertising policy of the publication. This enables you to assess the over-all quality and reliability of the articles and news reports. Some publications will not be influenced in the slightest by their advertisers while others, more hungry, will tailor their editorial content to show up individual advertisers in a desirable light or to encourage potential advertisers. You cannot always know this but you can sense much of it from the way in which editorial material is handled. If you get the impression that editorial policy is influenced by advertising considerations, you may be more careful in accepting things at face value.

2. Similarly, you should evaluate the publication's apparent policy and practice in trying to generate reader interest. If the publication is circulation-hungry, it might go all-out to bring in good editorial material, written by staff or by contributors, but there are cases, where there is not sufficient budget to acquire the best material, where the editors may try to make the most out of trashy headlines or sensational materials which have not been too well checked. This is more likely to be the case with independent publications than with those which are put out as official journals of professional or technical societies. Your experience in reading several issues and in acquainting yourself with the backgrounds of authors in such publications will help you evaluate the editorial content.

3. For a quick survey of what is included in the latest issue, scan the table of contents. Captions may or may not be properly descriptive, so, if one attracts your attention, you should turn to the article itself to see if it is really of interest. Where the table of contents is supported by article digests, you may not need to turn to the article to find out if you are interested. Sometimes the digest is at the head of the article itself. Remember that the actual article may cover much more information than seems to be indicated by the caption. On the other hand, you will have cases where the caption is misleading to the point where the article may be of absolutely no interest to you.

4. Don't overlook "departments" and "columns." They are usually written by people who have been selected as authorities in a particular field of interest. Sometimes they are the most important editorial items in a publication. Regular features might

include new products, new books and other publications, statistical or financial information important for the reader, etc.

5. Unless the publication is to be recirculated or has permanent reference value, tear out pages for further use. Sometimes reprints are available at a nominal charge.

6. Don't overlook the advertisements. They tell you about new products and services. Sometimes they tell you about helpful information which you can obtain by writing to the advertiser. Use the inquiry card if one is bound into the publication. Otherwise, mark the things you want and send for them or have a secretary do so.

Newspapers

A good newspaper is organized so that you can read its contents quickly in whatever depth you desire. As in the case of trade and technical publications, you should appraise editorial policy as a guide to the credence you can put in news stories. The following few, simple rules will help you take the most out of the newspaper within the time you have available for reading:

1. For the quickest survey of contents, read the news headlines and subheads. These are the very top of the news.

2. To cover the news in at least a little greater depth, read the lead paragraphs of specific news stories. They contain a summary of the story—a synopsis which answers such questions as who, what, why, when, and how. The main points in the story will be elaborated in succeeding paragraphs. In a long story this may be done in several stages, with some repetition, accordingly, in the process.

3. Distinguish between news stories and editorial material. News stories are supposed to be factual in their entirety. Signed stories may contain a combination of fact and opinion, while editorials usually express opinion.

4. The top of the news may, in some papers, be summarized in a box or section of the first page. Some newspapers, like the New York *Times,* will include an index of the news which serves also as a brief summary. The *Wall Street Journal* publishes news briefs and summaries of inside articles on the front page. More detailed coverage is then available in the inside pages.

5. Become thoroughly familiar with the special features, news

columns, and departments of the newspaper. Much valuable information may be overlooked by not being fully aware of what the paper contains.

6. Even the advertisements may tell you a great deal. From a traveling salesman I learned how important it is, when going into a new community, to learn about it from a reading of the local newspaper. The social notes, the display advertisements and the appeals that they use, and the classified advertisements all have stories to tell.

Books and Pamphlets

1. Read the various identifying and descriptive materials for a preview: the book jacket, the preface, introduction, table of contents, bibliography, and index.

2. Skim through the book or pamphlet for the highlights— the essence—in order that you may obtain an over-all view.

3. Read selectively or fully, depending on your knowledge of the material and your need for any of the information contained in the publication.

4. When reading on specific topics, not readily noted in the table of contents or index, the obvious thing to do is look for related or synonymous subject-matter headings. Don't overlook the clues that you can find in opposite topics. When you check them in the text, you may find leads to what you want more directly. Sometimes you must be a literary detective, projecting yourself into the mind of the author to see how he would be likely to organize his materials and under what headings he would be likely to cover specific items.

5. With long items, especially books, try to extend or limit your reading, as the case may be, so that you cover a single topic fully before you put the reading material away. Try not to end in the middle of a topic, for you will have to retrace too much ground when you pick it up again.

6. Make notes as you read. Don't be afraid to do so or to underscore items if you own the book or pamphlet and no one else will be inconvenienced by your doing so.

7. When you have finished going through the material, run through it once more, at least on surface, to make sure you

have not skipped anything. Also, by the time you have come to the end, you may have learned to see some things in a new light. These may have appeared much earlier in the book or pamphlet and now you may want to consider them again.

THE "TRUTH" ABOUT RAPID READING

Rapid-reading courses have been with us for many years, but only lately have they begun to assume fad proportions as people flock to them to find the secret of reading a great deal more in very much less time. The claims that are made for some of the courses are so amazing as to border on quackery. Because rapid-reading courses can be very important for you, it is essential that you know what they can and cannot do.

What the Courses Claim and Do

The average adult who has not had prior training in rapid reading can cover about 250 words per minute. It will take him about two minutes to read a page in an average book. Freshmen in college are a wee bit faster; they average out to about 260 words per minute. Now, moving up the scale, people with college educations will read about 320 words per minute. College professors average out at about 550 words per minute.

With training in rapid reading, adults and freshmen will raise their level of reading to about 500 words a minute, or about one page of a book every minute. The college graduates will make 600 or more, while college professors will have a little higher rate of reading increase or about 1200 words per minute.

These are average. Some people will not do as well while others will do much, much better.

These gains in reading speed are matched by modest gains in reading comprehension—the ability to understand what you have read. This is something apart from reading *retention*. We'll have more to say about both of these below.

Another thing to note is that the reading scores given above are based on standard reading tests using material of average difficulty. Light reading materials will move much faster, such as novels, while more difficult technical material will take more time for reading and comprehension. Bear in mind that we are reading not for words alone but for thought content.

But what of those reading records claimed for graduates of certain commercial schools which cite such spectaculars as 3000, 5000, 6000, on up to as high as 12,000 or more words per minute? That's a lot of reading, even for the relatively few who can attain such high rates, but the question is whether it is really *reading* or *skimming*. There's a big difference.

How Reading Speeds Are Increased

The most common cause of slow reading is word-for-word reading. The eye pauses at a word, takes it in, and then moves to the next word. At this rate the reader can take in about four words a second, which adds up to 240 words a minute, which is about the average of 250 that we mentioned above.

Each pause is called a *fixation*. Obviously, if you can cover more words per fixation, you can increase your reading speed. *Phrase reading* is therefore the basic technique in rapid reading.

Other bad reading habits which can slow you down to reading speeds much lower than the average of 250 include *subvocalization* and *regressive reading*. Subvocalization may be actual or mental sounding of the words. You have certainly seen people who move their lips when they read. Some may not move their lips but you can see their throats tensing and flexing as they sound the words through silent muscular contractions. The regressive readers are the ones who must go back over the same material many times. If you study their eyes as they read, you would see a constant moving back as they move forward.

The main approach used in most courses, with variations in mechanical technique, is to force the reader to move at a greater pace. One device used is called the *tachistoscope*. This projection device allows the trainee to see words, phrases, or numbers for a fraction of a second. This forces him to recognize the exposed material in a single perception without word-for-word reading and without backtracking. A *reading pacer* accomplishes the same thing differently. It works by exposing one line at a time, on a page of reading matter. The pacer moves down the page at a predetermined rate, forcing the reader to keep up with the movement of the pacer. The timing of the reading pacer can be individualized, starting with just a little bit more than the reader's actual rate at the time he begins his training and then increasing up to his potential. There are variations of these devices but they serve the same purpose of forcing the reader to accelerate his perceptual pace.

Without the use of mechanical accelerators one can practice reading pretimed passages. A very simple technique which can be used by anyone to increase his perceptual span is to draw a line down the center of a newspaper column. Then, following the penciled line, the reader tries to perceive the entire line of type in one glance. This kind of self-training is made possible by the narrowness of the newspaper column. The training can be carried forward, however, to the wider book page where material can be read with a fewer number of fixations per line.

What the Courses Really Do for You

When it comes to actual *reading,* there is no doubt that the various courses can, for most people, at least double their rates of reading speed with improved comprehension. Also, it appears that the better readers can keep a higher rate of improvement than the poorer readers.

Some training programs can bring inherently good readers up to fifteen hundred words per minute and in a few cases as high as two thousand words per minute. It is doubtful whether anyone who claims to read at much greater rates of speed can do more than skimming which, as we will recall, is a surface kind of reading which picks up main ideas without actually reading all the words, even in phrase groups.

You may say, "Who cares, so long as you pick up the main ideas?" This brings us to the difference between comprehension and retention.

The chief reason that comprehension improves with more rapid reading is that you are able to see more of the idea content in less time and, in doing so, you can perceive more quickly the relationship of ideas. This, in itself, makes it unnecessary to backtrack over material already read but forgotten due to one's slow pace.

Comprehending or understanding at the moment of reading will not assure that you will retain or remember well what you have just read. While there are some facts and figures about improvement in comprehension, there is little, if anything, about what happens to your ability to retain what you have learned under the incredible speeds of thousands of words per minute.

If you want to read a whodunit for the plot, you may not care whether you retain very much. When it comes to really good literature, wherein the author tries painstakingly to develop situations, characters, themes, and philosophies, it is hard to see any real purpose in reading the novel if one is not to be able to soak himself reflectively and vicariously into each of the passages. Why should you sit for long periods of time gazing out toward the distant sea or the magical mists of far-off mountains, when a quickie glance should otherwise be sufficient? That's the difference between impressionistic skimming and appreciative reading.

As to retention, it is doubtful that any sound educational psychologist would accept a skimming substitute for the classically established laws of learning, which are the basis for remembering well. To learn and remember well, you must spend time with your material and you must think. The basic techniques for doing so were covered above—such things as pausing to reflect, spacing your reading, reviewing what you read previously, note-making, talking over what you have learned, and organizing the new materials in your mind, among other techniques.

There are exceptions, of course—people with so-called photographic memories—but for practically all the rest of us the short cuts to remembering are those of the nature described above and in Chapter XIV, "The Art of Concentrating."

One final note of caution: It has already been observed that, after training in a rapid-reading course, many graduates will regress, losing much of their newly-acquired reading speed. This happens, apparently, when the reading improvement is not maintained through practice. It should be obvious that the training of several weeks or even months must be augmented from time to time with additional practice if the habits of a lifetime are to be overcome permanently.

SUMMARY

Regardless of your rate of reading, you can cover more in less time if you learn to read selectively. This begins with the screening of the things which come to your attention. Even as to those things which pass your screening test, it may not be necessary that you read everything. You should be able to pick out, selectively, those things which serve a specific reading purpose, whether it be for the acquisition of information or for the taking of some kind of action.

The skilled reader looks for the clues to informational content. He finds them in prefatory materials, digests, tables of contents, headings in the body of the text, and in the material which precedes and follows certain verbal signals to which he attunes his eye.

When the reader wants to study his materials more intensively for greater understanding and retention, he must spend more time with his material. He courses through the paragraphs and pages with a sharpened reading purpose. He pauses to reflect imaginatively. He underscores key points, organizes and reorganizes his thoughts as he acquires them, makes notes, and talks over his ideas with other people. He avoids crowding too much into a single reading session, for he has learned that to retain more, he must space out what he has learned and he must review what he has learned earlier.

These general principles can be applied to the variety of special forms of communication that come across desks of business and professional people. While this will help, one must also study the special characteristics of the various types of communications so that he will know where and how to find the ideas contained in each of them.

XVI

How to Write More in Less Time

The time lost in poor business writing is incalculable. There is the time lost through a pick-and-hack method of drafting. There is time lost in endless correcting and revision of many papers. There is a tremendous amount of time lost in writing back and forth in the frustrating search for clarification that should have been achieved in the first instance. Who can measure the cost in time and money of poorly drafted communications which cause the wrong actions to be taken or deadlines to be missed or business to be lost?

I consider this chapter to be one of the most important in this book, if only for the reason that it offers the greatest opportunity for producing visible results! Every piece of writing serves two purposes: first, it is a communication of some kind of intelligence. Second, it is ambassadorial—an extension of self. This being the case, one finds it hard to understand why so few people seem sufficiently interested to want to do something about their own writing.

The central principle in good business writing is *preparation*. "Writing still is thought of as if it meant stringing words together," said Stephen Leacock, "whereas in reality, the main part of it is 'thinking.' People don't realize this."

With this in mind, this chapter will cover the following topics:

1. General suggestions for writing to the point, thoroughly and quickly.

2. Techniques for turning out correspondence and memoranda.

3. Techniques for writing a variety of other business communications.

4. Advice on how to dictate.

SOME GENERAL SUGGESTIONS

Times of great stress seem to bring out masterpieces of expression like the brilliantly succinct "Sighted sub, sank same" of World War II. Cutting through the camouflage of bureaucratic verbiage, Franklin D. Roosevelt set many examples of his own, such as the one which follows, quoted from the New York *Times* of March 11, 1942.

"The Chief Executive read to a press conference today a letter which Dean Landis had prepared for him to send to the Federal Works Agency on the subject of blacking out Federal buildings during air raids.

"'Such preparations shall be made,' the letter said, 'as will completely obscure all Federal buildings and non-Federal buildings occupied by the Federal Government during an air raid for any period of time from visibility by reason of internal or external illumination. Such obscuration may be obtained either by blackout construction or by termination of the illumination.'

"With a grin, Mr. Roosevelt hastened to remark that 'obscuration' was not his word, nor was 'termination of the illumination' his language.

"He read on.

"'This will, of course, require that in building areas in which production must continue during the blackout, construction must be provided that internal illumination may continue.'

"Mr. Roosevelt asserted that he knew some people who had had internal illumination, and after a roar of laughter subsided, he continued once more with the letter:

"'Other areas, whether or not occupied by personnel, may be obscured by terminating the illumination.'

"The Chief Executive stopped, turned to his press secretary, Stephen Early, and ordered a rewrite job.

" 'Tell them,' he said, 'that in buildings where they have to keep the work going, to put something across the window. In buildings where they can afford to let the work stop for a while, turn out the lights. Stop there,' he said."

The basic rules for clear, forceful, direct, economical writing are these:

1. First, get the facts.
2. Develop your approach.
3. Organize your thoughts.
4. Write for the recipient.
5. Use an active, crisp style.

First, Get the Facts

Because writing is preparation and thinking, you will save time in the long run if you get the whole story before you begin putting words down on paper. You won't be able to write smoothly, without interrupting yourself, if you must pick up the telephone or send for a file or have someone come in to fill a factual gap while you are in the midst of drafting. What's more, you will be losing time while you are waiting.

If this is not sufficiently evident to you, think back to those occasions when you had to write supplementary correspondence or documents which could have been avoided with a little more thorough fact-finding before you actually began to write the first communication.

You may have had the experience of feeling mentally frustrated because you did not have enough facts to enable you to develop a logical structure of thought—mental blockage which could not be relieved until you did more fact-finding and reflective thinking. Subsequently, when you were better prepared, you could see in retrospect just why you were unable to proceed.

Another good reason for being prepared before you begin to dictate is that you'll save the time of others, especially that of the secretary. She could be doing other constructive work instead of whiling her time away while you search through files or frantically call people on the telephone.

Develop Your Approach

Before writing, before even making an outline, you should have clearly in mind what it is you wish to accomplish with the written material. When this is clear, you can then examine your facts and with them begin seeking out the pathways of approach to your communication goal. Here are some self-analysis questions which may help you clarify your approach:

1. What is the need, expectation, or problem of the organization or the person who is to receive the written material?

2. What is demanded by the situation itself?

3. How are the situation and the possible courses of action related to other policies, procedures, precedents, and situations and how will they affect the content of your material?

4. What effect should you achieve with the present communication—long-term? immediately?

5. What should you emphasize first? second? What should you avoid? What limitations, caveats, exceptions?

Organize Your Thoughts

Thus far we have been concentrating on ideas and their sequence rather than on words as such. When you have organized your ideas, the words will take care of themselves.

One of the most powerful lessons I ever learned was from James F. Grady, presently American Consul General at Southampton, England, when he was "correspondence counselor" for the U. S. Department of Agriculture. Jim thought that any writing of more than a couple of paragraphs or so should be planned even if it meant only jotting down the sequence of the few paragraphs or the very few ideas on a small piece of scratch paper or on the back of an envelope. Now, more than two decades later, I still use this technique. For longer compositions, I use longer outlines.

Rarely will you need to prepare a very long outline. For most of your purposes you will not need to go beyond a few lines or even a single sheet of paper.

If you are uncertain of your materials or if they are of such importance or complexity that they warrant revision and polishing, it is more economical to do so in the outline form than in the final prose. You can make an initial draft of the outline and then set it aside until later in the day or until another day, if your schedule permits. In the meantime you may have done some subconscious thinking about the subject. You may be able to see the outline in a new light or additional facts may be recalled, thereby provoking new ideas and approaches. There'll be more on techniques of outlining later in this chapter.

The organization of your materials will be kept much simpler if you restrict them to the one-topic principle. As soon as you begin to cover more than one topic in a paper, you add to its complexity and to the likelihood that it will not be finished on time.

Write for the Recipient

You should first have thought about the recipient or the intended reader in the early planning stages. You should be thinking of him recurringly as you organize your approach in greater detail and as you actually write the final draft. This may seem so obvious, to the point of being labored, yet this is one of the greatest failings in writing.

The error we are prone to make is in assuming that what we think or want is identical with the point of view of the reader.

To convey our thoughts so that they will be understood, we must also write in a depth of coverage and in a style appropriate to the reader's grasp of the subject matter.

Use an Active, Crisp Style

For some strange reason, the businessman who would say in conversation, "Sam shot a 65 Saturday," would write the same statement something like this: "This past Saturday afternoon, a 65 score was made by Sam while playing golf." A more conservative writer might even have started out by saying, "It is reported that . . ."

"In business writing," said Glenn Kerfoot in *Supervisory Management,* published by the American Management Association, "things rarely get started any more. Instead, they are 'activated,' 'instigated,' 'initiated,' or 'inaugurated.' New policies are 'implemented.' Equipment is not used, but 'utilized.' . . ."

Kerfoot added that "a man is no longer paid for his work. Instead, he is 'compensated,' 'remunerated,' or 'reimbursed.' Things don't even end any more—they are 'terminated,' 'finalized,' 'completed,' or 'concluded.' "

He went on to quote Henry Watson Fowler, the great authority on English usage: "Those who run to long words are mainly the unskilful and tasteless. They confuse pomposity with dignity, and bulk with force."

We write like that, according to Robert Gunning, author of *The Technique of Clear Writing* and originator of the "Fog Index," because we try to "impress rather than express." It really goes deeper than that. In the context of business life we emulate what we consider to be acceptable style. If we could trace this style back to its early beginnings, we would find that it is the cumulative result of personal striving for protection against the insecurities of business life and public office. Pick up almost any piece of business correspondence and you'll find it clothed in protective phraseology—the limited commitment, permissive or discretionary language offering a way out, and qualified rejections or disapprovals to give oneself a way back in. In our business writing, we tend to use an impassive, impersonal, and indirect style. We seek shelter behind the corporate "we."

Here are a few suggestions for writing more clearly, directly, and economically:

1. Cut out the preliminaries. You'd be surprised how many introductory paragraphs, sentences, and even pages are totally unnecessary. See for yourself. Go through any batch of letters, memoranda, and reports and mark through the introductory material until you come to the first meaningful information. That's where the writing should have begun. In your own writing, when you review it, look for superfluous beginnings.

2. Write short sentences. They are easier for you to put down and they are easier for the reader to comprehend. If you get involved in long sentences, you must pause to worry through the correctness and logical sequence of your involved phraseology. Your reader will have the same difficulty and sometimes he will write you another letter asking for an explanation or for more information.

3. Use a direct, active style. Combine this with a reader orientation by adopting a "you" approach. The second person is most appropriate for any communication materials which have an action connotation for the reader, which tell him how to do things. Whether you write in the second or third person, you are more likely to be understood and you will get your writing done faster if you will follow a main style of beginning the sentence with the subject and following it with the predicate. Instead of saying, "The correspondence will be filed," write it more directly as, "File the correspondence." Instead of, "The report will be submitted in writing and will be mailed to reach the home office by June 18," say, "Mail the report to reach the home office by June 18." They both say the same thing.

4. Use specific, concrete, familiar words. Take the word *handles*. It is not specific. The messenger handles correspondence because he opens it in the mail room and delivers it to desk boxes. The secretary handles correspondence at different stages. So does the original drafter of the correspondence, who may initial it or send it to somebody else for signature. Anyone who reviews and signs correspondence prepared by others also handles it. The file clerk gets into the act also. The point, of course, is to use active verbs that express specifically what is being done or is expected to be done.

5. Omit irrelevancies and say-nothing language. Get to the point. The following item was prepared for inclusion in the Postal Bulletin of the U. S. Post Office Department:

> The Department has been advised by several postmasters that there would result some convenience to window clerks in filing chapter 2 of the Postal Manual in the front of the Directory of International Mail. The Department has authorized the selective distribution of chapters 1, 2 and 3 to window clerks where justified by postmasters. If window clerks find it more convenient to file chapter 2 of the Postal Manual in the front of the Directory of International Mail, they may do so.

This proposed statement began with unnecessary preliminaries and arguments which were irrelevant to the instruction contained in the last sentence of the paragraph. Everything else was cut out. Look the paragraph over. From the standpoint of the reader, did he really need any information other than that contained in the last sentence to which the instruction was finally restricted?

6. Stop when you have finished your message. In a letter you might add a final courtesy sentence, but don't go beyond this. In most writing it is not necessary to reiterate what you have said before and to repeat assurances and qualifications.

HOW TO PRODUCE CORRESPONDENCE

The general principles just given apply to most forms of writing. Of course, you need to vary your approach with each medium of communication. Correspondence deserves special attention because it is the substance of the daily conduct of business. It is action-oriented.

The first principle is to distinguish between routine correspondence and that which requires original treatment in each case. You can save a great deal of time by using a variety of short cuts for your routine writing.

Correspondence Short Cuts

One of the fellows at the office had been out for a few weeks, recovering from a serious injury sustained in an automobile accident. Upon his return he found himself so plagued by questions about the accident and his injury that he prepared a one-page mimeographed statement giving all details. Whenever someone approached him with a question about his misfortune, he reached into his pocket, smilingly, withdrew a copy of the statement, and gave it to his inquisitor. He saved a great deal of time for himself and so can you by boiler-plating your typical correspondence.

We are all familiar with form letters. These are preprinted letters which give a stock reply in response to routine inquiries. If you have a secretary or correspondence clerk, much of this kind of correspondence will be disposed of without ever reaching you. On some of the correspondence you receive, you may often save time by merely indicating to the secretary that she should send a certain form letter.

This is the general procedure, but now let us look at the other side of it. How many times have you received form letters which did not answer your questions? With a feeling of utter frustration you write another letter painstakingly explaining that you asked for certain information, received a form letter in reply, but it did not cover certain points raised in your original letter. As a result, both sides wind up with more work which could have been avoided in the first instance.

The first rule in using a form to answer correspondence, then, is to make sure that it answers fully the needs of the recipient. If it does not, you can often correct this by adding a postscript at the bottom of the form letter. If this is not adequate or if it is too long, both parties will be better off and save time in the long run if you prepare an original letter in reply.

This Is a "Quickie"

Dear

Sometimes we run into a peak load of incoming mail that taxes our ability to do full justice to our correspondence—and right now is one of those times!

That's why I'm sending you this "Quickie" to acknowledge your recent communication. It's not intended as a formal reply —only a fast means to let you know that we have received your communication and appreciate having it.

If a reply is in order, you may be assured that it will be on its way to you as soon as possible. In the meanwhile, I hope that you will understand why I'm using this quick means to speed an acknowledgement to you without delay.

Sincerely yours,

Guide letters will also save you a great deal of time while preserving the outer appearance of individually-typed letters and memoranda. These are stock replies to specific inquiries or comments. They are similar to "precedent letters" used in many organizations. The idea is that when you have carefully worked out the details of a reply, often spending hours in drafting and in review, you get extra mileage out of this effort by use of the same information to take care of similar situations in the future. For occasional letters where this technique can be used, it is sufficient to go to the file for a carbon copy of a model letter. Where you have frequent use for certain stock letters and paragraphs, both you and your secretary might keep a set of these in a loose-leaf book at your respective desks. As with the form letter, however, make sure that the reply is fully applicable to the recipient's needs. At least you have the advantage of tailor-making the reply with a few changes since it will be typewritten completely. Be careful about notes that you put on the incoming correspondence and make sure that they are removed when the reply is sent out. Remember the famous anecdote about the hotel guest who sent a complaint to a hotel. With his reply he also found a note written by the manager to his secretary: "Send him the bedbug letter!"

Standard attachments are another way of saving time. You take care of the recipient's feelings by sending him a brief, individually-typewritten letter which may also contain any special remarks pertinent to his needs. For the standard, boiler-plate portion of the reply, you refer to an attachment which contains the information which the recipient desires. The attachment may cover more than he asked for and, if so, you merely indicate in the letter that he will find what he needs in certain marked-for-reference paragraphs or pages.

Thus far, we have been discussing boiler-plate short cuts. Not in this category, but deserving of mention, is the *speed letter*. Typically, this is a three-part, snap-out form into which the carbon paper is already bound. You write or type your note to the recipient and then you send him the original and one copy. The second copy is placed in your files. The recipient also writes or types directly on the same form. He sends you the original with his reply and keeps his carbon copy, which now contains both your note and his. Speed letters are used increasingly in intracompany correspondence. They are also finding greater usage in external correspondence.

In addition to using speed letters to hasten replies, the Public Personnel Association, as an example, uses "multigrams." These are multi-addressee communications carrying this red-bordered notice: "This is a 'Multigram.' It was duplicated so that you and others would get it quickly. Please give it early attention."

The simple referral slip is another timesaver for anyone who works behind a desk. It can be used by the man with a secretary, although it is of greatest benefit to those who must do their own desk work. When you are working late or when you do not want to bother your secretary on a spot item, it is handy to be able to pull out a preprinted referral slip—in effect a small form letter—and merely fill in a line or two of identification. Doctors especially can use referral slips to direct their patients to other physicians.

Individually-Composed Correspondence

The following suggestions should save time by (1) getting you through correspondence faster, (2) minimizing rewrite work, and (3) reducing the second and third rounds of returned correspondence because of a lack of clarity or completeness:

1. Put all related letters and memoranda together before answering them. Often, the reply to one can be used as the basis for a reply to the others. Also, if you glance at all of them before replying to any, you may get ideas from one for use in replying to the others.

2. Underscore or note the key points in each. If you can write on the incoming document, make marginal notations on any of the points. Otherwise, jot down your key points on a piece of paper. In this way you begin fixing the main ideas in your mind before you write. You also give yourself quick points of reference which sometimes eliminate the need for making up a jiffy outline, as suggested below.

3. Dictate or write the simple replies—the very brief ones— on a sight basis. For most of your correspondence, you can use "jiffy" outlines. A jiffy outline is merely a brief listing of the main points you wish to cover in your reply, in the sequence in which you will treat them. By taking them out of your mind and putting them before you for visual referral on a piece of paper, you free your mind for concentration on the words immediately to be put down, without the need for retaining the imagery of the sequence of the entire communication. (More detailed outlines could be used for the structuring of long or complex communications, as explained below.)

4. On the important items you might hold the outline, if time permits, until the next go-around. Doing this gives you a new perspective out of which may come new ideas and a recognition of gaps and irrelevancies. This is especially important when you write anything under emotional tension.

5. Don't quote the incoming letter back to the addressee other

than to refer to his communication by topic and date. He should know what it was that he wrote you about. In certain special situations, however, such as in legalistic determinations, it may be necessary to pin down specific phraseology as used by a claimant so that a reply could be prepared on the specific point.

6. Before signing, check over these points: Are the addressee's questions answered? Will he be satisfied with the reply? If the reply is to be disappointing, have you expressed yourself as considerately as possible? Is the matter left sufficiently open so that he will write for more information or explanations which can be avoided in the first instance?

7. On correspondence initiated by you, have you explained so clearly what it is you want and why, that there will be full understanding on the part of the recipient? After all, he has his preoccupations and points of view and they may not afford him insight into your problems unless you explain them clearly. Finally, if there is a previous history to the matter, have you given him all necessary reference data, thereby making it easier for him to speed a reply to you?

HOW TO WRITE A VARIETY OF PAPERS

In business communication you may be called upon to prepare various special kinds of papers. Some of the most common ones—staff papers and reports, memoranda for files, minutes of meetings, and statements of duties and assignments—I have described below, giving suggestions for simplifying the task of draftsmanship. Before going into them, however, we should first cover two important techniques: (1) the techniques of outlining (in somewhat greater detail than given above) and (2) the techniques of rough drafting.

Tips on Outlining

Most people freeze at the idea of writing longer compositions of any kind whether they be letters, memoranda, reports, staff studies, features, articles, or books. The long paper really need hold no terrors. The "secret of success" is to break the longer paper into smaller parts. If you drive from Washington, D.C., to New York City, the five-hour journey behind the wheel seems long in prospect. If, however, you drive from Washington, D.C., to Baltimore, Maryland, and from there to Wilmington, Delaware, and then to the first Howard Johnson's on the New Jersey Turnpike, and so on until you reach the streets of Manhattan, the journey has been subdivided into a sequence of small trips, each of which is tolerable or digestible—as you would prefer. The topics in an outline correspond to the small-trip destinations.

While I have touched on the value of outlining earlier, I would like to summarize and extend a little. The outline approach to writing has these advantages:

1. The outline enables you to plan with an economy of effort because you are working with a structure of ideas rather than the more cumbersome sequences of final prose.

2. Omissions or gaps, inconsistencies, and irrelevancies are more clearly brought out.

3. It is easier to move items from place to place in an outline, as a technique of revision, than to rewrite or rearrange written paragraphs.

4. The outline can be used as the basis for preliminary discussion with a reviewing officer, colleague, or adviser before time is spent (or wasted) on writing a final draft.

The first step in making an outline is to get all your notes or ideas down on paper. If it is to be a relatively short outline, you can list all of your ideas on a single sheet of paper where you can see them together. For a longer outline going into considerable detail, you may need to use three-by-five file cards or paper slips on which to record individual items of information or individual topics. When you have finished, examine all of your notes and, on another sheet of paper, list the main topics or ideas in the tentative order in which you think you will present them. To test the validity of this tentative outline, expand each topic by filling in under it the appropriate subtopics or subsidiary ideas or information. If you had a lot of notes before setting down your tentative outline headings and these notes then cannot fit under one heading or another appropriately, you know that the outline is defective in some way or that you may have more than you really should cover. If all of your notes are pertinent for inclusion, you just keep on reshuffling your major headings until everything has a proper niche and everything is in balance.

When you think you have the outline shaped up, put it aside for a cooling period. When you look at it after some moderate lapse of time—at least a day—you see the outline in a new light. You may make some changes. You may also decide to do some supplementary fact-finding before writing, based upon the need for this as suggested by your outlining experience.

This process of outlining can be carried on in any degree necessary, consistent with the length of the paper you are going to write. If it is as long as a book, your first outline would consist of the chapter headings. If it is as long as a chapter, or if you take a single chapter of the book and expand it, your first outline of the chapter would consist of the several main headings in that chapter and so on. Let's take this book, as an example. Each chapter is divided into only a few main parts, identified by headings in the center of the page, not counting the over-all chapter headings. Under each center heading you will note a series of side headings. These are the ones which begin flush with the left margin. The side headings represent further subdivisions of thought. In some instances you will find even further subdivisions.

There is more to an outline than the mere subdivision of thought. Your paper must have a strategy. Sometimes the major outlines of the strategy may be laid out for you, as in the case of a staff paper where your organization has a prescribed format. Even within the body of the discussion, however, you still have latitude for choosing your own sequence of ideas. In the preceding chapter on reading techniques we covered a variety of the methods used in presenting ideas. They were given there so that you could anticipate the other writer's line of presentation. You can use the same listings for your own compositions.

How to Write Rough Drafts

In many cases the outline will serve as a rough draft if it is prepared in sufficient detail. From it you may be able to go directly to a finished draft.

When you have any difficulty in expressing yourself in writing, the rough draft serves as a good ice-breaker. You can put down almost anything that comes to mind, knowing that you can revise it with equal freedom. When you come to a blockage in your thinking, or when you find yourself in need of more facts, you leave blank spaces and proceed to the next thought.

"When I write a rough draft," said Maurice H. Stans, president of Western Bancorporation, "I use paper more freely than time, because the paper is obviously so much cheaper. When I dictate, my secretary triple-spaces the copy. When I write long-hand, using a scratch pad, I also triple-space. This makes it so much easier to make corrections and insertions."

There seems to be a certain psychological advantage in having lots of space in the margins and between the lines of your draft. You feel more expansive and expressive. When you do not have much writing space, you tend to make fewer changes because of the greater physical difficulty in doing so, whether or not you are aware of it.

Two final suggestions: (1) Number or date all pages of all drafts so that you will know what the latest ones are as you preserve parts of earlier drafts to go into the latest one. (2) To make it easier to reshuffle material or to carry parts of earlier drafts forward, put new thought divisions on separate sheets.

Staff Papers and Reports

Staff papers and reports often follow a prescribed format which may run like this:
1. Purpose or problem.
2. Brief summary.
3. Facts or background.
4. Discussion.
5. Conclusion.
6. Recommendations.

This format provides you with your first physical outlining of your paper. You must still develop an effective organization of your ideas under each of the headings, as appropriate. For this, refer back to the section on outlining.

Typically, the staff paper that calls for any kind of action or policy determination is circulated among a number of people for comments and concurrences before being presented to an executive or committee for decision. This process of review engenders the writing of successive drafts and redrafts, in many cases. To keep this time-consuming process to a minimum, the writer should anticipate the problem requirements, points of view, informational needs, and probable questions of the various reviewers and decision-makers. In doing this he need not necessarily change his own point of view or recommendations—unless this thorough analysis in itself prompts him to do so.

The built-in appendix should be avoided. This may be an extended statistical, factual, or analytical presentation in the body of a staff paper or report. You will render the staff paper more digestible and more likely to be read if you consign these extended treatments to the back of the paper as separate appendixes, recognizable and identified as such. You can cross-reference to them in the body of the paper and list them at the end as attachments. Besides, you will find both the staff paper and the appendixes easier to draft if they are split up in this manner.

Work Assignments and Duties Statements

The losses due to misunderstanding of instructions are incalculable. It is sufficient for this point that each of us reflect on his own experiences in receiving instructions that could not be understood or in giving instructions that were not carried out as intended. Herein lies one of the most important areas for preventive timesaving.

1. Be complete but do not go into detail inappropriate for the level of responsibility or comprehension of the recipient. Make clear what it is you want accomplished, who is to do it, under what circumstances and—sometimes—how.

2. Use an active voice—the second person imperative: "You do this or that." Don't say "is responsible for correspondence," because this does not make clear his specific responsibility. Say, rather: "drafts replies to complaint letters" or "prepares purchase letters." Use transitive rather than intransitive verbs to express responsibility.

3. Make clear the recipient's specific responsibility as part of a broader assignment. Tell him when he gets into the act and who carries the ball when he is finished. State any reviews or approvals that he will need to obtain as well as any exceptions

to or limitations upon his authority. Tell him what resources he has: what he can spend and upon whom he can draw for assistance. State the performance goals: how much is to be accomplished and by when.

4. Bear in mind and provide for any anticipated reactions of the recipient whether of emotion or habit. If the reader's needs, feelings, convenience, or desires are affected, he may seek means of resisting the instruction or interpreting it for his own convenience. Anticipate these reactions so that you may be expressly clear as to what is desired.

5. When people are being asked to change what they have been doing, they may not resist the new so much as they may tend to continue the old merely because of habit. It is quite common for the new to be installed alongside of the old and for the two of them thereafter to be done! This happened in banks when adding machines were first installed. The clerks continued to make manual additions. I recall one IBM payrolling system that had been installed and, long after the break-in period had been successfully concluded, a parallel payroll continued to be done by hand. Therefore, when you provide for the new, provide also for the disposition of the old.

Memoranda for File

File memoranda should be written when you wish to recall precisely at some time in the future the gist of a current conversation. Details and even main points are very quickly forgotten unless they are so recorded. Because of the amount of time consumed by drafting, they should be used in the following circumstances:

1. Previous relationships with the person with whom you talked have taught you to confirm in writing any agreements, instructions, or critical information used as a basis for taking action or for refraining from action.

2. The information ordinarily should be the subject of a written communication, but in the interest of speed you are proceeding on the basis of oral communication.

3. The information has historical or future reference value and you do not wish to trust to your memory.

4. You need to add to a case file.

The memorandum should include the date, time, names of parties to the conversation, subject of the conversation, and how it came about, if pertinent.

If direct quotations are used, put these in quotation marks. Otherwise, it will be assumed that your statements are summaries or paraphrasing. Cover only the essential points. A blow-by-blow recital is essential only under unusual circumstances.

Unless you have a particular reason for not doing so, you strengthen the validity of your file memorandum if you send copies to the key parties, at least, to the conversation. If you are in error or if you misunderstood in any way, they thereby have an opportunity to correct your memorandum. The facts of this distribution should be noted on the bottom of the memorandum.

Minutes of Meetings

Minutes of meetings should be prepared in much the same way as file memoranda. Particular attention must be given, however, to policy or position determinations and decisions to take action. As with file memoranda, you should be careful to avoid excessively detailed reportage unless uniquely required by the situation.

Cover the following:

1. Topics discussed.
2. Specific conclusions or decisions.
3. Optional: what key positions were taken by whom?

Be succinct!

4. What is to be done by whom and when.

A terse, telegraphic style may be used. Specific action assignments and deadlines should be underscored or they can be brought out to the margin or listed separately under the item reported.

Your note-taking during the meeting deserves some comment. Conversations do not always proceed logically or in accordance with the prepared agenda. Topics may be discussed within other topics. People branch out from what was originally intended to be discussed to something else which is very much on their minds.

Hence, leave plenty of space between items and in the margins so that you can go back to an earlier item to add additional points and, also, so that you can have room for unanticipated topics and discussions.

HOW TO DICTATE

The opportunities for timesaving in dictation are threefold:

1. The greatest opportunity for timesaving is avoiding the re-do of work because it was poorly dictated.

2. By planning your dictation more carefully, you often can get work out in the same day's mail without it having to go over until the next day.

3. You can save time for both yourself and your secretary if you are able to arrange uninterrupted preplanned dictation.

Your Mode of Dictation

You can dictate in person to a secretary, use a dictating machine, or a centralized transcribing service. What you do may be partly a matter of your personal choice and partly a matter of the facilities available to or prescribed for you. Each has its advantages and disadvantages.

Obviously, having a secretary or stenographer at your side while you dictate is most convenient for you because you can have her read things back to you without the necessity for manipulating mechanical controls. This is the most expensive way of dictating because you must count in her waiting time as you rummage through your papers and as you hem and haw. For this reason, you must be particularly conscious of the need for saving her time and, hence, this will receive particular attention in this section.

There are many different kinds of dictating machines on the market: belt recorders, tape recorders, disc recorders, with subcategories of each. This is no place to deprive you of the experience of having a parade of sales representatives convince you on the relative merits of a variety of machines. Your choice—if you have one—will depend upon your physical preferences and convenience. In use, the dictating machine is often kept "hot" by busy people. With the switch on and the instrument warmed up, you can add notes at any time in the day that something occurs to you. Keeping the machine open in this way eliminates any self-conscious resistance to turning it on just to dictate a sentence or two, even though they may be very important sentences. When talking into a machine, you must be careful to enunciate difficult words and figures clearly. Of course, the same goes for your dictation as a whole, because the person who transcribes will not be able to ask for a restatement. She will simply give to you whatever she takes off the tape, right or wrong.

Telephonic dictation may be to a live secretary or it may be to one of a battery of dictating machines hooked into the telephone system. If it is to a stenographer, the ordinary rules for stenographic dictation are applicable, with one exception. You can't give her things to copy and you can't show her particular things in a form or table. You would have to send these down to her, so this arrangement may be somewhat awkward. Of course, you cannot do this with a dictating machine, either. When dictating over the telephone to a machine, you need to follow the same practices as when dictating to an instrument in front of you, with the same requirements for careful enunciation.

On the whole, good dictation is something that comes with experience. "Unfortunately," said the U. S. Navy Management Office, "some people just aren't comfortable when dictating. They get the same feeling they had the first time they were cajoled onto a dance floor.

"Call it self-consciousness or mike-fright—it is a common symptom and does not in any way reflect on the would-be dictator's intelligence, executive potential, or linguistic abilities."

Check List for Dictation

1. Do you set aside a definite uninterrupted period for dictation?

2. Do you combine small bits of dictation, especially when they are unimportant, into worthwhile work sessions?

3. On mail that you want to get out that day, do you dictate it sufficiently early to enable the secretary to transcribe it, get it back to you, and then get it into the mail?

4. Do you clearly dictate priorities, and when you need anything that is "special?"

5. Do you identify the nature of the material, whether a letter, memorandum, report, etc.?

6. Do you tell whether the job is to be a rough draft or finished work, how many copies you will need, and whether there is any special spacing?

7. When you come to unfamiliar words and names, do you spell them out?

8. Do you speak clearly, facing the secretary, without a cigar in your mouth, and without your chin in your navel?

9. Do you adjust your rate of dictation to your secretary's ability to keep pace?

10. Do you make it easy for the secretary to ask you questions when she wants something clarified?

As to being considerate of your secretary, think also of *her* time being *your* time. If you waste it, she can't do other things. Governor Michael V. DiSalle of Ohio said: "In my own business I felt many times that it was money wasted for an associate to have a secretary sitting at his desk taking dictation while he was on the telephone. No more than she had finished refreshing his memory as to what he had been dictating by reading the last two pages, the telephone rang again and he would be off on another conversation. So often a few minutes dictation would usually take two hours and then turn out to be very unsatisfactory for both parties."

SUMMARY

If there is one main secret of how to write more in less time, it is to think through beforehand what you should say. You will have a better product and you will save time for yourself as well as for your readers. While time can be saved in the actual mechanics of writing, the greatest opportunities for timesaving lie in making unnecessary the second and third rounds of back-and-forth communications resulting from a lack of clarity. Hence, in your writing you should always have the recipient's reaction and probable understanding in mind. On the mechanical side of writing, most business writing calls for a direct, active, crisp style. Avoid cumbersome phraseology that clarifies nothing, impresses no one, and expresses little, if anything. Avoid tiresome preliminaries and endings. Your reader wants to get to the heart of the matter. In general, follow the specifications for the bikini: "Short enough to make the subject interesting, but long enough to cover it."

XVII

How to Do More Than One Thing at a Time

Most people who drive have had the experience of being so deep in thought while driving that upon arrival at their destination they had no idea of how they ever got there. They had performed two separate acts simultaneously—a thinking act and a doing act.

You can combine one *thinking* act and one *doing* act within the same time-space, but you would be hard-put, however, to perform more than one thinking act or more than one doing act at the same time.* This is one of the topics to be covered in this chapter. We shall cover here, also, certain related topics, including how to derive side benefits from your main activity, how to increase your productivity through multiple projects, and how to put your subconscious to work.

* There may be seeming contradictions to this, in which two thinking or two doing things occur simultaneously. A micromotion analysis would show an alternating of attention from one to the other which might not ordinarily seem apparent.

THE MIND AND THE HAND

In an earlier chapter we covered briefly how thinking and muscular activity go together. We noted that to do good thinking, you cannot be fully relaxed. You must, rather, be in a state of physical alertness and tension.

Here, we can go a step further, examining how you can engage in one activity of a physical nature while thinking of another activity, both consciously and subconsciously.

How the Hand Unlocks the Mind

Just how physical activity releases the mind for creative effort is not definitely understood. What matters is that you can put this phenomenon to work for you.

If you want to find examples in your own experiences, think back to occasions when you thought of solutions to your problems while you were mowing the lawn, raking leaves, sawing wooden boards, pounding nails, turning a lathe in your workshop, painting a wall, or taking a shave. Now think of some of the people you know who simply cannot talk unless they wave their arms around in broad gestures. Watch some people engaged in animated telephone discussions in which they display facial expressions and make gestures with their hands. If these people were conscious of their hands being tied down, they probably couldn't express themselves well.

There has been much speculation as to what constitutes the mind—whether it goes beyond the brain itself. In any event we seem to proceed best when we use as many of our faculties as possible—sight, sound, and touch; even taste and smell, when appropriate.

Hence, it is plausible that any aggressive or manipulative activity may prime the mind for conscious creative activity. Recent research findings, for example, indicate that intelligence and manual dexterity go together. This was brought out, for example, in a canvass of the hobby interests of a highly creative group of people, working together as management analysts. Most of them, in this case, had handcraft and related hobbies such as woodworking, metalworking, electronic construction, model building, etc. Very few of the creative staff did not have some kind of manipulative hobby in which they engaged at home.

Suggestions for Physical Activity

Naturally, if you are doing work at home, you can find many opportunities to release your mental blockages, whether this be through working on creative hobbies or through performing any of the limitless chores in and around the house—including dishwashing.

But what if you are not working at home or, if you are and wish to express yourself solely through work? In such cases you can turn to any neutral, externalized activity. That is, it should be something which does not divert you into other areas of concentration, for if this were to happen, your thought processes could become short-circuited so far as the main problem is concerned. You can straighten your desk, arrange your papers, straighten the bookshelves, look for a missing file, or even pace the floor.

If you are able to do so, take a walk outside—and think.

Mental Activities That Stimulate

Next to physical activities, you might engage in a variety of other activities of the mind that may overlap your main area of interest. These should be nondistracting. That is, they should not send you into other lines of thought and concentration which might divert you from your principal interest. The idea is that you work on a variety of these, engage in some manipulative activity, and also are exposed to related facets of your subject matter which may throw light upon the original problem.

Thus, you can work on related correspondence, read related reports, and riffle through trade journals and technical literature.

You might also involve yourself in the physical interaction of visitors and telephone calls where these have a subject-matter involvement that would be both compatible and stimulating.

THE TAKING OF SIDE BENEFITS

When you are engaged in other activities, the ideas that come to you spontaneously are not necessarily pertinent to the things on which you most want help. They may be useful ideas but not for the moment. You may encounter them when performing any of a variety of tasks, in your reading, in your conversations, or in your reflections on other matters. You cannot stop to go into these good ideas at the time, but you can be prepared to capture them for later use.

Capturing the Stray Idea

"Ideas are the most elusive things in the world. I have actually had one escape me while I was rushing to my library to get it down on paper," said advertising man James R. Adams. "If you are creative, the closer you stay to paper and pencil the safer you will be. . . . I have a special pad and pencil that open out of a metal drawer beside the steering wheel in my car. For some reason, my mind is especially active and productive when I drive. The little pad I mentioned salvages any ideas I may have at the wheel."

The first thing you must do is to put note-making materials wherever you are likely to be: in your automobile, beside your telephones, at your bedside, and wherever you may read or relax. You will also want to carry note-making materials on your person.

Ordinarily, you should not jot down more than one topic to a card or note-page. Then, if the notes are for deferred attention, you can put them away by date or by subject matter. Thus, John Gunther, who wrote the "Inside" books, told how he would collect thousands upon thousands of notes during his journeys, putting each separate idea or topic on a separate slip. Then, he would organize or arrange these by subject matter as seemed best.

The procedures of note-taking are well pointed in the following anecdote from H. Allen Smith's *The Compleat Practical Joker**:

* Garden City, N.Y.: Doubleday and Company, 1953.

"Max Schuster, the book publisher, is the champion memo-writer of modern times. Most of his memos are written to himself. He starts the day with a supply of paper slips in the left pocket of his jacket. All day long he jots down maxims, ideas, bits of conversation, book ideas, clever phrases, and so on, transferring the written memos to the right-hand pocket of his coat. At the end of the day he studies his supply of memos, and files them away. It is said that he contemplates producing, someday, a huge history of the world's wisdom.

"One afternoon Max Eastman was in Mr. Schuster's office. He managed to sneak a slip of paper from the publisher's left-hand pocket. On it he wrote a single word, 'Dinkelspiel.' Then he slipped it into Mr. Schuster's right-hand pocket.

"That night Mr. Schuster stayed up late, puzzling over the one-word memo. He was unable to remember why he had written it. He couldn't go to sleep. He worried about it for days, repeating it over and over to himself, sometimes aloud, confusing people in his office by pacing up and down the floor and saying, 'Dinkelspiel, Dinkelspiel, Dinkelspiel.' After about a week he gave it up, choosing to lose that bit of wisdom rather than drive himself mad."

If you prefer to list your notes consecutively on a sheet of paper and if you have a secretary, you might have her transcribe them on separate cards or slips for further disposition, apart from those on which she is expected to do something immediately.

Hunting for Side Benefits

In the preceding section we noted the importance of being alert for ideas that spontaneously flash across your consciousness. You need not be passive about this. You can actually put yourself usefully into a variety of situations of immediate benefit which may also produce a variety of side benefits.

For example, you are invited to deliver a paper at the annual meeting of a professional society or trade association. The preparation of the paper will in itself have a secondary benefit because information you have to pull together may later form a basis for an article for a professional or trade journal. Having decided to make the trip, you plan to stay a day longer so that you may hear other papers and so that you may also interact with other attendees. From this one trip, then, you derive the following: (1) the writing of a paper that is likely to be of professional value to you and others in the future, (2) ideas for one or more other projects you might do in the future, (3) ideas about aspects of your work to which you had not previously been exposed, (4) specific topics and ideas that you can put to use currently, (5) suggestions for the broadening of some of your career interests and opportunities, and (6) a number of new professional or business friendships.

While I use a meeting as an example, you can put yourself into a variety of situations which will be of benefit to you in themselves in the expectation that they will be productive, also, of aid to you in your search for other ideas or materials. I mention conferences and conventions, particularly, because of the many opportunities for stimulating interaction. You may encounter useful ideas and material in related reports, files, and publications. The technique is to look for overlapping spheres of involvement. Some one fact, some one analogous situation, some one parallel experience—any of these might provide for you the flash of recognition or insight that will help you in your own situation.

Some people, recognizing the value of this kind of exposure, will budget for it in their time schedules. They limit this, however, to activities or reading materials which in themselves will be useful but which will also give them broadened exposure in their own fields.

HOW TO MANAGE MULTIPLE PROJECTS

Blindfold chess consists of playing against an opponent without seeing him or his moves and without seeing the chessboard at any time during the game. To play one such game is, in itself, a great feat, for you must keep in mind, simultaneously, an image of how the pieces are laid out on the board, the apparent strategy of your opponent, and your own strategy, changing all of these after each move by either party.

The origins of blindfold chess go back at least to the eleventh century, when it was exhibited by Arabian and Persian players. Among modern chess players, it was considered incredible that François Philidor of France was able to play, toward the end of the eighteenth century, three blindfold games simultaneously. This record was surpassed by the great American master, Paul Morphy of New Orleans, who, about the middle of the nineteenth century, played with great success on several occasions against eight strong players. Truly, this was an accomplishment.

When you consider the skill of playing one blindfold game, you must marvel. Three games seems amazing or incredible and eight games seems fantastic, especially when you work out the mathematics of all the combinations that must be remembered. In the twentieth century, to match the great feats of the new era into which the world was entering, unbelievable records were established. In 1929 the world's record reached twenty-nine, in 1933 it rose to thirty-two, in 1937 thirty-four games were played simultaneously, while in 1943, in Buenos Aires, Miguel Najdorf, a great tournament player, exceeded all previous records by playing forty blindfold games simultaneously!

Now, the word *simultaneously* should be examined. While all the games being played can be stored in the mind, they are recalled selectively and played one at a time. The games are played in sequence, not simultaneously. The player shifts from one to the other, dropping the image of one game and calling up the image of the next.

We do this sort of thing every day as we approach the countless situations in which we are involved at work, in our communities, at home, and in our conduct of correspondence. Each new situation that demands our attention brings forth its own game board. Our play, then, may be an instantaneous response or one that is calculated in the light of an anticipated series of moves.

Since all of us become accustomed, as a condition of ordinary living, to keeping many things in mind, one may wonder why many people go to pieces at the mere thought of having to manage "simultaneously" more than one project. Multiple-project responsibility need really hold no terror, provided you master certain basic approaches discussed elsewhere in this book, mainly in

Chapter IV, "How to Save Time By Looking Ahead." The essence of multiple-project management is planning, scheduling, and control. In the context of doing more than one thing at a time, some additional suggestions are given below.

When It Pays to Run Multiple Projects

There are at least four reasons for increasing the number of projects you are managing at the same time.* These are:

1. *Common elements.* The simplest case is of projects or activities that constitute more of the same. The pattern of one serves as a basis for doing the others. Next come the different projects which have overlapping elements in common. They might be the same facilities, equipment, planning formats, ideas, personnel, etc. Thus, if a visiting expert is with you only for a short time, try to bring up as many different things as possible which can be done or solved with his assistance. Then, there are projects which are not very much the same but which offer mutual challenges. The ideas you develop for the one may have been stimulated by your findings in the other. In this respect, of course, there is also some element of overlap.

2. *Waiting sequences.* Projects that involve the performance of a sequence of steps over a period of time also run into sequential delays and blockages. You may be waiting for information, materials, the results of experiments or tests, the approval of others, or the availability or repair of equipment, among others. You might even be waiting for a mental blockage to be dispelled in order that a new flow of ideas may bring with it a new spurt of progress. While you are waiting, you can do other things.

3. *Parallel development.* When two or more projects *must* be done at the same time, you ordinarily have a situation of mutual dependence. That is, the multiple projects must jointly contribute to a larger common purpose. In this situation, typically, you will be directing the work of others or, if you are working by yourself, your attention will alternate from one to the other.

* You can actually *manage* a number of things simultaneously, even though you may not be able to work on two or more separate things at the same moment. In this sense management implies responsibility which can encompass many things at the same time.

4. *Multiplication of self.* When you have employees to do your bidding, one measure of your effectiveness is the extent to which you can add to your scope through the assistance available to you. If there is room within your span of attention and control for additional activities, you can add new projects or expand the scope of existing ones.

Techniques of Operating Multiple Projects

The common element in being able to carry on a number of things at once is the *even distribution of pressures.* You will note these in the following suggestions:

1. Do things that are related to each other. If you undertake unrelated projects, avoid diversifying too much or you will increase the pressures on your attention as you switch from one to the other.

2. Add new projects only after you have existing projects under control. Don't start two or more important projects at the same time because this may put too great a strain upon your attention and capabilities. Remember that the greatest effort in getting something done usually occurs in getting it started on the right track.

3. Schedule projects so that they come to a head and culminate at different times. Too often we underestimate the amount of time and the last-minute crisis activity that goes into winding up a project.

4. Identify the critical junctures of individual projects and try to schedule them so that only one will require attention at a time. Of course, this holds true only for the things you can anticipate; unscheduled crises will arise whether you plan for them or not. Also, identify "long-lead" items and begin their development or procurement as early as possible in order to avert later crises.

5. Set up a control system that keeps you posted as to critical due dates.

HOW TO PUT YOUR SUBCONSCIOUS TO WORK

Do you have difficulty thinking up ideas? Do you know that when you are stumped, or blocked, you might find solutions to problems by assigning them to your subconscious? Of course, you must have a storehouse of information in the subconscious. This same informational reserve can also aid in the immediate production of ideas.

How to Use the Past

Ideas must come out of prior knowledge and experience. If your mind is a blank on a given topic, if you know nothing at all about it, if you've had no parallel experiences or exposures to knowledge, you can look at the problem all day and not come up with any ideas. You must have an *organized* body of knowledge and experience stored away in the mind. The word *organized* is emphasized because mere informational input alone is not sufficient. There must be an interval of time during which the mind absorbs new information and integrates it with related information and experience already stored away.

One implication of this is that you are more likely to be a good idea-producer in the least time if you are well-informed on your subject. Upon perceiving a new problem you can draw immediately upon your well-organized inputs. Another implication of this is that you can excel in competition with a person of greater intelligence if you have had better inputs over a period of time.

The obvious course for you is to fill your mental stores with as much information and knowledge as possible about the subjects with which you will be concerned. While this includes reading, seeing, and listening, the most vigorous commitment to mind will occur when you come into some manipulative interaction with the material of your interest. It is better to work out a problem or come into physical interaction with a situation than to read about it or talk about it.

As your mental stores become more and more enriched in this way, you will notice a curious thing. When you are confronted with new situations, you will find that you need fewer and fewer clues to prompt the emergence of ideas. One can draw, here, a parallel to the way a beginner attacks a problem as compared to the performance of a master. The beginner painstakingly embraces all the information he can obtain about the situation, point by point. Then, he studies it through and imagines the various conclusions he can draw and just as painstakingly begins to verify each of them in turn. The master comes into the same situation, looks around appraisingly, asks a few key questions, and then delivers an opinion which usually is correct.

Assignments to the Subconscious

The technique of making assignments to the subconscious works best when you have an excellent fund of knowledge already assimilated and organized within the mind. Then, when a new problem arises, you take all the pertinent information about it and consciously feed it to the mind. You give it a sense of direction by consciously working this material over, actively seeking solutions. If this does not bring forth the answers you desire, you should continue to a point of evident frustration, but not beyond. That is, if the answers are not forthcoming after a reasonable effort, don't strain at it. Turn to other activities or, if you are working at night, go to bed.

Once having assigned the problem to the subconscious, you cannot tell when the flash inspiration might come. It might be the next morning, and certainly it is worth a try to see what happens when you take a new look at the problem, consciously this time. Again, if nothing comes forth, drop the matter unless you have additional information to feed to the subconscious. Then, once more, proceed to other things. If the information you desire is to come, it will find its own good time and occasion. It need not be while you are shaving, although this seems to be a favorite, ranking with driving as an occasion when ideas emerge.

Recognizing the value of this technique, some people will consciously organize a problem situation before they go to bed; having pursued it to the point of frustration, they then let the subconscious take over as they sleep.

SUMMARY

In the literal meaning of doing two things at the same time you can do something physical while at the same time you are doing something mental. The two need not even be related. The only requirement would be that the physical operation not make such continuing demands upon the mind as to be competitive with independent thought processes.

When working at home, you can turn to creative or physical hobbies and while engaged in them, you can let your mind run freely over any other thoughts with which you want to preoccupy yourself. This may well be productive of good ideas. At the office you can relieve mental blockages by turning from the work before you to a variety of other manipulative activities—things which keep you busy, especially in the handling of things, so that your mind will have free play at the same time.

The active personality will discover useful ideas and information under a variety of unanticipated circumstances. In a passive sense he should be prepared with pencil and paper to note these ideas on paper for future use while he continues with his current activities. In the more active sense it may be worthwhile to budget some of one's time to engage in useful activities which are likely to be productive of desirable side benefits in the form of new ideas, auxiliary uses for information, and new acquaintanceships in one's own field.

One of the most common ways in which to do things "simultaneously" is in our management of more than one project at a time. It is obvious that we should be working at full capacity, but another reason for undertaking a number of projects to be consummated together is that you encounter delays and intervals of inactivity during which you should have other constructive work to do. The procedural approach to multiple-project management is effective planning, scheduling, and control. To this must be added an even distribution of critical times so that you will be least likely to be confronted with too many crises at any one time.

Sometimes you can find ideas and solutions to problems while you are working on other things or while you are sleeping. On a continuing basis you should be constantly storing information and experience on the matters with which you are concerned. For the specific problem, you give attention to the immediate facts, mull over them, and then assign them to the subconscious for attention there while you are engaged in other things. The flash inspiration may come when you least expect it or when next you address yourself to the problem.

XVIII

Time on the Move

This is a chapter for people who travel. Some may travel in the same city area. Some go from city to city and some may take themselves to the remotest corners of the world. Within the context of this book travel may seem to be a primary consideration. Indeed, speed *is* important but our emphasis will be as much on other considerations as on your rate of travel.

In this regard Elmo Roper, the renowned pollster, to whom I had addressed the question "Time for What?", said: "I suspect a great many people would have difficulty answering that. In my case I think the thing desired is leisure for reflection. For example, I don't try to save time going to the West Coast by flying. I take the New York Central's Century to Chicago, transact a little business in Chicago, and take the Super Chief on to the Coast. I find the trip very conducive to reflections and thinking in general, and I find myself thinking of the train trip which takes nearly three days not as a waste of time but as my reward for having properly managed my time over the previous several months!"

Other topics to which we shall address ourselves in this chapter include your activities in transit, other than your main business; planning your schedule and preparing for your trip; and some aspects of your face-to-face contacts with the people whom you have journeyed to see. These last two are perhaps the most important.

By far the greatest single traveling group consists of outside salesmen. While we will cover the interests of people of all occupations who travel on business, the sequence of topics will accommodate the main interests of the sales group.

HOW TO GET THERE

Intercity Transportation

If there is any one rule in planning intercity transportation, it is this: Each trip is its own problem. Sometimes air might be the fastest, sometimes rail is most practicable, and sometimes the bus is the only way. An important factor is the time of day. If you're to go from New York to Chicago, leaving in the evening, and if you have no late-evening engagement in Chicago, you might consider the advantages of taking the train, provided you are able to sleep on a train.

The modern bus, traveling over superhighways between major cities, may often be better suited to your needs than either rail or plane. The deluxe buses operate on reservations, are air-conditioned, and offer pillows, box lunches, and the services of a hostess. They have obsolesced the old humor about the comfort stops because now they offer built-in washrooms.

The automobile may be your best bet under some circumstances, especially if you're to make many stops en route. It may also be first choice if you are carrying bulky merchandise or equipment or if several people travel in the same car. On the other hand, there should be other advantages if only one person is to travel by car, considering time, mileage, toll charges, and the inability to use one's time constructively en route.

The lower costs and greater convenience of motels offer other arguments in favor of automobile travel. Besides saving time and costs, you are able to get in and out of a motel much more quickly than in the case of an in-town commercial hotel. There are fewer formalities, often you can leave most of your things in your car, and usually there are fewer "opportunities" for tipping, a not-inconsiderable part of your budget.

One special burden of the automobile traveler is the condition of his car. He cannot afford to have his car break down in the middle of nowhere. His entire schedule can be thrown off and it usually costs much more to have a car fixed en route when you are in a hurry.

Additional Suggestions for Air Travelers

There are many things about air travel which even the experienced traveler might overlook. I am indebted to the public-relations department of American Airlines for preparing the following "Hints on Saving Time by Air" for use in this book.

"One of the most important ways to save time is to have a validated ticket when you arrive at the airport. If you 'carry on' your baggage, this means you can proceed directly to the gate in most cases and board your flight without waiting behind somebody buying his ticket. Alternatively, you can go directly to express baggage-checking counters.

"There are several ways of obtaining your ticket in advance besides picking it up at a downtown ticket office. If you can plan your flight sufficiently in advance, you can have the ticket mailed to your home or office and pay by check. Or you might want to investigate the Air Travel Plan which provides, for a small deposit, a travel charge account good anywhere in the world. Under this plan an arrangement can be made by which you or somebody in your firm can hold a batch of blank tickets, and fill one out when needed right in your own office. Even easier is the write-your-own-ticket concept, such as American's Air Check, which can be completed as easily as a personal check and for which billing is made after completion of travel.*

"Then, for larger firms, there is Teleticketing, developed by American Airlines. When your company's call for a reservation has been made, the ticket is transmitted by Teletype and automatically printed in your office on a special machine.

* Don't forget the services of your travel agency for making reservations expertly and at least cost of time for you. The agency may mail or deliver the tickets to you—all at no extra cost. Check your airline, also, for other means of obtaining mail delivery of your tickets.

"Airlines have gone a long way toward eliminating delays in baggage claiming. But if you are in an extra hurry, you can carry some luggage off and on. In most airliners a bag measuring no larger than 21″×13″×8″ can be placed under the seat. On some airliners like American's Electra IIs and Convair 240s, there are baggage racks accommodating luggage of almost any size.

"Don't wait until you arrive to arrange for a rented car. Ask your airline to do it for you and the car will be waiting when you arrive. Your airline will also arrange for air-taxi service to off-line airports, if needed, and don't forget that such cities as New York, Chicago, Los Angeles, and San Francisco have helicopter service to downtown and to nearby airports.

"Even some experienced travelers overlook the time that can be saved by a shrewd choice of airports. Depending on exactly where you live or work and where you are headed, you may save time on a New York to Chicago trip, for example, by taking an Electra II from Newark Airport or LaGuardia Field to Midway Airport, rather than a jet from Idlewild to O'Hare Field, both of which are farther from downtown.

"Before you leave for the airport, incidentally, you might want to make a last-minute telephone check on your flight, especially if the weather looks a bit threatening. Your airline will call you if there is a major delay or cancellation.

"If you can, you might take advantage of the free meals aloft provided by your airline on mealtime flights. Don't overlook the fact that you can catch up on paper work while airborne. A meal tray or even a briefcase in your lap will usually suffice, but the stewardess can frequently supply you with a table. Make sure you have a fountain pen that will work and won't leak at higher altitudes. Take along a portable dictating machine if you have one and want to catch up on letters.* And don't forget that an electric razor is always available from the stewardess if you need one. This is especially good for saving time on overnight flights.

"If you are a businessman, don't overlook the time your company can save by use of airfreight, including speedy new jet-

* Although the Federal Aviation Agency has prohibited passenger use of FM radio receivers aboard aircraft, it has not prohibited use of portable dictating machines, as of the time this book was written. Some airlines may not permit their use as a matter of company policy. Therefore check beforehand with the individual airline.

freight carried in the holds of the big passenger-carrying jets that criss-cross the United States. If your plant is not located near a major airport, there is a nationwide system called "Truck-Air" that links smaller cities with big airfreight terminals by highway and speeds your shipment aloft. Finally, if you are traveling with a lot of luggage, you can save on excess-baggage charges by shipping most of it at lower airfreight rates."

Aside from the few deserved references to American Airlines, the suggestions, as intimated throughout, are applicable to most other airlines.

Travel by Day or Night

Travel by night offers the advantage of leaving the day free for the conduct of business. This may be very attractive to the man whose livelihood depends upon seeing as many people as possible in the shortest period of time.

It's a good objective, from the economic point of view, but like other good things, it must not be abused. The most important consideration is that you *must* get enough sleep. Anyone who has missed successive nights of sleep will know what it may do to his mental alertness, appearance, temper, and energies.

As a general rule, when you are going from city to city or when you are making a one-day trip, where the period of travel is about two hours and not more than about three, it is good economics to use either the very early morning or the early evening for travel. On the really long trip, travel by day may be unavoidable. If you are flying from the East Coast to the West Coast, you can leave in the afternoon and arrive in time for an early dinner. The time-zone differences make this possible but they also "lengthen" your trip on the way back.

Going to the West Coast, it scarcely pays to try to take a night plane unless you have no other alternative. Going to the East Coast, unless you sleep comfortably in an airplane seat, an early morning plane should be considered. Some travelers will take sleeping pills but as to this one's physician should be consulted.

Travel within the City

In some cities, like Los Angeles, the only way to get around is through driving your own automobile. In other cities, notably New York, an automobile is something to put away until you are ready to leave town.

Partly, it depends on how much you need to have with you of bulky materials and equipment. If your load is heavy and if a taxicab is not practicable, using your own vehicle may be your only course. You may not like to use parking lots, because of the expense, but this may be very much cheaper than tiresome cruising in search of a public parking spot. If you're going to be getting in and out of parking lots all day, you might be much better off to use taxicabs. In dense, rush-hour traffic it might pay to walk unless it's raining. Incidentally, if you pick up a taxicab at a waiting stand, the driver might not appreciate a short haul even though legally he is obliged to take you.

In cities that have subways these usually offer the quickest in-town transportation. During rush hours you should be mindful of the inconvenience of carrying bulky hand baggage.

ACTIVITIES IN TRANSIT

When writing his "Inside" books, John Gunther and his wife Jane would make many stops in the lands they traveled, to see countless people, in order to get firsthand impressions which they could weave together to form their fascinating reports. You can get the feel of his pace from the following paragraph describing how he managed his work during his trip to Africa to gather material for *Inside Africa*.

"Take Nairobi. In a day we might have a schedule which included meetings with at least twenty people, ranging from African nationalists to government officials to white settlers. In between there would have to be sandwiched in time for shopping or sightseeing or to go to the dentist, an hour with a travel man to fix up the safari we were planning later, telephone calls to confirm plans or invitations, interviewers to see, letters to write, and arrangements to make for getting off to our next country, Uganda.

Then, at midnight, notes to take. When the time came to totter onto the Uganda plane, we were more dead than alive. But the minute the seat belt was fastened, out would come my briefcase so that I could glance through my Uganda dossier before we touched ground at Entebbe. And always there were unending lists to make—people seen, people to see, questions to ask—and always an infernal backlog of memories to write down of conversations and impressions of countries which we had left behind."*

John Gunther was very much a man on the move. In his case his principal commodity was intelligence, so he learned the absolute necessity of recording information as soon as possible after it was acquired. You will note, however, that he also took time out for personal activities.

Work Activities

All of the following should be obvious. They would deserve no mention except that they are usually overlooked!

1. *Stationery.* Take along writing materials, including notebooks, note cards (three-by-five or four-by-six), postal cards, stamped envelopes, air-letter sheets (eleven cents for international correspondence anywhere in the world), writing paper, envelopes for bulky materials, and enough postage to cover airmail and special delivery. Estimate postage weights beforehand by noting how many sheets of your stationery plus an envelope make one ounce and two ounces. Do the same with any special forms that you may fill out en route. Carry adequate supplies of such forms.

2. *Reading matter.* Take along reports, memoranda, trade and technical literature, and books. Apart from catching up with your necessary business reading, use this as an opportunity to cover things that will help in your own personal development. Also, provide some recreational reading.

3. *Waiting-time work.* Some of your stationery and reading matter should be pocketable. Then, while waiting for transportation or for the person you are to see, you can do something constructive.

* John Gunther, "Writing the 'Inside' Books," *Harper's Magazine,* March 1961.

4. *Paper work*. Use travel time to catch up with paper work held in reserve. Try to keep current with each day's paper work or you will become mired in the accumulation. If you delay making notes, you will quickly forget many details. Do your writing by hand if you prefer or use a portable dictating machine. Mail your belts, discs, or tapes home to be transcribed.

Developmental Activities

While they may not be directly related to your business calls, there are some things you can do which will be of future use or which will assist you indirectly in carrying out your local business.

1. *Newspapers*. Read one or more newspapers, particularly if you are visiting the city for the first time. Read particularly the local civic, political, business, and social news. Read both the display and classified advertisements. All of these give you a feeling of how the people in that city live and work and what they think about things. More directly, you might get important business ideas.

2. *Mealtime*. Try not to eat alone unless you are terribly rushed. Use the time for relaxed discussion with a business contact or prospect. Look up an old friend or someone in your own business or profession. Don't overlook breakfast meetings. They give you a chance to see at least one additional person without losing time since everyone knows that breakfasts must be brief because they are followed by business.

3. *New business opportunities*. For the same visit or for future reference, do some research on new business opportunities. Check the local chamber of commerce. Talk to the local banker. Scan the classified section of the telephone directory. Make mental notes as to community, industrial, and economic trends and developments. Acquaint yourself with dominant industries.

Personal Activities

Don't overlook personal activities that may be enriching, enlivening, and relaxing. They are important physically. They also provide the moments of detachment which enable you to get a better perspective on your business activities during travel.

1. *Cultural*. In the evening visit the local library. Attend live

theater. Listen to a concert. These provide quiet, wholesome relaxation. Visit the local museum, although you might need to do this during the weekend.

2. *Sight-seeing.* Brochures at the hotel will list the various local attractions which can be seen both at night and during the day. Daytime sight-seeing is not usually feasible for people traveling on business unless it occurs over the weekend. Take along a camera to record interesting sights and scenes.

3. *Hobby materials.* Take along things to work on in your hotel room—a stamp collection, an electronic kit, portable handcrafts, etc. They compel a complete relaxation. They help dispel the loneliness of travel.

SCHEDULE PLANNING AND PREPARATION

The man on the move has many more things to arrange within his schedule than the man who leaves his home each morning for a desk at the office. The desk-based man knows that some things which cannot be done today can be accommodated the next day or the next week. The traveling man knows that he has certain business or professional objectives to achieve within a limited time and that if he does not utilize this time well, important opportunities may be lost—sometimes irretrievably.

While advance planning and preparation are important, there is some tendency for them to be built around the major activities. It is important, also, that we not overlook the details of the day. If we do not give attention to them, their careless handling can nullify all of our best intentions. An issue of the trade journal *Farm Chemicals* carried an article on organizing time by O. C. Merrett in which was included a check list which clearly points up the details of personal management that make up much of the day. The check list is intended for use in organizing your work of the next day.

1. What time will I get up?
2. How long will it take to shower, shave, dress, breakfast, brush teeth?
3. How long will I read paper—listen to news?
4. When will I leave home?
5. How long will it take to get to the office?

6. How long will I spend at the office?

7. What will I do at the office?

8. What time will I be face to face with my first prospect?

9. Is my appointment sheet filled?

10. When will I use telephone?

11. How long will I use telephone?

12. Do I have a substitute in mind in case of a canceled appointment?

13. Are my appointments planned close together?

14. Am I squeezing in that one more call before lunch?

15. Am I going to stop for coffee? If so, how long?

16. What time will I stop for lunch?

17. Am I eating alone? If so, why?

18. How much time will I spend eating lunch?

19. What time will I face my first after-lunch appointment?

20. Will I stop in the afternoon for refreshments or coffee?

21. What time will I make my last call?

22. Could I make just one more call?

23. Do I have any evening calls planned? If not, how will I spend the evening?

24. When will I analyze today's calls; if I closed, why? If not, why not?

25. When will I plan tomorrow?

26. When will I read and study up on my product?

27. When will I organize my portfolio—my demonstration?

28. When will I research my prospect?

29. When will I go to bed?

30. When will I study my advertising?

How Much to Schedule

The key to getting the most return from a trip is this: *Plan your schedule around the most important calls*. There are only so many hours available to you during the day and sometimes you may have special hours available at night with people you want to see. Into those hours you must fit the calls you *must make,* arranging them with due regard to the time they will take, the convenience of the person upon whom you are calling, and the time it will take to get from one place to the next.

Having accounted for your key calls, you next can plan for

things you would like to fit in. These should be the calls you are ready to sacrifice if the more important ones should take more time. It is important that you not *commit* yourself to too much because when you are on the move, you run into many unforeseeables. Also, it is in the nature of much of your business that you may not be able to control the disposition of your time by the people upon whom you call. Hence, if you are over-scheduled, you will tend to be apprehensive of time and you may tend to rush things which require a little more time than you seem inclined to give to them. The person upon whom you are calling may sense your apprehensiveness about time and he might also interpret it to your disadvantage.

When you try to crowd too much into a day, you also add an additional burden—that of being unusually conscious of your schedule and spending a burdensome amount of time trying to maintain it.

In short, your schedule should assure that you take care of your main business, while at the same time being sufficiently full to keep you moving briskly.

Arranging Calls and Appointments

Lewis Nichols of the New York *Times Book Review,* writing of a scouting visit to America by Andre Deutsch, head of the London publishing firm of that name, said: "His firm publishes forty-five to fifty titles a year, 20 per cent usually of American origin. The logistics of his pursuit of these 20 per cent sound like the onslaught on Carthage. In his London office he has a large map of New York, in his briefcase a notebook listing publishers and authors' agents by region—Park Avenue South, Madison Avenue midtown, etc. Before leaving home, he writes everyone he can think of, making appointments. Trick is to get a full day's appointments in the same region, thus avoiding the stagnant air of taxicabs."

At least as to your key appointments you should try to arrange them in advance for specific hours. Do so by letter or by telephone. Professor James H. Davis, in his study on *Increasing Wholesale Drug Salesmen's Effectiveness,* found that the most efficient salesmen spent only 7.5 per cent of their time waiting for interviews while the least efficient spent 20.5 per cent or almost three times as much. When you make an advance appointment, it is more likely to work out as intended if you pin it down to a specific time. Avoid being approximate. If you say "the morning," your party will not be able to plan specifically. Just when you arrive, he may be engaged in something which he cannot put aside, so that you will have to wait after all. In other words, you did not make a real appointment.

The importance of the prearranged appointment, as opposed to the "drop-in" call, has been emphasized by many. John C. Emery, Jr., vice-president of the Emery Air Freight Corporation, said, ". . . We know that our salesmen will have greater success if they make appointments in advance of their calls, so we insist upon two appointment calls per day."

Additional suggestions: Have other appointments tentatively in mind in case previously-made appointments are broken. Work out a routing for your calls that enables you to cover the maximum number of calls with the least time spent in travel. Know your prospects and their work habits, especially those who do not like to receive salesmen by appointment.

Advance Preparation

The more you do beforehand, the more likely you are to use your time well at the point of call. When you are prepared in advance, it gives you a feeling of confidence, as you approach the call itself. Advance preparation gives you time for improvement.

With respect to your travel arrangements, take along time-tables and road maps, as appropriate. Know beforehand how to get out of the town at different times of the day as well as how to get into the town.

Go through your files and study them for any notes on your past relationships with people upon whom you are to call. Some people keep individual cards on each sales prospect, covering prior experiences, analyses of the customer and his likes and dislikes, his competition, his past business, etc. A study of this information enables the selling man to develop his strategy beforehand and to arrange any special materials he will need to assist in putting across his ideas.

Then there are all the samples, catalogues, fact sheets, visual aids, and other selling tools, all of which should be checked out beforehand to make sure they are complete, up to date, and in good working order.

Don't overlook information you can send out in advance to the party upon whom you are calling. Bear in mind that he receives material from many other people. What you send him must be arresting. He must see in it a special "angle" which suggests advantage to him. A "gimmick" may arrest his attention but it will not necessarily hold it if it is not supported by real substance.

FACE-TO-FACE

The purpose of most business travel is to get things done, usually with people. What a tremendous loss in time and money a trip can be if it is not productive of the results you need and desire. The art of handling face-to-face relationships is a topic worthy of extended discussion in itself. Here, we should cover at least those main aspects which pertain to your most effective utilization of time on the road.

Talking to the Right People

Although the salesman may be marketing products or services, in an indirect sense he is selling time. All that we have said about effective planning of one's travel and effective preparation for the face-to-face contact is merely preliminary to that contact. The pay-off must come out of what the salesman is able to derive from the interview.

One of the first questions with which he is concerned is: "Am I talking to the right person?" When you are selling to someone in an organization this means: "Am I selling to the man who has the authority to buy?" Perhaps he is not that person, but this does not mean that you should not spend your time with him. His task may be to screen and to recommend. Somehow you must find this out so that you will be able to develop your selling strategy leading toward an engagement with the person who actually does have authority to make a purchase. You may not be able to tell this the first time you call upon a prospect but, through continued interaction, you can get to know where the power lies.

A related question is: "Is this a good prospect or am I wasting my time?" The experienced salesman learns to organize his presentation in successive stages so that he can cut off at any time that he thinks further activity is useless. This is sometimes called "qualifying the prospect." In each field of selling there will be individual clues for which one might be on the alert. They all add up to the same thing: What are the probabilities that this person will buy—not necessarily on this first try, but after a reasonable amount of cultivation by the salesman? Among the aspects of this question from which we should seek clues are the discernible need of the prospect, his interest, and his financial capabilities.

Waiting Activities

Ted H. Lazar, sales manager of the Union Underwear Company, Inc., said in a round-table discussion of *The American Salesman* on the subject of "How to Be a Good Manager of Your Own Time": "You can save time when calling on accounts by having an understanding with the customer. Our salesmen, after they have opened up an account, usually try to make an arrangement with the customer to be permitted to enter the customer's stockroom, take the inventory, straighten up the stock, and write an order for whatever merchandise they feel is necessary. They then show this order to the customer, giving him the opportunity of either increasing or decreasing it to the amount which he feels he needs, and then they take a little additional time to talk to the buyer to introduce any additional numbers which he might not now be carrying. Our men also are trained to note on the customers' performance sheets any unusual characteristics or personal problems of the account so that during their conversation they can make mention of these to create a better feeling between buyer and seller."

Mr. Lazar recommends this as normal practice but it is also a recommended way in which salesmen can use their time to good purpose when they are waiting to talk to the buyer or dealer. My friend Jack Black told me that when he would call on photographic dealers he often would have to wait while the dealer attended to a customer of his own who, naturally, would receive the dealer's first attention. Jack would use the same technique of checking inventory but, in addition, he made quite a specialty out of checking the book rack for titles that should be reordered, since this was something to which the typical photographic dealer did not seem to give very much attention. In this way Jack built up a very big volume in photographic books, as compared to other salesmen.

How Long to Stay

The astute salesman never overstays his welcome nor does he let others keep him longer than it pays for him to stay. He does not initiate small talk but enters into it only at the instance of the buyer, getting away from it and back to business whenever he feels it opportune to do so. If he overstays his time, it will be at the risk of getting himself typed as a time-waster. If this should happen, he will meet with resistance the next time he comes around. His prospects will give him the "busy routine."

There will be occasions when the salesman feels that he needs additional time. It is up to him to induce the prospect to want him to stay longer. Joseph Focarino of the editorial staff of *The American Salesman* said: "If the buyer has given you more time or if he hasn't and you want more time but you have really captured his interest, let him be the one to extend the time. The trick is to get him really intrigued and to see his own self-interest. In fact, you should start making a move to terminate. Then, if he gives you more time, the responsibility is with him."

SUMMARY

The art of making good time on the move consists of knowing how to use the best means of travel, how to use one's time in transit, how to prepare for the appointments one has scheduled, and how to best manage one's face-to-face contacts.

The mode of transportation you select need not necessarily be the fastest. Each of the common means of transportation—air, rail, bus, and automobile—has its own advantages and disadvantages. You must take into account traffic conditions into and out of your points of departure and destination. Within the city the automobile may be best if traffic conditions permit. You should consider taxicabs in preference to moving your automobile in and out of garages. Sometimes, you might as well go by foot when your next point of call is not too far away.

The time you spend in public conveyances as well as the time available to you in the evening and over weekends, while away from home, can be put to constructive use. You should take with you business reading matter and papers as well as stationery so that you can keep current on your paper work. You must also look to your own personal relaxation and recreation. Some things, such as books, a camera, and hobby materials, you can take along with you but you might also be alert to cultural, recreational, and sight-seeing opportunities that might be available locally, consistent with your off-hours schedule.

In planning your actual schedule you should build around the key calls that you must make, allowing enough time for other business. To the extent possible, your appointments should be arranged in advance. Also in advance, you should brief yourself on past relationships with the prospect. Be sure you are prepared in depth with whatever informational and selling materials you might need.

Finally, in your face-to-face contacts, you must learn to sense whether you are talking with a prospect who can and might buy. One of the hazards of selling is the time spent in waiting. You should have activities in reserve—activities of your own as well as such things as inventorying the customer's stock of your merchandise. Finally, one must not overstay his welcome. If more time is needed, the effort must be to induce the prospect to *want* you to stay longer.

XIX

How to Work at Home

People work at home for a variety of reasons. Some make their headquarters at home but work away from home, returning to do their paper work. Some set up actual offices in their homes, apart from their living quarters, if possible. Some, like writers, use their homes to do part-time work in addition to holding down regular jobs. Many come home from an outside office to do some additional work after dinner or over the weekend. They work under a common disadvantage: somehow, a home does not seem like an office and hence it invites intrusions upon one's time. Moreover, the opportunities for relaxation at home also operate against productivity. Hence, in this chapter we will concentrate on how to overcome interruptions that are peculiar to working at home and on the particular problems of getting down to work.

INTERRUPTIONS AT HOME

The obstacles to getting any work done at home come from the family, visitors, and the telephone. It may be unreasonable to call all of these "sources of interruption." After all, the family does have a claim upon your time. So do other people, in moderation, for none of us is a thing apart from the rest of society. The word *moderation* is the key, however, for if your work dictates that you *must* do some things at home, it is not unreasonable to expect others to defer to your own needs.

The Family

Doing work at home is probably one of the important sources of conflict within the family, especially with one's wife. It has not always been this way, for in years gone by, families were quite accustomed to longer work weeks and workdays for most people. Be that as it may, the family looks with envy at neighbors who keep to regular schedules and never do any work at home. That's just wonderful for those who are able to live that way but for millions of others, including the probable readers of this book, the eight-hour day is something of a fiction.

At the very least, even if time at home is not spent in writing or in catching up with business reading, some of the time is used in constructive reflection upon one's problems.

"I am . . . convinced that a creative man's best work is done during those times he isn't supposed to be working at all," said advertising man James R. Adams. "I refer to evenings and weekends and his various and sundry holidays. Thinking back over my own work in creative advertising, I am sure that the things I can point to with greatest pride have been the products of my so-called leisure hours. Unless you have this capacity for carrying your creative problems around with you until you happen upon their solutions, you will scarcely succeed in this demanding business. The man who can leave the office and 'turn it off,' so to speak, hasn't much to turn off. You might show this to your wife and family. It could conceivably help them to understand certain of your preoccupations which are difficult for a family to endure!"

Nevertheless, the desire of the wife to have her husband participate fully in family life and to exercise his responsibilities as husband and father inevitably comes into conflict with the preoccupation of the man with his business or profession. A survey conducted by *The American Salesman* indicated something of a fifty-fifty division of opinion among those replying on whether they have conflicts between worktime and family time. Every shade of opinion, for and against, was expressed.

This problem came up once more at a round-table discussion sponsored by *The American Salesman* at which John C. Emery, Jr., vice president of Emery Air Freight Corporation, said: "It's probably heresy, but I believe that home and motherhood have been placed too high in the life of the typical salesman. What many wives don't realize, and what their husbands should help them realize, is that their standard of living—where they are located, the type of house they have, the furnishings they enjoy, how the family is fed and clothed—is incumbent upon the success of the salesman. Until greater recognition is given to the importance of the man, I think we are going to have this problem of wives not fully understanding their part in the salesman's work."

Well, that's one point of view. The more important thing is what to do about the situation. In the same round-table discussion, Robert E. Massa, sales representative of the Knickerbocker Brewery, said: "Conflict can probably be lessened simply by showing appreciation. For instance, if the salesman makes his wife feel that he really appreciates what she contributes by her understanding and sympathy, she'll respond by giving sympathy instead of argument."

Better communications between husband and wife as well as an opportunity for the wife to participate in her husband's interests was recommended by John G. Campana, sales manager of the Shaw-Walker Company. He said: "I think discussion between a husband and wife is one of the best ways to reduce conflict. In the old days, the wife never knew what the man was doing in his job. Today, wives are better educated and better able to understand a man's business problems. I know this is true because I discuss my problems with my wife and she comes up with some pretty good answers for me." Summing up this discussion, David R. Lindsay, editor of *The American Salesman,* said: "So we might say that a good way for a salesman to reduce the conflict between his home and his job is to do as good a job in explaining his work to his wife as he does in explaining his products to his customers."

Quite apart from this constructive approach, another hurdle to be overcome is the fact that a man working at home is a kind of "attractive nuisance." Paul R. Reynolds, the well-known literary agent, said: "As he is at home, it is difficult for his wife not to bother him to turn the mattress, let out the dog, answer the doorbell or the telephone. Some writers sleep in the daytime and work from 10 P.M. to 5 A.M. to avoid interruption. Some have an office and keep regular office hours. Some have a perceptive, well-trained, angelic wife. Many succeed despite all kinds of interruptions."*

The problem is not with the wife alone. There are the children, especially when they advance into those school subjects in which father's assistance is desired. Father must come across, even though he has long since forgotten his algebra or solid geometry for, if he does not, he is something lower than a heel. Explaining your own preoccupations to teens and subteens is not very easy, for they simply do not have what we might call economic empathy.

One way out is to put aside certain evenings exclusively for your own work. Another approach is to allow certain periods during a single evening as free time for the children after which a cutoff puts you into your "office hours."

Friends, Neighbors, and Relatives

The scheduled incursions upon your time by outsiders, whether they be friends, relatives, or neighbors, are a matter for self-control. The unscheduled, "drop-in" visits and interruptions are a matter for great tact.

Let's take up the first one. If you are socially in demand or if you know lots of people and like to be with people—the gregarious type—you are apt to find yourself in a round of partying, visits, and return visits. You can engage in such pursuits to such an extent that you will have little time for anything else, let alone some work at home. There is only one answer here and that is to budget your time. This means that you must space out your social involvements. In addition to limiting your own invitations, spreading them out, you must do the same with invitations that you receive. If you accept too many, you will be

* *The Writer and His Markets* (Garden City, N.Y.: Doubleday and Company, 1959).

back where you were because you will then be preoccupied with reciprocating.

The bigger problem is the unanticipated "drop-in" guest. If he or they should call on the telephone before coming over, you have at least some measure of control because the mere fact of the call leaves room for a polite declination. The challenge to your ingenuity comes when your guests appear at your front door without having given you the courtesy beforehand of declining to be in.

Because drop-in guests have time on their hands, they may not realize that you do not. Home is thought of as a place in which to relax. It is not thought of as being a place in which you are trying to continue the business of making a living. The unanticipated drop-in may not realize that he can ruin completely any plans which you may have had—and not just plans, but commitments to others based on your expectation of an uninterrupted evening.

Your problem now is to figure out some way of continuing with your work or else to look forward to being up half the night. Whatever you do, you are most anxious not to hurt your guest's feelings. An acquaintance offered the following seven suggestions for heading off a drop-in neighbor or for working in spite of him. They seem to be measures of desperation. Some people would prefer to be frank, in the first instance, about their being busy.

"1. Let one of the children answer the door. A child can get away with much more than an adult. He can say, 'My daddy is busy but I'll tell him you're here.' This *may* disturb the visitor but at least it will pave the way for your letting him know that you have other things to do.

"2. The wife can answer the door and graciously invite the visitor in while explaining that her husband is very busy. The wife can continue entertaining the visitor without calling her husband.

"3. Graciously invite the visitor in, offer food and drink, and then, as some people have done successfully, tell the visitor that you are in the midst of something which will keep you for a little while and won't he busy himself in some book or the television.

"4. Have whoever greets the visitor at the door explain that you are in the midst of some work and then bring the visitor down to your actual workplace. The idea is that the visitor will see you in a nonsocial environment in your home and may get the hint.

"5. Greet the visitor with delight. Tell him that he's just the person to help you with some of your work and then give him something to keep him busy which will not conflict with what you need to do.

"6. Go to the door yourself carrying a pile of papers and a pencil in your hand. Invite the visitor in to partake of your hospitality while you never let go of your papers. Continue working on your papers in front of the visitor, explaining that you're up against a terrible deadline.

"7. Install a one-way peephole in your front door and simply refuse to be home even though your car is out front."

The Telephone

If you let it, the telephone can become the complete master of your evenings. At home you do not have a secretary to fend off callers but, with a little training, your family will be able to do just as well, if not better.

The first rule is not to answer the telephone yourself. Have your wife do it or some other member of your family or the maid, with instructions to say that you're not in. Have a message taken. You can call back if it is a call you really want to take.

The second rule is to tell your family about any important calls you expect and ask them to divert any other calls.

Train your children in how to take calls. Teach them not to cry out, loud enough to be heard over the telephone, "Daddy, are you in? Someone wants you on the telephone."

If you're in a clientele operation in which you want calls restricted solely to your office during regular office hours, have your telephone unlisted or put it in your wife's name. Another possibility is to use a telephone-answering service to pick up your listed telephone calls. Then, you can decide which ones to return.

GETTING DOWN TO WORK

If you have the room, it is a good idea to set aside a part of your home which would be equipped and furnished as though it were an office, with desk, file cabinets, and other office paraphernalia. There are certain other advantages that go with this, which are good for your own productivity as well.

Your Office at Home

The main value of an office area within your home, if you have enough use for it, is that psychologically it takes you out of the more informal atmosphere of your home. When you step into your office area, it is an unspoken reminder to your family as well as to yourself that you have withdrawn from family interactions for the time that you are at your desk. If the children interrupt you, you can more easily explain that you are now busy with office work.

The environment of your workplace should be as simple and neat as possible. There should be very little décor and as few distractions as possible. Music may be quite all right but television should be taboo. If you have a telephone on your desk, you can have the ring quietened completely.

The conventional picture of the man at home in lounging robe in a deep, cushioned chair should be associated with relaxed reading of a newspaper, a book, or a magazine. It is not a chair in which to do hard, crisp thinking. It is too relaxing. For creative, incisive thought, you need a chair which, while comfortable, is not so relaxing that it induces you to go off into a reverie or into a visit with Morpheus.

Your Work Procedures

At the office or during the day, on the go, you tend to be conditioned to a nine-to-five alertness. Your manner of dress itself suggests business. You are not ready to relax. At home you are naturally inclined to relax. After all, that is one of the things for which you have a home. However true this may be, it is not consistent with your desire to get a little work done.

As a matter of fact, it is probably less important to dress a certain way than to work in the right physical environment and under a good schedule. In other words, you can get into old clothes, lounging pajamas, slippers, sport clothes, or any other getup you prefer, but don't make yourself comfortable to the point of being too relaxed.

The hours remaining to you for work in the evening are very few. When you come home and have dinner, you might feel a little groggy. If you can do so, take a brief nap, for it will refresh you. After the nap you may find new energies which will support your working effort. In any event, reserve the earliest part of your working time for tasks that require the most critical thinking.

If you find it hard to get down to work, set aside a certain time on one or more days which you identify clearly as working time. For example, you might set aside every Monday evening to get at least a certain amount of paper work done. When Monday evening comes along, if you have made this part of your habit structure, you will find yourself drifting to your work quarters and you will have little trouble getting under way. Moreover, your family and friends will get to know that on Monday evenings you should not be interrupted. This carries over to one of the values of having your own work area. If you build a habit of using the area solely for office work at home, when you move into it, you will immediately tend to associate your efforts with productive work. That is, you will need much less effort to get under way.

Working Full-Time at Home

The man who works at home part of the time is mindful of the incursions upon his time by others. The man who works at home regularly on a full-time basis must be mindful of himself as a source of time diversion. He must acquire habits which take account of the special work environment of the home. These fall into three categories:

1. The need for regular office-type hours and practices.
2. Separation from the domestic activities of the home.

3. The need for activity outside the home.

At home there could be a tendency to work under irregular schedules. A late start might be the more comfortable way, especially after a late night, but this irregularity would interfere with a necessary rhythm of productive work. Moreover, it is apt to run afoul of the domestic schedules of the house. The man who must go to the office, however, will maintain his regular schedule—ordinarily—in spite of the night before. This does not throw out the permissibility and advantage of serving your own moods occasionally, but these should be recognizable exceptions.

Personal grooming and personal attire can also be what you want them to be, but there is something more businesslike—and more conducive to being productive—about being dressed almost as though you were going to an office. A necktie may not be an imperative but the clothes should be good enough for visitors.

There should be a clear separation of the man's activities from those of his wife. This is a two-way street. While it is so convenient for the wife to use her husband as a porter, chauffeur, repairman, or disciplinarian, a frank recognition by both parties will bring out the economic disadvantage of using his time in this way. On the other hand, the husband should not intrude upon his wife's privacy and domestic procedures. He should not monitor her telephone calls or interfere with her treatment of children at home. When she has visitors, he should disappear from the living room; the chances are that the visiting ladies don't want any man-talk anyway.

The home-based man needs to make a point of getting outside the home. He does not go to and from an office, nor does he usually go out to lunch. Unless he has constant callers, he misses face-to-face interactions.

Hence, except during inclement weather, he should make a point of getting out of the house each day—perhaps for a walk or even for lunch, preferably with an outsider. His sedentary pattern calls for a more pronounced emphasis on physical recreation. His vacations, obviously, should not be spent at home.

SUMMARY

The main problem in working at home is that it is a place for family activity and relaxation and, as such, it is difficult for family and visitors to take your work efforts seriously. Moreover, your wife and family feel, rightfully, that your evening and weekend hours should be theirs.

As regards the family, the most constructive approach is to take the wife and children into confidence—to make them part of your enterprise—up to a point of noninterference. Beyond this, another fruitful procedure is to set aside definite work schedules which enable you to honor family responsibilities while the family learns to recognize your "not-in" periods.

Visitors who drop in can frustrate your ordinary schedules as well as special commitments. A variety of techniques can be used to discourage drop-in visitors, or at least to let you continue working, but you should not offend the visitor who has merely assumed that a home is to be visited. The telephone can be more easily controlled. Don't answer it. Train the family in what to say. Use an unlisted phone. Use an answering service.

Your workplace at home should, insofar as possible, be set up as a place aside. It should be businesslike and free of distractions. Dress as comfortably as you desire but don't make yourself too comfortable in your chair. Keep alert. If you can, take a nap after dinner, before working. Do first those things which call for the clearest mind.

The man who works at home full-time must keep regular hours, for maximum productivity, as though he were going to an outside office. Variations should be the exception. His work routines should be kept sacred by his wife, in her own economic interests. Reciprocally, he must resist involving himself in her own domestic procedures, telephone calls, and guest interactions. He must make up for his seclusion and restricted physical activity by getting out of the home for some purpose each day. He needs a planned program of outside interactions.

XX

Time for What?

For what is Time? Who is able easily and briefly to explain it?
Who is able so much as in thought to comprehend it so as to
express himself concerning it? And yet what in our usual dis-
course do we more familiarly and knowingly make more mention of than Time? And surely we understand it well enough
when we speak of it; we understand it also when in speaking with
another we hear it named. What then is Time? If nobody asks me I
know; but if I were desirous to explain it to someone that should
ask me, plainly I know not.

ST. AUGUSTINE

When Gulliver was captured by the Lilliputians, one of the
things which evoked their particular interest was his pocket watch
—not merely the timepiece itself but its role in Gulliver's life and,
symbolically, in Everyman's life. Said the Lilliputians through
their narrator, Jonathan Swift:

"Out of the right Fob hung a great Silver Chain, with a
wonderful kind of Engine at the Bottom. . . . He put this
Engine to our Ears, which made an incessant Noise like that of a
Water-Mill. And we conjectured it either some unknown Animal,
or the God that he worships: But we are more inclined to the
latter Opinion, because he assured . . . that he seldom did any-

thing without consulting it. He called it his Oracle, and said it pointed out the Time for every Action of his Life."

It might seem that this book, also, is dedicated to regulating the use of time for every action in business or professional life. We have examined the uses of time from many different stand-points, mainly to obtain the best productive use of our time. We have addressed ourselves to such questions as: How can I get more done in the same time? How can I get as much done in less time? How can I avoid distractions and diversions? How can I do more than one thing at a time? And so on.

In the preface we noted that how you use any time-savings is a matter of personal choice: whether to release time for greater productivity or for a fuller personal life. Of course, this is far from an original preoccupation. The savants and philosophers of the ages struggled with the values of time. Closer to our own day, Lord Chesterfield wrote, in one of his famous *Letters to His Son:*

"There is nothing which I wish more that you should know, and which fewer people do know, than the true use and value of time. It is in everybody's mouth; but in few people's practice. Every fool, who slatterns away his whole time in nothing, utters, however, some trite commonplace sentence, of which there are millions, to prove, at once, the value and the fleetness of time. The sun-dials all over Europe have some ingenious inscriptions to that effect; so that nobody squanders away their time without hearing and seeing daily how necessary it is to employ well, and how irrecoverable it is if lost."

In Chesterfield's day, those who had a surfeit of time to be "slatterned away," were more likely either to be the gentle-men, for many of whom work may have seemed odious, or the indolent and the dispossessed. For the masses, such leisure as they had was devoted to physical rest and to religion. Leisure in the more modern sense of pleasure is a recent phenomenon in Western society. (For most other peoples, leisure as we know it is a rarity.) Only recently has society given organized attention to problems of what to do with our leisure time.*

Despite the focus on "high culture," creative arts and crafts, and participation in community activities, various surveys have

---

* See *Mass Leisure,* by Eric Larrabee and Rolf Meyersohn (Glencoe, Illinois: The Free Press, 1958).

brought out that as much as 90 per cent of the leisure time of most people is spent in eating, visiting, reading, sports, radio and television, motoring, clubs, etc.

These people, however, are not our main concern, nor is it our task to suggest the best cultural and recreational mix for them. Rather, we are concerned here with those whose work hours spill over into what ordinarily should be regarded as time for family and self. To provide a diversified viewpoint on this area of our concern, I put the problem of "time for what" to some very busy people.

"Time is a tyrant," said John W. Macy, Jr., a distinguished educator and professional civil servant, chairman of the United States Civil Service Commission. "It controls the life of any person of far-ranging interests and desires for human association. One of the first steps in managing time is to recognize the existence of this tyrant. In order to achieve a balance in the allocation of time to the conflicting demands of work and of people, one must first look within himself to find the value judgments which will give him guidance.

"What is important? To which duties or interests should one commit the treasured minutes and hours? Unless we find within ourselves the answers to these questions, the tyranny of time will reign. We will find ourselves consuming precious time on relative trivia while significant effort must be deferred or never reached. In the final analysis each human being must gauge his capacity, identify his aspirations, and plan the commitment of precious time accordingly."

Let us take this idea a step further. As we mature in the community as citizens and as parents, and as we assume greater responsibilities in the business world, we find that the pressures on our time come not from work alone. They come from our families and from the innumerable agencies of the community, both formal and informal. How does one accommodate all these demands upon his time?

"It depends upon each individual's personality, abilities, position, philosophy, interests, and even his health and metabolism," said Ellsworth C. Alvord, a distinguished legal counselor. "Each of us has interests outside of business for which time has to be found and allocated—such as public service, charities, educational matters, recreation, social activities, and perhaps even family matters!"

What we are getting to here is the need of finding for ourselves, individually, a socially useful way of life. When we have identified the real things of importance, we can assign relative values to them, thereby finding the priorities that will give us guidance in making individual allocations of time.

The aim of such self-programing is the broadened fulfillment of the individual. Thus, time saved at work, through better self-management, could well be put to getting ahead of oneself—to obtaining a perspective on self. "That opportunity is best used," wrote Maurice H. Stans, president of Western Bancorporation and former Director of the U. S. Bureau of the Budget, "if it is applied to looking ahead, to planning, to thinking, to probing just a little deeper into one or more of the aspects of one's activities." He urged, often, that at least 10 per cent of one's time be devoted to such thinking.

A liberated slice of time could be invested in new and different activities rather than in more of the same. While our industrial system demands specialization, there is a growing awareness that this spawns a narrow vision. A deliberate effort must be made to see one's contribution within the framework of the larger needs of one's organization and of society. The specialist should learn about the work methods and problems of others who perform related tasks. The generalist, for his part, will find it rewarding to explore in depth one or more of the specialized areas which come within his view.

Time saved—or reallocated—should be given, also, to broadening one's social exposure. We tend to become absorbed in inbred social circles which may parallel our business relationships. The attraction of like for like may be seen in engineers seeking out engineers, lawyers congregating with lawyers, and administrators associating with other administrators. These social patterns are often reinforced by the wives, whose "get-togethers" parallel those of their husbands. The conversion of business contacts into social ones may be beneficial, up to a point, but this could fail to provide genuinely relaxed companionship. When you mix with people of varying interests, apart from your regular work, they may serve as windows into many different philosophies and experiences, thereby enriching you and broadening your perspectives.

Some measure of relaxed withdrawal can also be enriching: time spent in reading and reflection, time given to creative interests, and time merely for the appreciation of beauty. Many a weekend painter has found within himself an unsuspected talent —and his name need not be Dwight D. Eisenhower or Winston Churchill. A manual hobby, moreover, may stimulate a free flow of undirected thought, sometimes serving as the medium for finding solutions to great problems.

Music as a background remains just that, but if you play an instrument or listen actively to sonatas and concertos and symphonies, you'll hear tonal riches you may not have noticed before. Have you ever heard the birds awakening the world? When did you last see the sunrise sweep away the night?

Somewhere in this edifice of personal values and pursuits to which we give thought, we must find room for people. Of course, this includes some devotion to community responsibilities, but I mean a deeper, more personal involvement that goes beyond people in general, people in the abstract, people upon whom you cannot cast your eyes. Rather, I mean people with whom you can converse directly, people whom you can see as flesh and blood, people with joys and sorrows, victories and defeats.

When did you last take time for a relaxed conversation with a neighbor—something more than the surface exchange of amenities?

It is a peculiar phenomenon that many great reformers, leaders of great causes, doers of great good for the masses, could find little room in their hearts for one man at a time. They have found it so convenient to rationalize their aloofness in the belief that they are committing their time for the greatest good.

Do you have time for people whose business may be important for them but not for you? True, a little of this could go a long way, but do you find time even for the little bit that will help you preserve your own human touch?

A thought-provoking commentary on the importance of the individual, even for those who think of the masses, came to me from Bishop James A. Pike of San Francisco. He said: "How does one settle the priorities as between, for example, meeting a deadline on an article for a popular magazine and seeing a given person in trouble? If the article is well done, it will help many,

many people solve their problems—or perhaps stay out of trouble. But this particular person is at your doorstep. I know it seems illogical, but I always choose the latter.

"Even if the former would seem more important," he continued, "in the end one has more to say that is useful in mass-communication when one continues to see and work with individuals in their distinct problems." Here, Bishop Pike underscored an important thought: "If one ever chose to give his time to individuals merely because doing so would provide experiences that would aid communication to the masses, the experience would not be fruitful and the aid to the many would be faulty!"